CRIME AND THE HUMAN MIND

PATTERSON SMITH REPRINT SERIES IN
CRIMINOLOGY, LAW ENFORCEMENT, AND SOCIAL PROBLEMS

PUBLICATION NO. 43: PATTERSON SMITH REPRINT SERIES IN CRIMINOLOGY, LAW ENFORCEMENT, AND SOCIAL PROBLEMS

CRIME AND THE HUMAN MIND

By DAVID ABRAHAMSEN, M.D.

Department of Psychiatry, Columbia University

Montclair, New Jersey

PATTERSON SMITH

1969

62554

SBN 87585-043-X

Library of Congress Catalog Card Number: 69-14906

To My Wife, Lova

WHOSE INDOMITABLE SPIRIT AND
WARM FRIENDSHIP HAVE BEEN MY
CONSTANT SOURCE OF INSPIRATION

FOREWORD

THIS BOOK introduces the reader to the present day psychologic viewpoints on criminology through the medium of a
comprehensive historical review of the development of this subject
as it has occurred in several countries and schools of thought.

Such a work as the present one should serve the purpose of fixing
attention upon the attitudes, concepts, and methods that will make
for a better understanding of the criminal and for a more intelligent
way of solving the problems involved.

In dealing with the individual criminal in terms of his immediate acts we do not deal sufficiently with the problem of causes,
nor with the question of prevention. Although everyone recognizes
that peculiarities of the human mind enter the picture, this factor
has been sadly neglected.

Among the numerous problems that confront society in modern
times, there are probably few of greater importance than that concerning the criminal classes. There are so many elements in this
complex situation that solutions to the problems will not all come
from any one type of approach; however, it is obvious that psychiatry must play a major role, as the necessity of evaluating the mental
status and the personality factors along with the criminal act is becoming recognized more and more by all concerned.

The criminal, like other people, has lived a life of instinctive
drives, of desires, of wishes, of feelings, but one in which his intellect has apparently functioned less effectually as a brake upon
certain trends. His constitutional make-up deviates toward the abnormal, leading him into conflicts with the laws of society and its
cultural patterns. The act which leads to a prison sentence is the
result of a life of distorted viewpoints and of standards of conduct
which are out of keeping with what the rest of us consider as normal
and right.

The subject of criminology is in an unsettled state, and there
are many diverse opinions about some of its important aspects.
This is to be expected as various workers have different special
interests and possess different degrees of information; therefore,

the classifications and interpretations of the material presented in this volume may not be acceptable to all readers. As many things are not yet settled in this field, differences in opinion should serve as a stimulus to additional research. Enlightenment will come finally through the combined efforts of several professions, including medicine, law, anthropology, and sociology.

Since criminology continues to be one of the principal problems confronting legislators, educators, physicians, those working in the psychological and sociological disciplines, and the private citizen, it is hoped that the days of the military conqueror will soon be past so that the scientist and the physician may direct the full force of their abilities and interests to the task of studying and correcting the elements that make for crime and criminal careers. During the past fifty years the activities of scientific men have served to greatly increase the happiness and longevity of mankind. Some solution of the crime problem would benefit mankind in quite as tangible a way as have the conquering of pathogenic bacteria and the control of communicable diseases.

Many problems are discussed in these pages in a manner that should give those members of the medical profession who have not specialized in this field a better understanding of the problems confronting the psychiatrists and the judges of courts as well as those involving the unfortunate victims of circumstances that make for a criminal maladjustment.

The laws governing the trial and punishment of criminals will not and should not be expected to change just to accommodate new ideas, however sensible they may seem to be, but the laws and methods of procedure will be modified when once the legislators are no longer uncertain about the facts, and the public demands such action. It is the task of all concerned to accumulate and demonstrate the facts from research in a scientific manner that they may be thus evaluated and become convincing.

This book offers information regarding the factors in crime from a psychiatric-psychologic viewpoint. The material has been presented in a very interesting way by one who has had a wealth of experience and who is well qualified to write on this subject. The author was born in Norway in 1903 and obtained his medical degree in 1929 at the Royal Frederick University of Oslo, Norway.

He studied with Professor Monrad-Krohn and others at the University Clinic in Oslo and later in Copenhagen and London. At the latter place he worked in anthropology with Professor Malinowski. In 1938 he was appointed psychiatrist at the Department of Justice, Oslo, Norway. For a time he studied psychology and philosophy at the Royal Frederick University with Professor Anathon Aall. He has numerous published works in several languages, including articles on science and its future, mass-psychosis, the psychiatric-psychologic background of murder, the dynamic connection between crime and personality, and the function of language and its development.

Dr. Abrahamsen was in the midst of the conflict when the Germans invaded Norway. He established a field hospital and stayed until the end of organized resistance, when, fortunately, he was able to leave that country.

In the autumn of 1940 he worked at St. Elizabeth's Hospital in Washington, D.C., and in 1941 as a psychiatrist at the Illinois State Penitentiary. In 1942 he lectured in psychiatric criminology at the postgraduate courses of the Psychiatric Institute, Columbia University. In 1943 he was research associate on the staff of the Menninger Clinic, Topeka, Kansas, following which he was appointed to the psychiatric staff of Bellevue Hospital. He has served as a psychiatrist at the Psychiatric Clinic, Court of General Sessions, New York City. Through funds granted by the Josiah Macy Jr. Foundation, he was appointed this autumn as a research associate in the Department of Psychiatry, Columbia University.

The volume deals comprehensively with many aspects of criminology and should serve the purpose wherever an authoritative book is desired for the general reader and college and university students.

NOLAN D. C. LEWIS, M.D.,
*Director, N.Y. State Psychiatric Institute and
Hospital, Columbia University, New York, N.Y.*

PREFACE

CRIME is a many-headed monster. Its tentacles reach far and embrace all walks of human life. It presents a problem not only to the public, the judge, and the lawyer but also to the psychiatrist, the psychologist, the sociologist, the anthropologist, the social worker, and, last but not least, to the criminal himself.

It is the lack of understanding of the criminal himself that makes the problem of crime so complicated. Yes, so complicated that one who tries to solve it may soon feel himself lost as in the midst of a jungle. And yet it is necessary that everyone interested in this field, laymen and teachers, students of medicine, law, sociology, economy, and social work, be given a substantial amount of information about the criminal from the psychiatric-psychologic point of view. I therefore deemed it important that a single book be written treating the psychiatric-psychologic aspects of the criminal and his act. Such a book should help to dispel some of the confusion attendant on the problem and serve to orient the reader who otherwise would have to delve through a number of unrelated volumes.

It cannot be stressed too much that if we are to understand the offender, then we ought to know the forces that drive him into crime. Such an understanding can be arrived at by considering the psychiatric-psychologic aspects of the criminal and his deed. Psychiatry is in its implications a social science, and its foremost task is to interest itself in all social phenomena pertaining to the mind. This includes criminal conduct. Only a realistic approach can give us an understanding of antisocial behavior and lead us to more intelligent management of the offender.

This book is based on lectures given at the postgraduate courses of the Psychiatric Institute of Columbia University. My studies with Professor Malinowski at the University of London, my work as psychiatrist at the Department of Justice in Norway (State Penitentiary and County Jail, Oslo), at the Illinois State Penitentiary in Joliet, at the Menninger Clinic in Topeka, Kansas, and at the Psychiatric Clinic of the Court of General Sessions in New York City have been sources of my experience in this field.

I wish to pay tribute to three scientists of my native Norway, devoted to medicine and the study of social problems: my former teacher, G. H. Monrad-Krohn, M.D., Professor of Neurology at the Royal Frederick University, Oslo; Johan Scharffenberg, M.D., Chief Psychiatrist at the Department of Justice, Oslo; and Hartvig Nissen, Ph.D., Warden at the State Penitentiary, Oslo. Their understanding and deep knowledge of medicine in particular and of social problems, including crime, in general have laid the foundation for my research in this field.

This book could not have been undertaken if it were not for the many people in the United States who have met me with a spirit of friendship and cooperation. I am grateful for the support and encouragement extended to me by Dr. Nolan D. C. Lewis, Director of the Psychiatric Institute, Columbia University; Dr. Winfred Overholser, Superintendent of St. Elizabeth's Hospital, Washington, D.C.; Mr. Austin H. MacCormick, Executive Director of the Osborne Association, New York City; Dr. Israel S. Wechsler, Professor of Clinical Neurology, Columbia University; Dr. Peter Bassoe, Professor of Neurology, University of Illinois, Chicago; Dr. Paul L. Schroeder, Superintendent of the Institute of Juvenile Research, Chicago; and by Martin L. Reymert, Ph.D., Director of the Moosehart Laboratory for Child Research, Moosehart, Illinois. I am also grateful to Dr. S. Bernard Wortis, Director of Bellevue Psychiatric Hospital, and Mr. Irving A. Halpern, Chief Probation Officer, Court of General Sessions, New York City, for their interest in my work. I wish, too, to acknowledge permission from the following publishers to quote material: G. P. Putnam's Sons for Gina Ferrero-Lombroso, *Criminal Man,* and for Oscar Wilde, *De Profundis;* and W. W. Norton & Co. for D. K. Henderson, *Psychopathic States.*

I also express my thanks to various libraries for their kind assistance, in particular, the New York Public Library, the library at the Menninger Clinic, Topeka, Kansas, and the library of the Russell Sage Foundation, New York City.

Finally, I am grateful for the cooperative spirit shown to me by everyone at Columbia University Press who assisted me in transforming the manuscript into the present book.

DAVID ABRAHAMSEN

July, 1944

CONTENTS

TABLES

We are not ourselves
When nature, being oppress'd, commands the mind
To suffer with the body.

—KING LEAR, ACT II, SCENE IV

I

CRIMINOLOGY AS A SCIENCE

CRIMINAL HISTORY reflects the prevailing attitudes of mind that have characterized men at various stages of human culture. In a book concerning the psychiatric aspects of crime it may therefore be well to introduce the subject by giving a retrospective survey of this development and its psychological significance.

As far back as human history goes several elements such as the union of blood and the search for food have tied men together in unity under some authority which all members of the tribe had to obey.[1] In the course of time the custom of the tribe, partly because of fear, became the accepted principle of conduct to which there was more or less passive submission. When a higher social organization was reached, the custom, according to Westermarck's view, became a law, and the law itself became an order of nature to which all had to yield.[2]

This acquiescence of every member to the tribal rules, learned in childhood, was a fundamental formula of the primitive order. Malinowski found in his investigations among the inhabitants of the Trobriand Archipelago that the motivating force behind this adherence was reciprocity of services among the respective members of primitive communities.[3] This principle of give and take was the result of the inner transactions, both mental and social, without which primitive and modern society could not exist.[4]

Because of certain customs and rules of law within the community, it was but natural that a complex of behavior arose, a complex that has had repercussions up to our time. It was characteristic of the life of savage tribes that an infraction of the laws of taboo

---

[1] In Australia it was in certain cases the fire by which food could be cooked that bound the savage people constituting a tribe.
[2] Edvard Westermarck, *Origin and Development of the Moral Ideas*, I, 162. See also Westermarck's, *The Goodness of Gods*.
[3] Bronislaw Malinowski, *Crime and Custom in Savage Society*, p. 24.
[4] *Ibid.*, p. 25.

upon which the whole society rested was a crime. Breaking a taboo automatically brought punishment so that investigation of the crime and of the criminal would have been superfluous. Primitive society was not concerned about why the criminal behaved as he did. Its only interest was in punishing the culprit so that the people would be satisfied. Such procedure was based upon the belief that man's behavior occurred through the action of fate or divine interference. While today we have the sequence: crime—investigation—finding the criminal—punishment, primitive society followed the sequence of crime—punishment.

Although they punished the culprit, the members of the group felt that they also were responsible for the crime and that they would suffer. Partly because of this they came to believe that when a crime had been committed, it had to be counteracted by a system of magic. The tribe acted as if with a collective mind, calling forth punitive measures against the offender and protection for itself.

Keeping these factors in mind, it is not so surprising that the enormous quantity of legal records and texts collected from the earliest days contains little information about the criminal himself and reveals a peculiar lack of understanding of him. However, the one feature that stands out in sharp relief is the group reaction which gives the impression that the tribe acted as a whole. There is hardly any aspect of human life in which a people's emotions and resentments have been more colorfully expressed than in their attitude concerning crime and the criminal. When law-abiding citizens react with harsh feelings toward a crime which they mutually condemn, it is not only because they want to see the law obeyed but also because the deep unconscious load of impressions and experiences collected through successive generations links them together and gives rise to the common reaction. It is as if each people had a "soul in common," [5] differentiated from that of others not only through economic, social, or agricultural conditions but also through the psychological peculiarities of the different races. Such a "common soul," assuming that it exists, has been formed by unknown processes, probably related to what Freud called identification.[6]

[5] David Abrahamsen, "Mass-Psychosis and Its Effects," *Journal of Nervous and Mental Disease*, XCIII (Jan., 1941), 65.
[6] Ives Hendrick, *Facts and Theories of Psychoanalysis*, p. 159.

If we study the collective mind more closely, it appears to be related to or identical with the concept which Jung called the *racial* or *collective unconscious*. This type of unconscious—in contrast to the individual unconscious—represents the sum of experiences of the race or nation, though these experiences may be quite distinct from those of the individual.[7] We might say that this collective unconscious is a part of our inheritance, built up of instincts and archetypes. The latter appear in the form of superstitions and myths, in dreams, and in the thoughts of the psychotic.

In determining the motivation of crime it is important that our attention be directed towards elements related to the collective unconscious, in whatever form they may appear.

This fact is illustrated by the following case where superstition seemed to play a fatal part. A thirty-year-old Negro murdered his wife after a party. He accused her of having danced with another man; they quarreled, and he stabbed her. On the surface this murder would appear to have been instigated by jealousy and committed under the influence of alcohol. The life story, however, revealed the following facts. This man had had a child by a woman whom he had refused to marry. Five years later when his mother lay on her deathbed, she extracted from him a promise to marry a woman of her choice—the woman who had borne him the child. Fearing that his mother's evil spirit would follow him if he did not keep his promise, he married the woman. He also believed that only in this way could his mother (symbolically) continue to live. For a time his marriage went along fairly well, but he eventually tired of his wife and so killed her. Among certain tribes in South Africa a superstition exists that a man has to marry a woman of his mother's choice.[8] The case seems to show that similar superstition formed an unlucky constellation of circumstances where external imaginative forces injected fear and anxiety into the individual.

Since crime reflects the cultural development and the mind of the race, it is interesting to note that certain "crimes" were prevalent among primitive tribes—incest (not universally taboo, however), other sexual offenses, and witchcraft, which originated from the conception that the culprit could influence evil spirits.

[7] See C. G. Jung, *The Psychology of the Unconscious.*
[8] Personal communication from Bronislaw Malinowski.

It is in the code of Hammurabi 1927 B. C. (?) that we first meet the *lex talionis,* the principle of punishment which demands retaliation for the crime committed and is expressed in the old words, "an eye for an eye, a tooth for a tooth." [9] This principle later appeared in the Mosaic law, and has influenced Christianity and civil and criminal law up to our time. This demand for revenge for a crime was an expression of the instinct of self-preservation within the group, which considered every infraction of the rules as an attack upon its authority.

Criminal law has also felt the powerful force of the Hebrew and the Christian religion. Religious thoughts and fears concerning the fate of a man's soul led to the belief that human justice should to some extent mirror the punishment or reward that a man's soul would receive in the afterlife. The belief of the depravity of man did not make one concerned about the fate of the criminal. Since man was considered evil by nature, it made no difference if he were sentenced to die for some trivial offense. The doctrine of freedom of the will implied that crime was the result of the criminal's free will, acting independently of other causes. Naturally, then, it seemed superfluous to inquire into any deep-seated reasons for the crime. The offender had perpetrated the crime because his will was directed toward accomplishing it. This belief bolstered up faith in retaliation as the guiding principle in punishing crime and encouraged very severe penalties.[10]

In the latter part of the eighteenth century the problem of whether or not a criminal was different from other human beings first came under debate. Influenced by such contemporary humanitarian writers as Voltaire, Montesquieu, Condorcet, and Rousseau, Cesare Beccaria in 1764 wrote *An Essay on Crimes and Punishment,* in which he violently protested against the cruel and inhuman punishment inflicted upon criminals and the arbitrary way in which sentences were imposed. He stated that the punishment should be the mildest permitted in a given case, that it should be in proportion to the crime, and be determined by law.[11] This concept of the

[9] The Danish philosopher, Harald Höffding, historically found this to be the case.
[10] Even the philosopher Kant, who was considered to have a liberal mind, once said: "Before the earth perishes the last thief should be hanged in the guts of the last murderer."
[11] Beccaria, *An Essay on Crimes and Punishment,* p. 133.

Classical School was based upon the idea that the criminal was a free moral agent who might choose to commit a crime. If the criminal chose the bad rather than the good act, he should be judged by his act rather than by his intentions.

Faulty as this utilitarian doctrine might appear, it was embodied into the French Code of 1791. But, in practical effect it became a compromise between Beccaria's ideas and the medieval system of penology. While it simplified the legal process and placed emphasis upon the crime by inflicting the same measure of punishment upon the first offender as upon the recidivist, it completely disregarded the personality of the criminal and failed to consider whether he was a minor or an adult, feeble-minded or insane.

Because such a conception is based upon theory rather than upon the real facts, the Neo-Classical School asserted that the quantity of punishment should be in proportion to the crime and determined in accordance with the personal make-up of the criminal. Although such a view was put into the new revised French Code of 1810, the criminal as such remained in the background, still unrecognized.

Since the new humanitarian ideas exerted influence upon the punishment of the criminal only, another concept was necessary in order to view the whole problem of crime more realistically. This was hastened by scientific discoveries of this period: Lavoisier discovered the nature of the elements, Dalton found new proof for the atomic theory, and Wöhler synthesized organic material from inorganic, thus proving that the organic and inorganic world were not two entirely different worlds, as was heretofore believed.[12] These and subsequent discoveries shook many old beliefs about humans and the world.

Scientific investigations opened new perspectives, new fields were examined, new cultural life was investigated and adopted, new insight achieved. The knowledge accumulated through scientific research stimulated investigation of the human mind and the social relations of man. In the first instance the search was directed toward the sociological manifestations, and in the latter case toward man himself who, as a result of the new sociological conception, was viewed in the environment to which he belonged.

[12] Wöhler synthesized the organic urea of inorganic ammonium salts of cyanic acid.

This fruitful thinking stimulated the statistician L. A. J. Quételet to examine human conduct in relation to surroundings; he found that man's behavior varied with environmental conditions.[13] Partly influenced by him, partly by Philippe Pinel, "the liberator" of the insane, Morel in 1857 stated that the criminal was a product of mental, physical, and moral introgression.

At this time a powerful factor appeared which gave quite another characteristic not only to the conception of human life but also to that of the criminal. This was the evolutionary theory of Charles Darwin, first published in 1859 in *Origin of Species*. He held that physical and psychological functions gradually evolved through express adaptation to environment, and held as corollaries, that man was intimately connected with other animals and was motivated by the same biological drives.[14] These doctrines were destined to make a tremendous impression at a time when all seeking knowledge within the criminological field found themselves halted by a barrier of fixed and limited ideas. This theory impressed the mind of one of the most distinguished physicians and anthropologists in the criminological field, Cesare Lombroso (1836–1909), the founder of medical criminal research. He tried, as did Herbert Spencer [15] with his scientific philosophy, to apply Darwin's biological theory to the criminal and to crime. In a little pamphlet entitled *The Criminal in Relation to Anthropological Jurisprudence and Psychiatry*, published in 1876, he stated that the criminal behaved as he did because he was born so and thus did not act, but merely expressed his inner nature.

Lombroso's pamphlet later grew to be a work of three volumes called *L'Uomo delinquente* (*Criminal Man*). However much one disagrees with Lombroso's findings and conclusions, even his most ardent opponents must admit that he made the first attempt to establish a new scientific criminal psychopathology. This is Lombroso's undying reward. Although his theory of the born criminal has now been put aside, one must not forget the fundamental contribution which he made through his investigations of the

13 L. A. J. Quételet, *Physique sociale.*
14 Here it must be said that the normal mind differs strongly from that of the animal, but both have in their basic structures and in their principal disposition mutual mental elements.
15 See M. Guthne, *Spencer's Formula of Evolution.*

scientific characteristics of the criminal and the causes of crime. In addition he has shown us the continued peril to society if delinquents are permitted to follow their antisocial tendencies.

One cannot but admire the fearless and outstanding efforts he made to bring scientific order and understanding to a problem which was vital to society, in spite of the surprising lack of self-criticism in his conclusions and generalizations. The twelve years that Lombroso spent on his theory were days and nights of work, excitement, hope and anxiety. An army physician in 1864, Lombroso in his leisure began to study the condition of the soldiers. He believed that some vicious soldiers were different from good soldiers by reason of their being tattooed and by the indency of the figures on the skin. Two years later he called attention to the idea that the study of psychiatry should be based upon medical experimental methods. Shortly afterwards while studying Italian prisoners he became acquainted with a hardboiled robber, one Vitella, notorious for his impudence and vicious and cunning behavior. After his death, Lombroso performed an autopsy and found in the fossae cranii posterior a depression similar to that found in rodents and other lower animals instead of the protuberance which is present normally in the human skull.

Lombroso was struck by this discovery and became convinced that the explanation of criminal traits was to be found in atavism. The criminal had reverted to a primitive type and was biologically a savage. He was thus a distinct anthropological type with certain cranial characteristics.

But, let us see what Lombroso himself says about his discovery.

This [his discovery] was not merely an idea, but a revelation. At the sight of that skull, I seemed to see all of a sudden, lighted up as a vast plain under a flaming sky, the problem of the nature of the criminal—an atavistic being who reproduces in his person the ferocious instincts of primitive humanity and the inferior animals. Thus were explained anatomically the enormous jaws, high cheekbones, prominent superciliary arches, solitary lines in the palms, extreme size of the orbits, handle-shaped or sessile ears found in criminals, savages and apes, insensibility to pain, extremely acute sight, tattooing, excessive idleness, love of orgies, and the irresistible craving for evil for its own sake, the desire not only to extinguish life in the victim, but to mutilate the corpse, tear its flesh, and drink its blood.

I was further encouraged in this bold hypothesis by the results of my studies on Verzeni, a criminal convicted of sadism and rape, who showed the cannibalistic instincts of primitive anthropophagists and the ferocity of beasts of prey.

The various parts of the extremely complex problem of criminality were, however, not all solved thereby. The final key was given by another case, that of Misdea, a young soldier of about 21, unintelligent but not vicious, although subject to epileptic fits. He had served for some years in the army when suddenly, for some trivial cause, he attacked and killed eight of his superior officers and comrades. His horrible work accomplished, he fell into a deep slumber, which lasted twelve hours and on awakening appeared to have no recollection of what had happened. Misdea, while representing the most ferocious type of an animal, manifested, in addition, all the phenomena of epilepsy, which appeared to be hereditary in all members of his family. It flashed across my mind that many criminal characteristics not attributable to atavism, such as facial asymmetry, cerebral sclerosis, impulsiveness, instantaneousness, the periodicity of criminal acts, the desire for evil for evil's sake, were morbid characteristics common to epilepsy, mingled with others due to atavism.[16]

In his theory Lombroso said that the criminal lacked insight, felt no remorse, was unstable and vain, and that nature had created this individual with the subhuman anthropological and anatomical features of a criminal *a reo natu* (the born criminal). His investigations consisted of measuring the skull and various other organs in post-mortem observation and of examining living criminals in regard to blood pressure, emotional reactions, hearing, taste, smell, and even handwriting. Thus Lombroso transferred the method of anthropological science to the field of psychiatry, which was a great achievement, even though his measurements lacked accuracy. In our time this type of anthropological study has been used in several investigations of criminals, recently in the extensive investigation by Earnest A. Hooton.[17]

Although Lombroso's data on anatomical characteristics of the criminal proved to be inaccurate and not at all conclusive, his description of the psychological traits which the criminal manifested was more nearly correct./Lombroso showed intuition when he pointed out that instability, impulsiveness, meagerly developed affections, vanity, lying, gambling, and lack of restraint were out-

[16] G. Ferrero-Lombroso, *Criminal Man*, pp. xiv–xvi.
[17] *The American Criminal*.

standing features in the make-up of the criminal, and men who have dealt with criminals agree with this general description.

However, when Lombroso launched his ideas they were sharply criticized and caused considerable discussion. Because of new investigations and additional knowledge he eventually began to modify them. The prominence of his great idea—the born criminal —obscured the fact that he recognized three other classes of criminals: the insane criminal; the criminal by passion; and the occasional or accidental criminal.

It is important to mention these three types because this was the first attempt to classify them scientifically. These types are known and reckoned with today, although our classification has been broadened.

Among the group of insane criminals he described various types of insanity that might lead to crime. It is interesting to note that Lombroso recognized the "criminal by passion," meaning a person who was characterized by unusual affectibility which under certain conditions might lead him into crime.

The occasional criminal he divided into three types: the pseudo criminal; the habitual criminal; and the criminaloid.

The pseudo criminal was a person who committed a crime under extraordinary and irritating circumstances, or one whose crime was only a technical violation of the law that did not involve any important moral issue.

The habitual criminal Lombroso characterized as one who was normal at birth, but who from early childhood had been repeatedly exposed to detrimental environmental influences which in due course produced a deviation in conduct from that of a law-abiding citizen.

The criminaloid was a transitional type between the born criminal and the occasional criminal; he was not actually a criminal but a person who was tempted into crime under unfortunate circumstances.

As a result of vigorous attacks on his ideas, in which his critics often showed as little judgment as did Lombroso himself, Lombroso tried to find proof for his theories. True, he was wrong in his basic idea of the born criminal but he showed foresight in his view that criminals were infantile, which later investigations have proved to be correct. Today we find that many criminals are immature in their judgment and that this is reflected in their antisocial behavior.

Above all, Lombroso will be remembered for disproving the assumption that a criminal acted as he did because the human will was free and that he was responsible for his act. Further, by his insistence that the personality of the criminal be examined, he paved the way for the idea that the criminal was the cause and crime the result. Finally, Lombroso realized that future research in criminology had to be built upon a new basis; he constructed the framework for the investigations upon which our understanding of the criminal has largely depended.

While Lombroso called attention to the anatomical and psychological factors in the criminal, Enrico Ferri [18] stressed the sociological elements which contributed to making the criminal. Such influential factors were the constitution of the family, the age and occupation of its different members, the industrial, economic, and political conditions, and the country's climatic and geographical conditions. Ferri incorporated his thoughts in studies called *Homicide* and *Criminal Sociology,* published in 1884. His view was based on what he called "the law of criminal saturation," stating that if people and their surroundings remained constant, crime would remain stable regardless of the methods of punishment used. Keeping in mind the failure of punishment, he proposed preventive measures—exclusion of juveniles from the courts, better education, better marriage and divorce laws, shorter working hours, and so on.

Closely related to Ferri's views were those of Raffaeli Garofalo (born 1852) who regarded crime from the psychological rather than from the anatomical or sociological viewpoint. He emphasized studying the criminal's personality and the circumstances under which the crime had been committed.

It was but natural that the new ideas advanced by the Italian School should spread and give impetus to new concepts not only of the criminal, but also of how he was to be treated. In Germany, Lombroso's scientific colleague, Emil Kraepelin, in 1880 published a pamphlet, *Die Abschaffung des Strafmasses,* bearing the motto,

---

[18] Enrico Ferri (1856–1929) had in 1879 become a pupil of Lombroso at the University of Turin and was later a professor of criminal law at the Royal University of Rome.

Pro Humanitate. This created a stir which resulted in the shelving of the policy of retaliation for one aimed at improving the criminal. The criminal was not to be given a fixed or flat sentence, but an indeterminate one.

This new idea in penology was also adopted within the ranks of lawyers. In 1881 Professor Frantz von Liszt (one of the most illustrious figures in criminal law, as illustrious in science as was his cousin in music) and Professor Adolf Dochow founded the periodical, *Zeitschrift für die gesamte Strafrechtswissenschaft.* All the contributors, regardless of their nationality or their conception of criminal law, agreed to work for the progress of criminology and penology. Though he met great resistance from the old Classical School, Liszt worked slowly until his ideas won much sympathy, particularly in France. With youthful enthusiasm he challenged the classical philosophy of crime and its treatment. The main task of Liszt's school was therefore to introduce the method of investigating the causes of crime; it emphasized that crime should be examined as a social-ethical phenomenon and that punishment should be regarded accordingly.

Liszt, together with G. A. von Hamel of Amsterdam and Adolphe Prins of Brussels, established on New Year's Eve, 1888, the International Association of Criminal Law (*L'Union Internationale de Droit Penal*). The association contended that crime and punishment should be considered as much from a sociological as from a judicial point of view. Such a conclusion did not imply that Liszt was unaware of the possibility of finding some of the causes for antisocial behavior in the criminal's own personality. His close friend, the psychiatrist Richard von Krafft-Ebing, sharpened his awareness of the intimate relationship between psychology and psychiatry and criminal law.[19]

In the pamphlet *Zur Vorbereitung des Strafgesetzentwurfs,* Liszt maintained that the lawmaker who wants to go to the root of crime must know not only its exterior appearance but also the deeper, interior layers. Without a scientifically founded etiology of crime a rational philosophy of crime is impossible.[20]

[19] K. V. Lilienthal, "Frantz von Liszt," *Zeitschrift für die gesamte Strafrechtswissenschaft,* XL (1919), 535.
[20] Frantz von Liszt, *Strafrechtliche Aufsätze und Vorträge,* II, 412.

Of more importance than this pamphlet was Liszt's *Lehrbuch des deutschen Strafrechts* (*Textbook of German Criminal Law*), which first appeared in 1881 and later grew to be an invaluable work. Being widely distributed in translation, it made Liszt well known outside Germany. K. V. Lilienthal said that there were other good textbooks on criminal law but that Liszt had written *the* textbook on criminal law.[21] Liszt may well be regarded as the founder of the German criminal-sociological school.[22]

Some twenty years after Kraepelin demanded a reform of the criminal law, a young psychiatrist who was bound to exert a tremendous influence upon the development of the philosophy of crime came to the front. Gustav Aschaffenburg of Cologne had gained valuable experience as a psychiatrist at a large penitentiary, and as an expert in court cases collected considerable material. In 1902 he published *Das Verbrechen und seine Bekämpfung* (*Crime and Its Repression*), dedicated to Kraepelin. There was no doubt, Aschaffenburg said in his introduction, that the new trend in criminal law was intimately connected with the advances being made in medicine and anthropology. In order to stimulate investigation and discussion of the causes of crime, he founded in 1904 *Monatschrift für Kriminalpsychologie und Strafrechtsreform* (*Monthly Periodical of Criminal Psychology and Criminal Law Reform*). Publication was discontinued in 1936, when at the age of seventy, he was forced to flee the Nazis. In his article "Rückblick und Ausblick" (Retrospect and Prospect) in the last number, he pointed out that the psychiatrist had to make a decisive contribution to the problem of crime—this was one of the reasons that prompted him to edit the periodical. It is gratifying to know that Aschaffenburg continues his fruitful research in this country. Hardly another besides Lombroso has furthered the development of criminology into a science so much as he.

English investigators directed the most severe and comprehensive criticism against Lombroso's born criminal. In 1901, an English prison physician, Charles Goring, began extensive examinations of 3,000 English prisoners and a like number of normal Englishmen.

[21] Hartvig Nissen, "Strafferetsutviklingen i Tyskland," *Tidskrift for rettsvidentskap*, 1938, p. 249.
[22] For the development of the criminal law see Chapter IX.

The results were tabulated by Karl Pearson in 1908, but it required another five years to interpret the findings, which were published in 1913 in *The English Convict*. In comparing the cephalic measurements of the criminals with those of normal persons, Goring found only a slight difference, which in no way could warrant a decisive conclusion. He then compared different groups of criminals, burglars, forgers, and so on, but could find no difference among them. "Our inevitable conclusion," he said, "must be that there is no such thing as a physical criminal type." [23]

Goring thought that poor physical condition combined with defective mentality made the criminal.[24] Although he seemed to disregard Lombroso's concept of the born criminal, nevertheless he outlined the idea that there was a physical, mental, and moral type of normal individual who tends to be convicted of crime.[25]

It is essential to add that neither Goring nor Lombroso thought that physical stigmata caused crime. Against Goring's conclusions was the fact that his measurements were inaccurate (in spite of anthropometrical methods superior to those of Lombroso), and that he took none of the social or economic causes of crime into consideration. Also, when tracing the mental traits in the criminal, he depended upon subjective rather than objective data.

To recapitulate, the Classical School emphasized the rights and the liberties of the individual, punishing him with an unvarying penalty; the Neo-Classical School made the penal system flexible and excluded children, the feeble-minded, and the insane from punishment; the Lombrosian School, with the aid of anthropological knowledge, tried to find an explanation of the criminal's behavior in his anatomical and, to a lesser extent, his psychological make-up.

A study of all the possible factors related to crime first began in our time. Such studies have been intensely pursued in this country, and it might be appropriate to describe briefly the most outstanding of them.

It is perhaps surprising that the interest of American criminologists did not originally center so much about the behavior or personality of the criminal as about his being isolated from society. This was, I think, mainly due to a basic character trait of Americans—

[23] *The English Convict*, p. 173.   [24] *Ibid.*, p. 263.   [25] *Ibid.*, p. 370.

they think and act in practical terms. The American criminologist was interested in learning how to deal with the offender; he was therefore concerned with his imprisonment which resulted naturally in a development of the prison system. This may also be one of the reasons why the American prison emphasized custodial care rather than treatment. Once the criminal had been identified as a victim of his environment or of his constitutional make-up, he was incarcerated, thereby fulfilling the main purpose.

Criminal anthropology was not recognized in this country before E. P. Fowler's article appeared in 1880,[26] followed the next year by his translation of Benedict's book. However, as early as 1786, Benjamin Rush, "America's first psychiatrist," at a meeting of the American Philosophical Society had observed that criminal behavior was accompanied by a certain state of mind.[27] He reiterated this statement in his lectures on the study of medical jurisprudence at the University of Pennsylvania in 1810.[28] Isaac Ray in 1838 distinguished between a criminal and an insane individual.[29] Although these facts intimate that American physicians were keenly aware of the difference in behavior of the criminal and of the normal person, criminal anthropology in this country had no original leaders comparable to Rush and Ray in legal psychiatry.

Since Benedict's investigations had their starting point in the study of the criminal brain, it was reasonable that psychiatrists in America also began with this type of study. It is interesting to note that in 1886 the well-known psychiatrist, Charles K. Mill of Philadelphia, held that it was wrong to build a theory on the anatomic basis of crime since crime in reality was a violation of the law.[30] In the following years post-mortem studies of the criminal brain were made by James Weir,[31] Professor H. H. Donaldson,[32] Charles W. McCorkle Poynter, to name a few, who doubted that a criminal

26 E. P. Fowler, "Are the Brains of Criminals Anatomical Perversions?", *Medico-Chirurgical Quarterly*, I (1880), 1–32.
27 "An Inquiry into the Influence of Physical Causes upon the Moral Faculty."
28 *Sixteen Introductory Lectures to Courses of Lectures upon the Institute and Practice of Medicine*, p. 380.
29 *A Treatise on the Medical Jurisprudence of Insanity*, p. 52.
30 "Arrested and Aberrant Development of Fissures and Gyres in the Brains of Paranoiacs, Criminals, Idiots, and Negroes," *Journal of Nervous and Mental Disease*, XIII (1886), 523–50.
31 "Criminal Anthropology," *Medical Journal* XLV (Jan., 1894), 42–45.
32 "The Criminal Brain," *Journal of Nervous and Mental Disease*, XII (1892), 654.

brain existed. Such a view did not prevent others from making further investigations. An outstanding contribution was made by Hamilton D. Wey, prison physician at Elmira Reformatory.[33] His studies were followed by those of another prison physician, W. A. M'Corn of the Wisconsin State Prison (1896), and of the psychologist, George E. Dawson, who examined delinquent girls and boys from reform schools in Massachusetts.[34] The most extensive investigations on the criminal brain were carried out on murderers and recidivists at the Illinois State Penitentiary at Joliet by Drs. G. Frank Lydstone and Eugene L. Talbot. Their findings were published in 1891 and later included in Lydstone's pamphlet, *The Diseases of Society* (1904). All data showed some deviation from the normal form of the head, which seemed rather striking.

The first book written on the American criminal from an anthropological and psychobiological viewpoint as well was by August Drahms. In *The Criminal* (1900), which contained a preface by Lombroso, Drahms concluded that the criminal type did not exist.

Many of these investigators dealt with the physiological and psychological make-up of the criminal. J. B. Ransom, for instance, found in an examination of over 2,000 prisoners that 25 per cent had a heart lesion or a disease of the vessels,[35] and George E. Dawson found that over 30 per cent of the delinquent boys had defective vision. Drahms observed in many offenders an unbalance of the autonomic nervous system, pointing to a preponderance of some physical defectiveness in the criminal.

Eugene Talbot described the criminal as an irritable, frequently incorrigible, and stupid fellow.[36] Brower confirmed Lombroso's findings that criminals were frequently tattooed, while Drahms pointed out that this tattooing was no more than that seen in sailors and soldiers. The most complete description of the criminal was given by Lydstone, who pointed out that intelligence varied with the type of criminal and the criminal ability. Equally important were G. Stanley Hall's examinations in which he focused attention

[33] "Criminal Anthropology," *Proceedings of the National Prison Association*, 1890, pp. 274–91.
[34] G. E. Dawson, "A Study in Youthful Degeneracy," *Pedagogical Seminary*, 1896, 232–33.
[35] "The Physician and the Criminal," *Journal of the American Medical Association*, XXVI (1896), 788–96.
[36] *Degeneracy, Its Causes, Signs and Results*, p. 18.

on the fact that criminal children were of a neurotic character.[37]

This necessarily brief discussion of America's contribution to criminology would not be complete without mention of such names as William Healy, William A. White, Sheldon and Eleanor T. Glueck, Winfred Overholser, Paul S. Schroeder, Franz Alexander, Gregory Zilboorg, Karl A. Menninger, Bernard Glueck, Benjamin Karpman, A. A. Brill, Austin MacCormick, Paul Schilder, E. H. Sutherland, Thorsten Sellin, and Earnest A. Hooton. Several periodicals, besides the purely psychiatric and sociological ones, also deserve mention, particularly *The Journal of Criminal Psychopathology*, edited by V. C. Branham, *The Journal of Criminal Law and Criminology*, edited by Robert H. Gault, and *Federal Probation*.

The few investigations mentioned indicate that the criminal and his behavior have been studied intensively,[38] and we will see this confirmed in our later discussions. Some of this research, however, even up to this time, has inclined to produce unfounded conclusions. Lombroso and his followers held that there was an absolute correlation between bodily form and criminal behavior. They disregarded the fact that such a correlation had first to be proved absolute, not only for a selected part of the population, but for the whole of it. They further disregarded the fact that this criminal behavior did not take place when the anatomical types differed.[39] Finally, it had to be proved that the theory of the anatomical type would imply a certain kind of behavior.

The one-sidedness of the early criminological investigators is remarkable. They did not think that a plurality of factors caused crime; this limited thinking delayed, even hampered, progress in a field which was—and still is—of the utmost importance to society. Criminal behavior is complex, more complex than a certain form of the skull, inherited traits, or environmental influences can account for. The normal man's conduct is a result of the interplay among several interrelated factors. The same must be realized of criminal behavior.

This complexity necessitates, therefore, that the field be divided if a scientific approach through research is to be possible.

Since it is impossible to cure diseases without knowing their

---

[37] *Adolescence*, pp. 335–37.   [38] See A. E. Fink, *Causes of Crime.*
[39] Franz Boas, "Race and Progress," *Science*, 1931, p. 74.

causes, it is reasonable to assume that this is also true regarding crime. How then are we to approach the investigation of crime? Criminological research must consequently be divided into: (1) the etiology of crime, that is, the knowledge of the causes of crime; and (2) the philosophy of crime, how to treat the offender and counteract crime.

The etiology of crime is many-sided and is principally related to man, his environment, or both. This field of research must be divided into:

1. Psychiatric criminology, which deals with the personality of the criminal, precipitating events of the crime, the criminal's experiences, inherited traits, and the causes of crime as they pertain to to his mind
2. Biological (or anthropological) criminology, which is concerned with the criminal in relation to his body build
3. Sociological criminology, which investigates all aspects of environment as causes of crime

The philosophy of crime can be divided into three subgroups:

1. Penology: the knowledge of punishment, its type and its adaptation to each criminal
2. The science of prisons: the knowledge of the execution of the punishment
3. Statistics of crime: the number of criminals and their recidivism.[40]

Criminology has now developed into a science with many ramifications, all of which aim at finding the causes of crime and thereby in a realistic way help to counteract it.

If we suppose that the human mind and behavior, including antisocial conduct, are intimately connected, or if we assume that much of crime is an expression of the individual's aggressions, this should be investigated by that physician whose profession brings him in daily contact with the personality and behavior of man—the psychiatrist.

This leads to the problem: What bearing have mental deviations or mental abnormalities on criminal behavior? Is there a relationship between the criminal's mental make-up and the crime? Can we in certain cases suppose that the criminal's personality is so far deviated from that of the normal individual's that underlying

[40] Statistics become an important guide in planning how to combat crime.

pathology is present which prompts the crime? This side of the criminological problem is of such importance that the establishment of a psychiatric criminology is more than justified.

Further, a psychiatric viewpoint is necessary so that the knowledge of the delinquent person can be translated into practical measures for treating him. Whenever new knowledge is acquired, it is gradually absorbed and used as a basis of treatment. This is one of the ways in which medicine works. In criminology also, we hasten to modify the method of treatment in accordance with newly achieved knowledge.

The methods of such a discipline are the same as physicians use elsewhere in combating disease. The cause of criminal behavior must be known before treatment for it can be adequately carried out. In finding these causes, we must ask:

Of what aspects of crime do we know the least and to which point must our attention be directed? In spite of extensive investigations it can be said with confidence that the area of crime of which we know the least is that pertaining to the mind, for the reason that the human mind, to say nothing of its relationship to anti-social behavior, is to a great extent still *terra incognita*. Thanks to the investigations of Lombroso and Kretschmer and to the genius of Freud, we are starting to probe the depths of the human mind and to look beneath the surface for the motives of human behavior and for the ultimate forces which carry man into crime.

II

THE MIND IN RELATION TO CRIME

THE HISTORY of mankind in all its diversity has always been a history of human behavior. Man's conduct was a source of wonder, sometimes of disgust—even, perhaps, of horror—when he transgressed the sacred rules, and when that was the case, he was regarded as an outsider and was subjected to punishment.

In the beginning there was the deed. But the deed could not be accomplished without the doer. That is to say, if a crime was committed, it was perpetrated through a man, and the act was to be regarded as an expression of his mental condition. This did not imply that the criminal knew more about the motives for his crime than anyone else. Indeed, even today in a homicide or other serious crime the criminal may be unable to give any information as to the real reason for his deed. Thus, one might receive the impression that there was little or no connection between the deed and the culprit.

Since the psychiatrist aims at evaluating the psychological processes in crime, he must ask: Why was the act perpetrated? In answering this question, we must bear in mind that man—paradoxical though it sounds—is not created just at the moment he is born. He is created before he comes into this world, before the egg cell and sperm fuse together, before the time of his parents and grandparents, created at the dawn of time. In man is ingrained more or less of the past as his forbears experienced it. Just as man's spinal column shows his connection with the past, so his mental qualities belong to the past.

Through man's attitude and behavior past experiences speak, experiences remote or recent, conscious or unconscious. No matter how much man wants to run away from them, they assert themselves and intrude upon him. It is impossible to rid himself of them. Past experiences follow the human in all walks of life in the same way as the shadow follows the path of light.

We believe that our reactions are directed by our intelligence, but there is no doubt that in most of our acts the emotions are not far in the background. Our acts may originate from several motives, although only one of these may be conscious. The psychological processes that underlie human conduct in general motivate the person's attitude and reaction to the prevailing situation.

These assumptions hold true also for those acts defined as criminal acts or crimes. Frequently it is only by penetrating into the deepest-lying layers of the human mind that we are able to trace the motives which link the criminal to the past—motives of which he himself has long been unaware. Individuals who are unable to adjust emotionally and whose conduct is determined by their inner conflicts rather than by social circumstances are more frequent than one might think. Even though we lack statistics on these types, it is not farfetched to assume that they exist in large numbers.[1] That we are able to catch only a few of these cases does not invalidate the assumption; this may be considered due to our inefficient method of tracing this type of criminal rather than to his nonexistence.

Observation of a criminal with only minor inner conflicts shows how these can lead him into crime. A boy of twenty was caught after three holdups and was sentenced to prison, where I saw him. In the first interview he was depressed, did not want to talk, and was unable to give any reason for committing the holdups. He spoke only of how drunk he had been and said that he did not remember anything until he awoke the following morning at the police station. In the next interview he was more accessible, greeted me in a friendly manner, and said before I had a chance to speak, "I think you can help me." He then stated that before the holdups he had been depressed, that his girl friend had left him, that he became nervous and took a few drinks. The following day he did not go to work. He felt lonesome and deserted, could not sleep, and decided to see a physician who after examination advised him to be hospitalized. This he could not afford; instead he took some sleeping tablets and slept through the night. However, he was still restless and did not return to his work. Soon his money ran out and one evening he committed the three holdups.

What did this young man's past reveal? In subsequent interviews I learned that his parents were poor; his father had been a hard

[1] Franz Alexander and William Healy, *Roots of Crime*, p. 7.

worker until he became disabled and lost his job; his mother kept house for the family, which included two younger brothers. The mother had become very attached to this boy and he to her until he had grown dependent upon her. He went through high school but then had to go to work when his father was disabled. Thus, at the age of sixteen he became the sole support of the family. For a short time he worked at night and during the next two years he held odd jobs. Every Saturday he brought home his earnings, taking only a small part for his own pleasure. Later he secured a job in a factory where he became acquainted with a girl. He fell in love with her but she did not want to go with him because he had to support his parents and brothers. Finally, she broke with him.

What took place in the mind of this young fellow? He felt depressed and in despair when the girl left him. But why could he not support a wife when he could support a family? His attachment to his mother and his dependence upon her were so strong that they determined his behavior toward the girl. He had not been aware of this strong attachment, but when he had spoken to me about his past history and about the meaning of his attitude, it became clear to him.

As we will see later, a comprehensive knowledge of the development of the personality is often one of the keys, or *the* key, to behavior which otherwise defies explanation. A person's behavior leading up to a crime can in many cases be understood only in terms of his past.

A man may not show gross mental abnormalities but still may be driven into crime by an unconscious urge. Although an offender may have a conscious motive in mind, unconscious motivation may also be present and it is this that in many cases is the driving force. We are too apt to be satisfied when it appears that a crime has been committed because of apparent gain, but this not always is the real motive. Indeed, in delving into the causes of certain types of stealing, such as shoplifting, or even into homicide, one finds motives which are beyond any comprehension of the culprit. One may find that stealing, which takes the form of a kleptomania, is an expression of a disguised wish for sexual intercourse.

All our acts are an expression of something within us. Our gait, habits of eating, our laughter, our tastes, all reflect our mental attitude. Our acts correspond to our whole personality, because they are an attempt to adapt the personality to the prevailing situation. True, this may occur in a way perhaps incomprehensible to the person, but still the acts take place so that the adaptation to the environmental situation can be accomplished.

This may also be said to be the case regarding a criminal act. Such an antisocial act represents attempts of the personality to adapt itself. A criminal becomes either a thief, an assailant, or a sexual offender, never an all-round criminal. He does not simultaneously develop into an embezzler, a drunkard, or a rapist.

Thus, to a certain extent each offender selects his own type of crime. One might say that such a selection depends upon the circumstances (for example, when a robber is frightened into committing a murder), nevertheless, the individual, within certain limits, brings about those circumstances of which he becomes a victim. Usually the crime chosen is typical of the person who perpetrates it. A person with a low I.Q. will in most cases commit a simple offense, like breaking through a window and taking some insignificant objects, or stealing a car, leaving it, and then running away. A more intelligent individual, one with experience in bookkeeping, for example, will by complicated manipulations embezzle funds. An exhibitionist will manifest his tendencies, but he will not commit other sexual offenses, such as rape. Even women seem to prefer certain criminal acts. It has been shown that the only crime in which females exceed males is shoplifting.[2] Even in those cases where circumstances seem to be determining, personality factors lurk in the background. This selection is to an overwhelming degree determined by the personality.

It is this unknown factor of personality that makes human behavior in general and antisocial behavior in particular so much of a riddle. The study of the personality was a task, first for the philosopher, next for the poet and artist, and now for the psychiatrist. When a human being achieves maturity, he does so as the result of a complicated sequence of actions which depend upon precipitating events, experiences, ingrained tendencies, and the more or less constant influence of social environment. This human being—or,

[2] According to the criminal report of the Court of Special Sessions in New York City, 1939, of the 829 persons charged with shoplifting, 517 were women.

in medical terms, this entire psycho-bio-functional organism—is planted in an external environment of the social and physical world and is linked to the past by innumerable ancestors.

What is the personality? It is the total individual expressing himself through an organization of ingrained ideational, affective, and conative faculties and inclinations which determine his behavior and characteristics. Personality integrates. the thinking, the willing, and the acting of the human being and represents the individual as a whole. We can say that the personality consists of four layers or levels. First, the anatomical or structural level, composed of the individual's skeleton, muscles, and organs. Second, the physiological level, which is concerned with the organs, their normal functioning, their interrelationship, and their ability to adjust to the needs of the personality. Third, the psychological level, which includes the ability to recognize, integrate, remember, and discriminate; in short, the mind of the individual. Fourth, the social level, has reference to the person's behavior, whether he is successful or unsuccessful in adjusting to his environment or whether he must make some compromise.

Personality then is a dynamic unit; upon its functioning the pattern of the person's behavior depends. When we seek to explain the riddle of human conduct in general and of antisocial behavior in particular, the solution must be sought in the personality.

Since there is a constant interplay between the personality and the environment, and since the surroundings change incessantly, the demand for the personality to adapt itself to the situation is a continuous one. If the individual is to succeed in adjusting himself, he must meet a wide variety of situations, he must be adaptable, flexible.

That different individuals are not able to meet the same situation is due not to the situation itself but to the individual, because not only does the personality vary in quantity, but also in the constellation of its different components. Each individual reveals a distinctive pattern of traits and behavior. In fact it is this manifest behavior pattern that we refer to when we speak of an individual. This pattern is made up of actual and potential traits which give impetus to two different types of impulses—constructive and destructive, or social and antisocial. These impulses are related to the erotic and to the aggressive drive. They are ingrained in all humans, so that the tendency to commit crime is a universal one. The fact that crime has been present in all stages of human development is further substantiation of this. That antisocial behavior is so widespread leads one to believe that the roots of crime extend farther than the particular social circumstances would indicate, and that they depend upon basic human tendencies which are present in all men. Goethe once said that there was no crime of which he could not trace the inclination in himself.

Since a tendency towards crime is present in all humans, criminals are not very different from many law-abiding citizens. If this is true, we may say they are more like normal individuals than different from them. In one sense, therefore, crime is an artificial thing, created by law. It would seem then that people become criminals not because the law raises a barrier against antisocial behavior, but primarily because they act according to their inner strivings.

We may assume that all psychological processes in humans are the same and follow the same psychological laws. It is unthinkable that one kind of psychological features should be present in one type of person and not in another. The essentially malicious, bad individual is rare—more rare than an essentially good human, such as Beethoven or Newton.

As long as we deal with human tendencies which are kept within social rules and the law, human behavior appears to be no problem at all. It becomes a problem, however, when the law is transgressed, because of its social implications.

It is necessary, therefore, to make a distinction as to how the term criminal is used here. The term *criminal* is not and should not be used in psychiatric terminology, since it implies that the individual is subject to imprisonment. However, because the term is in common use, it would be difficult to avoid it at present. Since the basic aim of all law is to protect society and to guarantee the individual his rights, a criminal is one who presents an antagonistic and antisocial attitude and behavior toward society. But such a conception of crime depends, as has been shown before, upon the ethical principles of society. Even if we say that the law is a custom determining what is right and what is wrong, we must recognize that customs vary greatly in different places. In certain primitive tribes it is the custom for a son to kill his parents when they are too old to carry on the strenuous nomadic life. In fact he is bound by honor to do so.

When we consider the founding of this country, we see that beside other factors it was established by men whose forbears fled from their native land because their liberty was at stake. But those men, whose ancestors were outlaws in their fatherland, gave expression to their belief in the Declaration of Independence: "We hold these truths to be self-evident, that all men are created equal, that they are endowed by their Creator with certain unalienable Rights, that among these are Life, Liberty and the pursuit of Happiness." In the strict sense of the word, their rebellion against the government of England put them outside the law, and therefore, subject to punishment. Were they criminals? Certainly not.

Because a man acts simultaneously as an individual and as a member of society, our concept of what constitutes criminalistic behavior has two roots. Since crime involves in great part human tendencies which are dynamic, one must say that crime is essentially dynamic in nature. The fact that it appears static arises from the ordinary concept of crime as founded on law. Attempts to solve crime have been focused upon the relation to the law, while correctly they should devolve upon the personality of the criminal. Because a deed cannot be performed without the doer, it should be pointed out that the personality make-up of the criminal must be taken into consideration if we are to understand his conduct.

Because criminalistic tendencies are present in all humans, a criterion of the criminal cannot be given. Even with the anthropological and sociological knowledge we have gained of the culprit, of his body, skull, height, face, the broken home situation, economic circumstances, and a thousand other things, the whole problem boils down to one question: *How does the mind function which reacts with antisocial behavior?*

Sociology and law have tried to solve the problem of crime. With due credit to the investigators in those fields, who have contributed valuable findings, we are still far away from a solution. Nor has psychiatry been able to solve the problem. Its main contribution has been in giving detailed descriptions of the criminal, but these have shed little light on the personality itself and its reactions.

True, psychiatry has speculated and compared the occurrence of crime to that of a neurosis or a psychosis, but with some honorable exceptions there has been no real psychiatric insight into criminalistic behavior. It is now time not only to describe the criminal adequately, but to interpret and to understand his behavior.

This leads to the questions: What creates the criminal impulse? What stimulates and gives it direction? In seeking answers to these questions we might consider why traumata in certain cases cause a psychosis, in other cases cause a neurosis, or perhaps a crime. Is it a difference in the personality structure that decides the outcome or is it the degree of the trauma?

Man's constant strivings, conscious or unconscious, to adapt himself to his environment may result in success or failure, or perhaps a compromise.[3] Possibly crime is a compromise, representing for the individual the most satisfactory method of adjustment to inner conflicts which he cannot express otherwise. Thus, his acting out the crime fulfills a certain aim or purpose. The same mechanism may take place in a psychosis where the person's delusions have a compensatory character and satisfy his inner strivings and needs. Crime may therefore be only a surface symptom or a symptom of mental illness which has existed for a long time.

In trying to discover what creates the criminal impulse, we must consider several factors. On one hand lie the individual's natural tendencies and the situation of the moment; on the other, his mental resistance against temptation. All humans have traits consisting of tendencies and counter-tendencies. A thought may give rise to a counter-thought; an emotion may cause a counter-emotion. These tendencies are more or less developed in all persons, but they are most purely seen in the compulsory-obsessional, schizoid, or schizophrenic person whose thoughts and deeds are counteracted to such an extent that he not only does not know what to think or do, but is inhibited. The Swedish poet, Strindberg, who himself undoubtedly went through a phase of schizophrenia, describes such a condition by asking: "Why shall I decide myself to do something when the decision in itself does not lead anywhere?"

Crime may then be considered a product of a person's tendencies

[3] Paul Schilder, "Success and Failure," *Psychoanalytic Review*, XXIX (Oct., 1942), 355–72.

and the situation of the moment interacting with his mental resistance. Letting C stand for crime, T for tendencies, S for the situation, and R for resistance, we derive the following formula:

$$C = \frac{T + S}{R}$$

We can assume that the individual's tendencies and his resistance against them have potential properties, extending either in a socially approved or disapproved direction. The traits, or tendencies, differ in strength from law-abiding to criminalistic, and vary inversely to the individual's resistance. One of the elements is indeterminate—the situation. When all the three factors, tendencies, situation, and resistance, are involved, it is obvious that a number of constellations might arise. Only one person can achieve a particular aim in a given situation, since his traits are peculiar to him alone. In circumstances which we call normal, the situation does not offer any temptation. If the person's traits and resistance neutralize each other so that there is no temptation, a transgression of social behavior will not occur. If the person's criminalistic tendencies are particularly strong, with consequent lowered mental resistance, he will show antisocial behavior.

It may be assumed then that it is not the tendencies and resistance embodied in the structure of the individual which carry him into crime, nor the situation as such, but the fact that he is functioning in the wrong set-up.[4]

Antisocial behavior is a direct expression of an aggression or may be a direct or indirect manifestation of a distorted erotic drive. The degrees of aggression vary—they may manifest themselves only as expressions of activity, or as protest reactions, rebellion, hostility toward one or more persons, or as projections. Aggressions may be merely fantasies or may express themselves in destructive behavior or in antisocial tendencies which take form as criminal acts. Thus aggression becomes transmitted as a pattern of behavior.

Generally speaking, aggression may be expressed directly or indirectly, directly as a self-defense or indirectly in the form of work,

[4] In order to clarify the intermediate causes, an "ideal type" of the criminal has been constructed; the "ideal type" would then respond to a certain situation in a certain way. See Max Weber, *Wirtschaft und Gesellschaft*, II, 9, and Ingjald Nissen, *Max Weber og den tyske kultur*.

play, or music, which are socially approved. Aggressions which do
not have social approval are lying and stealing. A more violent expression of aggression is lynching which, however, has a socially
ambivalent character. The most disapproved forms of aggression
are homicide, assault, and rape. Another direct expression of aggression is war. Even though it may have the approval of a people
it is still an aggression, though war in itself is not recognized in the
eyes of the law as a crime.[5] On this same level must be considered
indirect expressions of aggression like suicide, self-mutilation, and
alcoholism, which are the result of self-destructive tendencies.

The result of the aggressive drive produces in criminalistic behavior a certain characteristic mechanism. Individuals who have
irresistible impulses to commit crime cannot escape the revenge of
their own consciences. When such individuals have yielded to their
aggressive impulses, they are haunted by their own consciences
which lead them to seek punishment and to give themselves up.

Since crime is more or less the result of ingrained human tendencies, we must ask: Why do only certain people become criminals?
In answering this question I would ask: Why does war occur at
certain times and under certain circumstances? I think the reason
is that certain coincidences of internal and external relations are
necessary before a war can start. The same analogy may be applied
to the origin of criminal acts. Some experience in dealing with delinquent behavior will show surprisingly often how certain coincidences of situation may lead a person into crime. It is often said
that life to a large extent is accidental, that much happens by chance,
but I wonder whether this is always true. Is that not the case when
a person who has shown antisocial activities passes into a different
situation without being consciously aware of doing so, a situation
from which he could not get out? Think for a moment about the
boy whose alcoholic father refused to let him in the house in the
evening, thus forcing him to go onto the streets with the result
that he became a member of a gang. Or think about the married

---

[5] Malinowski in his investigations of the Trobriander tribes found that where
there was a patriarch, war prevailed, while in those tribes where there was a matriarch,
peaceful relations with other tribes existed. The same condition exists in China.
The Chinese peasants live predominantly in a matriarchal society, their religion being
called "taoism," which means road-peace; they live in peace with each other. On the
other hand, the upper classes live in a marked patriarchal society, in which disagreements, fights, and wars are common.

man whose nagging wife made life so intolerable for him that he murdered her.

If we were to delve into the personality of those individuals who by mere apparent external circumstances were forced to go into crime, we would in an overwhelming number of cases find some inadequacy in the mental make-up. That a certain coincidence of situation and antisocial tendencies must exist to lead to crime is another proof that a specific criterion for the criminal cannot be given.

Psychiatrists and sociologists have too long dealt with the so-called "bad environment" which leads man into crime. One has forgotten to ask why and how such a man came to be in such surroundings. One has been inclined to say in a case of unemployment that the man had to steal or commit burglary in order to live. Even in view of the fact that unemployment, particularly when it lasts long, cannot fail to affect the moral power of resistance against temptations, one should ask why he came to be unemployed. It is a fact that a man with a good education who is trained in a special field is less likely to be unemployed than one with little or no education. It is a peculiar thing that the records of burglars, robbers, and other people who apparently commit crimes for gain reveal that their usual excuse was that they did not have any work and so had to steal. There must be a reason why the man in question did not get further education, and we could guess that this was either because he was not too interested in school or because he had no opportunity to continue it. On the other hand, many poor boys and girls have worked themselves up against tremendous obstacles. This proves that persons with valuable personal traits will rarely yield to criminalistic tendencies.

True, it should be borne in mind that deteriorated neighborhoods, housing congestion, unemployment, malnutrition, and other factors of an economic nature play an important part in crime. One cannot possibly be unaware of the fact that much of crime stems from economic circumstances, but those economic circumstances are not economic as such, but have root in the particular organization of our society. That homes are dissolved and that the children's education is neglected may not be due so much to economic circumstances as to other factors, such as drunkenness or disharmony between the parents. In the latter case one will ask: Did disharmony between them originate from the mental make-up which caused the broken home and the neglecting of the children?

A decrease of resistance against criminalistic tendencies may be due to a primary or secondary insufficiency of the psychical activity, although we do not at present know how much the ego, superego, and id enter into this operation. Such an inadequacy of psychical activity may be seen in a number of mental diseases where blocking or repression is present, or in organic diseases, such as diabetes, chronic nephritis, intoxication by alcohol or morphine, encephalitis, and general paresis. When decreased psychical activity is present, social responsibility is lowered to such an extent that the person yields to his criminalistic tendencies. (For further discussion see Chapter III.)

It appears then that it may not be the situation in itself which leads a man to commit a crime but rather an accumulation of circumstances which in due course may cause different behavior. The outcome may be determined by a difference in the personality structure or by the degree of trauma the person experiences. It is obvious that the stronger the inclination is towards crime the weaker the precipitating events need be to elicit it; the less the criminal tendencies, the greater the precipitating events which would be necessary to call it forth.

Though aggressiveness hides inner weakness, still it may give rise to insecurity and feelings of inferiority. Such emotional factors combined with the aim of gain may instigate criminal behavior. However, if only one of those factors is present, it will not be sufficient to produce antisocial conduct.

It is basically an instability of the three factors—criminalistic tendencies, mental resistance, and situation—that leads man into crime. It is an alteration in the balance between what society demands and what the person is able to achieve. This makes it appear that criminality may be caused not only when a person has lived under favorable circumstances and goes into unfavorable conditions, but also when he has lived under poor circumstances and goes into favorable ones. In the latter case a person's committing a crime may be due to a maladjustment to his new situation; his personality may not be able to meet the demands which the new situation creates. In this connection, we might mention the findings in the examination of 9,958 consecutive prisoners who were seen at the Psychiatric Clinic of the Court of General Sessions in New York City.[6] These investigators found that those persons supposed to be normal included a number of types of unbalanced personalities. It would be logical to conclude from this that these criminals represent a personality problem.

Such an unbalance of the personality equilibrium is caused by an intricate interplay among emotional factors, precipitating events, and experiences. It may be assumed that before criminal tendencies arise in the mind certain ideas, thoughts, or fantasies about criminal acts may have taken place. However, a wide difference exists between the criminal fantasies and actual perpetration of a crime. Criminal fantasies are present in all people, perhaps most frequently in those suffering from a neurosis. In uncovering such fantasies, one would be inclined to think that one would discover the root of the criminal act, and thus ascertain the potential criminal. However, fantasies of crime may not actually lead to crime, although they often do so. In this connection, it is not farfetched to compare the criminalistic fantasies of perversions and their actual performance. A homosexual person, for instance, may indulge in fantasies but not actually transform them into acts; or a neurotic with homosexual tendencies may indulge in his fantasy and actually practice it. We see here that in the one case the person's fantasy life has not affected his conduct.

In these processes a certain intermingling between what Freud called the pleasure and reality principle occurs. This mechanism can be seen clearly in a simple situation. The little child's psychological processes are led by the pleasure principle, that is, by the tendency to receive immediate gratification and to avoid pain, while the adult must learn to endure the situation for the time being and to postpone certain satisfactions if he is to secure more important gratifications. Although the adult cannot transform his fantasies, they will live in his mind.

Thus, criminalistic fantasies may be assumed to be preoccupational ideas in which the criminal acts out his deed in detail. It has

6 W. Bromberg and C. B. Thompson, "The Relation of Psychosis, Mental Defect and Personality Types to Crime," *Journal of Criminal Law and Criminology,* XXVIII (1937), 70–89.

been asserted that this detailed elaborating of a criminal act hampers the actual performance of it. It is therefore doubtful whether psychological mechanisms which produce criminal fantasies are the same as those which produce the criminal act. This might indicate that crime would not be the same as a neurosis.

However, there is another point of comparison between neurosis and crime, and that is the sense of guilt. A feeling of guilt is an outstanding feature seen in a compulsory-obsessional neurosis, anxiety hysteria, and in schizophrenia or other types of psychosis. Some crimes are motivated not by the wish for profit but by an unconscious need to be punished.[7] In this case one would expect to find the same psychological mechanisms behind the performance of a crime as behind a neurosis or a psychosis. There is clinical support for the belief that self-punishment should be thought of as a cause of crime.

I am at times inclined to believe that this need of suffering or the unconscious need to be punished is much more prevalent than is thought. Yes, I am even disposed to think that many times this need to be punished seems to take place on a quite conscious level as seen in chronic offenders of certain types.

Some time ago I saw a case that concerned three individuals from three different cultural levels. The first one was from an old family, many of whose members had attained to important positions; the second was from the middle class; and the third, a woman, was from a low class. The first man, who was a lawyer, often drank heavily, and during one of his sprees became acquainted with the second man. A friendly relationship grew up between them, which included homosexual practices. This lawyer had been married for some time and his friend was on good terms with his wife. One night after the lawyer had been drinking, he asked his wife to have sexual intercourse with his friend while he was to be a spectator. She refused, but he forced her down on the bed, and his friend had intercourse with her while he looked on. The next day the wife reported the action to the police, and both men were arrested.

Details must be left out here. It should only be mentioned that in the interviews I had with the first man, he regretted, repented, and deplored his actions, wept and cried over his behavior. He gave

[7] Ives Hendrick, *Facts and Theories of Psychoanalysis*, p. 72.

a clue to his misbehavior himself by saying: "If I had been sentenced for fifty years, I could not have been more punished. I have punished myself."

It must be stressed that there are criminals who do not perpetrate crimes for this reason, for instance, certain types of murderers. On the other side it has been claimed that many times when a person commits a crime, he betrays himself afterwards by unconsciously leaving a clue for his detection. In studying this mechanism, it must be borne in mind that when a criminal has committed a crime two opposite inner forces struggle within him. One tries to get rid of all thoughts of the crime while the other proclaims the deed. This latter tendency is due to the fact that the criminal has an unconscious wish for punishment arising from unresolved strong unconscious feelings of guilt. Such wishes for punishment are expressed in all the faulty acts which the culprit performs after the actual crime.

This wish is one of the reasons why the criminal seeks to revisit the place where he committed the crime, an event that is most often seen in crimes where sexual elements are involved, such as in kleptomania, arson, and certain types of homicide. The returning of the culprit to the scene of his crime is a psychological mechanism which has not yet been sufficiently examined. Apparently a subconscious need for detection is present.[8]

Because of this deep-seated unconscious wish for punishment, the oft-mentioned perfect crime does not exist. A skillful perpetrator may be caught through a trivial piece of evidence because he involuntarily left this trace at the scene of the crime so that he might be apprehended. The fact that he might not be detected may be due more to external circumstances than to his lack of a nagging sense of guilt.

We have been hearing that the criminal lives in the underworld. It is now time that we recognize the criminal's mental underworld. All men live more or less in a mental underworld; our behavior is partly directed by unconscious motives. Since antisocial acts are partly conscious and partly unconscious, and since some criminal acts are primarily directed against society while others are primarily

[8] See p. 154 for a discussion of such a mechanism as described by Dostoyevsky in *Crime and Punishment*

an expression of an inner reaction or conflict, we may classify offenders into manifest, or into symptomatic or reactive ones.

To the first class belong those persons who perpetrate criminal acts which are primarily directed against society. The reactive or symptomatic offenders include those whose acts are primarily related to an inner conflict, and their acts against society are crimes only because certain social rules are violated. Typical of this group are kleptomaniacs, pyromaniacs, murderers (the latter only in some instances), and sexual offenders like exhibitionists, fetishists, and homosexuals. The grouping corresponds to that of Lindesmith and Dunham who from another point of view believe that criminals range from the social to the individual type.[9] It must be added that transitions between these two groups may occur.

What has to be emphasized is that crime must be regarded largely as symptoms in a personality with mental deviations or abnormalities. This being so, the attitude of society in inflicting punishment on the culprit must decisively alter.

[9] The prototype of the social criminal is the professional thief, who is the purest type, while the prototype of the individual criminal is the psychotic person. A discussion of the purest type is not possible here, but it is reasonable to think that the purest is the habitual criminal in the sociological group, while in the individual group it is rather doubtful whether the psychotic type is the purest. It may very well be that it could be the neurotic. A. R. Lindesmith and H. W. Dunham, "Some Principles of Criminal Typology," *Social Forces*, XIX (March, 1941), 307-14.

III

HEREDITY AND ENVIRONMENT AS CAUSES OF CRIME

HUMAN mentality is an elusive quality. Students of human nature may learn what a person will do under specified circumstances, and how and why he will react. But as science is lacking in knowledge of the normal make-up and since it certainly stumbles in probing the depths and recesses of the abnormal mind, our understanding and interpretation of antisocial actions is far from adequate.

This inadequacy is not the least called forth by the interplay among a number of factors, to a large extent unknown, which we can classify into: intrinsic factors—heredity; extrinsic factors—environment.

Let it be stressed that the problem of which has the greater influence in causing crime—heredity or environment—is an academic question. The author believes that ingrained human tendencies may be largely influenced by environmental factors. For the most part in the study of criminal activities it is surprising, as we will see later, how environmental influences may overshadow hereditary factors. This problem—the problem of the constitution—remains thus far an enigma.

The origin of crime as to hereditary or environmental elements may be so complicated that one hardly can say where the two types of factors belong. If a person born out of wedlock commits a crime, it is impossible to determine whether his being illegitimately born prompted his crime or whether he became a transgressor because nobody took adequate care of him. Further, it is a fairly well-established fact that people, generally speaking, with poor heredity form a poor environment while those having valuable traits create good surroundings. The human with a limited mental capacity or he who shuns work is unable to form a suitable home. Usually he raises many children in or out of wedlock. If they later become offenders we have no scientific method to measure the relative influence of their heredity and their environment.

We are justified in saying that nobody can say where heredity starts or environment ends.

In spite of the fact that some personality traits are established by the human germ plasm and therefore are to be considered as hereditary, while others are formed in the course of the life of the individual and therefore are to be regarded as environmental, biological research of today can theoretically not make such a division between hereditary and environmental influences. Practical purposes, however, make necessary a separation between the two, not only because of psychological reasons but also because of the social implications, of which the most important pertains to prevention of crime.

Biological science today maintains that heredity determines what a person can do, while environment decides what he does. This means that the individual inherits certain material that under certain conditions will produce a particular characteristic. This assumption leads us to think that certain inherited material establishes a predisposition within which frame environmental influences may work. It may also give support to our belief as to why persons to some extent select their crime. Where the soil is prepared by poor traits, such as emotional instability, strong or even abnormal drives, and more or less asocial feelings, environmental influences may easily elicit antisocial activities. This means that a number of men then are born to crime, that is their fate when certain constellations are fulfilled.

Because of the very nature of the personality some characteristics are determined by heredity, others by environment, others again by both. To the first types belong the human physique, such as height, weight, eye color. But even height and weight may be influenced by the environment, by nutrition and climate, for instance.

To the group affected by both heredity and environment belongs intelligence. Persons with a limited mental capacity may be brought up to an average mental level, while unusually endowed personalities, if circumstances are unfavorable, may retrogress.

More important than human physique and intelligence, and more decisive as to the outcome of a person's drifting into antisocial activities are two properties which are particularly influenced by the environment. These are the goal and the emotional strivings of the personality. Since life in general and crime in particular is largely an expression of the person's adaptation to conditions, it is obvious that the goal of the person must be directed and altered by his surroundings. It is this goal-obtaining activity with which the person is intensively concerned. Although the goal is basically stimulated by hereditary drives (the drive of self-preservation or the erotic drive), nevertheless, the achievement of the aim is conditioned by sociological circumstances previously present or formed by the individual himself. In achieving the goal, the individual may be hampered, he may or may not reach it. This produces conflicts and frustrations which if sufficiently pronounced may result in some deviation from normal behavior or in abnormality.

Closely associated with this goal-achieving activity of the personality are his emotional drives, his fears, hates, and loves. Though these strivings are basically conditioned by constitutional elements, their outcome is determined by environmental influences.[1] For the reasons mentioned we cannot speak of hereditary or environmental traits, but of traits conditioned by them.

When regarding the hereditary and environmental traits together, one characteristic comes to the fore—a general instability of all elements involved. There is a profound difference in the different types of crime. This makes it a great error to investigate the causes of crime under one heading. Crime is not a phenomenon produced by one kind of cause, but consists of different factors, whose origins have to be examined per se.

In order to prove that criminalistic tendencies were inherited great emphasis was placed upon the studies of families with these traits. Among such studies should be mentioned that of the European descendants of Ada Jurke and that of the Chrétien family, and in this country, the investigations of the tribe of Ishmael in 1888 by Oscar McCulloch, the Smoky Pilgrims by Frank W. Blackmar in 1897,[2] "The Jukes" by Richard L. Dugdale in 1877,[3] "The Kallikaks," in 1912 by Henry H. Goddard. All these studies claimed

---

[1] J. F. Brown, *Psychology and the Social Order*, p. 273.
[2] Oscar McCulloch, "The Tribe of Ishmael," *Proceedings of the National Conference of Charities and Correction*, 1888, pp. 154–59; Frank W. Blackmar, "The Smoky Pilgrims," *American Journal of Sociology*, Jan., 1897, pp. 485–500.
[3] Richard L. Dugdale, *The Jukes*.

that crime was due to hereditary traits, a finding which in view of our present knowledge is doubtful.

After investigating the family background of 1,000 juvenile offenders, Healy and Spaulding denied any evidence of a direct inheritance of antisocial inclinations. However, they asserted having found evidence of underlying existence of criminalistic tendencies through certain hereditary factors like feeble-mindedness and epilepsy.[4] In another study Healy and Bronner found that 46.8 per cent of the families of 675 young recidivists did not show delinquency, alcoholism, or mental abnormalcy. Of the remaining families 60 per cent were alcoholics, 45 per cent showed delinquent behavior, while 31 per cent were mentally abnormal. Healy and Bronner found that in 3,000 cases of delinquents (with families having more than one child) only 62 per cent had a delinquent child, while in only 4.4 per cent of the cases were all children delinquent.[5] In their latest investigation only 20 per cent of the parents in 133 delinquent families had a court record.[6] They concluded that there was no proof that criminalistic inheritance existed.[7] From my own experience I cite three cases where antisocial behavior was present among many members of the family.

X was born in 1905, the second of eight children. The father and his brother were chronic alcoholics and had been imprisoned several times. The patient's grandfather had been incarcerated for a sexual offense. His mother had been convicted of prostitution. His father's sister was committed to an institution for the insane, and his mother's brother was serving a life sentence.

X was brought up in a city slum and was supported by the community. His father was out of work and the whole family had only a two-room apartment. When the boy was eight years old he was sent to a school for the feeble-minded. At eighteen he was charged with theft, and having been on parole for a year for a similar offense, he was sentenced to one year's imprisonment. Later he was imprisoned for a robbery.

[4] E. R. Spaulding and William Healy, "Inheritance as a Factor in Criminality," *Bulletin of the American Academy of Medicine*, XV (Feb., 1914), 4–27.
[5] William Healy and A. F. Bronner, *Delinquents and Criminals, Their Making and Unmaking*, p. 103.
[6] William Healy and A. F. Bronner, *New Light on Delinquency and Its Treatment*, p. 28.
[7] *Ibid.*, p. 97.

Reviewing this case we find alcoholism, criminality, and insanity in the immediate family. The environment was so poor that one is not surprised that the boy turned out as he did.

Y was born in 1907. He was the first of eight children. The father was feeble-minded and died when the boy was ten years old. The mother was a chronic alcoholic. The father's brother was charged with robbery and murder and was declared insane. A third brother was an alcoholic. The sister of the patient was insane. When the patient was twelve years old he was charged with theft and was put under the jurisdiction of a private agency, from which he escaped. Later he became involved in robbery and murder and was finally given a long sentence and committed suicide in prison.

Z, a son of divorced parents, was put into a foster home where his education was neglected. His father was insane. His mother was an alcoholic. Two brothers were sentenced several times and imprisoned. Z himself was involved in theft and larceny when he was sixteen years old, having previously been charged with indecent behavior towards his female school teacher. When he was twenty he was charged with murder but was released because of lack of evidence. Later he became involved in a robbery for which he was given a long sentence.

These cases may show that there is a considerable tendency towards crime in the families, but one cannot say that there is an inheritance of this antisocial activity because the same heredity has produced an environment that has the potentiality to elicit criminalistic inclinations. One would be apt to say that where crime exists in several members of the family in several generations, the same criminogenic factors are present in the family, giving it a pattern of antisocial behavior.

The most significant evidence of hereditary influence was assumed established by Lange's investigations of twins.[8] As is known, human twins are of two types, identical (monozygotic) and fraternal (dizygotic). The former are two individuals who are developed from the same ovum and therefore identical, while the latter are developed from different ova and for this reason are no more similar than ordinary brothers. Lange secured the Bavarian prison records of 13 identical and 18 fraternal twins. Of the 13 sets

[8] Johannes Lange, *Crime and Destiny*, p. 41.

of identical twins, 10 had a criminal record for each twin, while the remaining three had one twin criminal and one noncriminal. Of the 18 fraternal twins, three were found to have a criminal record for each twin, and 15 had one twin criminal and one noncriminal. The results showed, according to Lange, that criminalistic tendencies were inherited. Investigations made by Stumpfl, Legars, and Kranz seemed to approve Lange's findings, but lately doubt has been raised as to the value of his investigations. One may doubt, first, whether grown-up twins can be determined exactly either as monozygotic or dizygotic, and second, whether Lange succeeded in reducing environmental influences; and third, it is a question whether there were criminalistic tendencies in all cases of the identical twins.

In 1934 Rosanoff [9] investigated 1,008 pairs of twins. He found that in 97 pairs one member was criminal, in 107 pairs one was a juvenile delinquent, and in 136 pairs one member showed behavior problems. He concluded that hereditary elements played an important role in establishing criminal behavior. Newman, Freeman, and Holzinger [10] have pointed out that identical twins, as compared with fraternal twins, are more like each other in physical traits than in personality traits. Thus, the twin investigations are not at all conclusive evidence that criminal tendencies are inherited.

We have, in Chapter I, pointed out the efforts of Lombroso's school to establish a correlation between the criminal and his physical make-up and we saw the shortcomings of such a theory. Kretschmer attempted to make a similar correlation between the mentally sick man and his body build, and established three types, the athletic, the asthenic, and the pyknic. Aschaffenburg, Kinberg, and others tried to apply Kretschmer's theory to types of criminals and concluded that the serious chronic criminals were largely of an athletic-schizothymic body build, while those with a better prognosis belonged to the pyknic-cyclothymic group.[11]

Painstaking work was done along these lines, but as would be expected, body build and its assumed relation to the criminal char-

[9] A. J. Rosanoff, L. M. Handy, and I. Rosanoff, "Criminality and Delinquency in Twins," *Journal of Criminal Law and Criminology*, Jan.–Feb., 1934, 925.
[10] H. H. Newman, F. N. Freeman, and K. J. Holzinger, *Twins: A Study of Heredity and Environment*, p. 352.
[11] Ernest Kretschmer, *Physique and Character*, pp. 24–35, 208–9.

acter could not furnish evidence for explaining the difference between criminal and noncriminal behavior. Lately there has been found a considerable discrepancy between the person's make-up and the objective measurements. In this country Frank and Cleland examined over 500 inmates of the New Jersey Reformatory at Rahway and found that there was no relation between the physical make-up and the type of crime.[12]

One of the most complete studies correlating the criminal with his physique was made by Hooton, who examined 13,873 American criminals and 3,203 noncriminals. He claimed that different types of offenses had their counterpart in different physical make-ups. Hooton revealed that there were differences in physical and morphological traits between criminals and non-criminals. He also discovered that criminals were inferior to noncriminals in nearly all of their body measurements,[13] an inferiority which he tentatively interpreted as due to heredity.[14] He deduces that it was from the physically inferior elements of the people that the native-born American criminal originated, concluding that criminality is the impact of bad environment on "low-grade" human organisms.[15]

Hooton has without doubt put much thought and effort into his extensive investigations. Unfortunately, the small number of non-criminals examined, only 3,203 in comparison with the 13,873 criminals, is a weak point in the study. One may also doubt whether the small deviations from the average person are really a basis for physical inferiority as Hooton claims. Perhaps worse is the fact that he concludes that this questionable biological inferiority is of a hereditary nature. From this assumption he goes on to claim that the weakest of the inferior yield to bad environment, thereby becoming criminals,[16] a claim which is far from true.

With regard to the physical make-up it has been asserted that there was a relation between endocrine dysfunction and criminality. Except for certain sexual offenses, such as overt homosexuality, where it cannot be denied that an imbalance of the sexual hormones may exist, it is at present hard to establish a relation between crim-

[12] Benjamin Frank and P. S. Cleland, "The Physical Capacity of the Young Adult Offender," *Journal of Criminal Law and Criminology*, XXVI (1936–37), 586.
[13] E. A. Hooton, *The American Criminal*, I, 229.
[14] *Ibid.*, I, 308.   [15] *Ibid.*, I, 304–9.   [16] *Ibid.*, I, 92.

inal behavior and the function of the endocrinal glands.[17] (See Chapter VI.) More important seems to be a possible connection between psychosomatic disorder and the origination of crime, a problem to which little attention has been paid.

However, some physiological states tend to expose the individual to crime; they therefore have a bearing on its perpetration. As the child approaches puberty, when sexual conflicts may prompt anti-social tendencies, he may be more exposed to the risk of committing crime than when he is mature. It is well known that most crimes are committed by young people. As a matter of fact the problem of crime is the problem of youth. It is at this period that the young must recognize and accept the influence of social factors.

TABLE 1. DISTRIBUTION OF ARRESTS BY AGE GROUPS IN 1941 [a]

Age Group	All Offenses [b]	Criminal Homicide	Robbery	Burglary	Larceny	Auto Theft
Under 21	17.6	13.0	33.0	46.6	33.3	57.6
21–29	29.2	34.8	41.7	29.8	30.0	29.9
30–39	25.9	27.6	18.2	15.1	20.0	8.8
40–49	16.7	15.0	5.7	6.0	10.8	2.8
50 and over	10.4	9.4	1.3	2.4	5.7	.8
Unknown	.2	.2	.1	.1	.2	.1
Total	100.0	100.0	100.0	100.0	100.0	100.0

a Federal Bureau of Investigation, *Uniform Crime Reports*, XII (1941), No. 4, 204.
b Not limited to specific crimes listed in the table.

The figures in Table 1 indicate that youth committed a large portion of the total offenses against property—robbery, burglary, larceny, and auto thefts. Most frequently arrested were those nineteen years of age, while those of eighteen were second. Disorderly conduct and drunkenness are offenses which continue into the older age periods. As it will be noted old age is not an age of crime; the only prevalent type is sex offenses.

If crime varies with age it also varies with sex. In 1941 only 9.2 per cent of the total arrested were women. It is easily understood that women, because of their body build, are not able to commit the more active crimes as well as men do. Another reason for the prevalence of the male criminal is his greater exposure to risk than the female. It should be noted that women rarely commit crimes in

17 A. W. Rowe, "A Possible Endocrine Factor in Behavior Problems of the Young," *American Journal of Orthopsychiatry*, I (1931), 451–75.

gangs as is often the case with men. Also, their crimes seem to be more directed against persons than against property, according to investigations made by Frank J. Curran [18] and others.

It has been asserted that there is a certain connection between physical diseases and criminalistic inclinations. As will be mentioned later (see Chapter VIII), a physical disease or a deformed body may affect a person's behavior and produce criminalistic tendencies. In an investigation Cyril Burt [19] found that 70 per cent of his delinquents suffered from bodily weakness or ill health, the conditions being one and a quarter times as prevalent among them as among nondelinquent children in the same community. He concluded that in 10 per cent of the boy's cases and in about 7 per cent of the girl's cases that their physical conditions were the main reason for the children's criminal behavior.

The extent to which a bodily disease may change the mind of a boy and elicit antisocial activity has not been sufficiently evaluated. To a certain degree such a result would not be due to the boy's disease but more to the effect of the surroundings. If he suffers from a disease which is of some significance to the surroundings, such as tuberculosis, making him more or less an invalid, he gradually receives the impression of being different from the environment, which may give rise to feelings of inferiority.

In this connection I cite here the case of a boy who had embezzled funds in an office.

The boy, I shall call him Eric, had an unhappy upbringing. His father died shortly after he was born, and his mother succumbed to tuberculosis when he was five years old. Fortunately for him he was in good economic standing, having inherited money from his parents. He was first reared in his aunt's family and went to a public school. When the boy was six years old he had an accident which made him a hunchback, the butt of other boys' teasing. He was overindulged and overprotected by his aunt. She let him have his own way in almost all his doings. Eric behaved rather well, was apparently grateful for what this home gave him, and made rapid progress in school. Becoming one of the best in his class, he was considered as a candidate for an academic career. However, the boy

18 "Specific Trends in Criminality of Women," *Journal of Criminal Psychopathology,* III (April, 1942), No. 4, 623.
19 *The Young Delinquent,* p. 249.

protested because he wanted to be a craftsman. But since his deformity prevented his doing this type of work he finally relented.

When he was ten years old his aunt discovered that his behavior had become queer. She did not know the reason for it but she thought that it was due to his comrades. In the course of time Eric became demanding; he wanted a steady increase of his weekly allowance which he gave to his pals in school. One summer he stole some jewelry from a home he visited. The butler was suspected and dismissed. Later it was discovered that Eric had taken the jewelry, but, defending his act, he argued that the butler had called him a hunchback. As he grew older he had to buy his way with his comrades and gave them money, candy, and the like. However, he could not avoid hearing them deride him.

When he was fourteen he was sent to a sanatorium in the mountains. After a short while he was transferred to a school in this mountainous region but his schoolmates, according to his explanation, behaved badly towards him and treated him as an inferior. At this time he decided to take up the fight against the boys and this he did in a cynical manner. He stole things from one boy and put them into the briefcase of another, giving the impression that the latter had taken it. On another occasion he stole material from the classroom and destroyed it by painting it over with ink. This caused so much upheaval that an investigation was conducted and Eric was caught. After half a year's stay in the school he received employment from the office where he later committed the embezzlement.

Eric's aunt was at this time greatly concerned about the boy's behavior and consulted a psychiatrist. In the examination Eric was defiant, argumentative, and showed great resistance, repeatedly saying that he had not wanted to come, that he could solve his own problems. He admitted that he had been isolated and lonely, which at times made him depressed. In later sessions he confessed that he wished to have friends but nobody wanted him because of his deformity. After having recovered from his depression he decided to treat people as he himself was treated. Eventually Eric discontinued his visits to the psychiatrist. Later he criminally attacked a girl, almost choking her to death. Last heard of he was in a penitentiary serving a long sentence for assault and robbery.

This case shows that even in good surroundings a diseased body may cause a change of mental attitude and so elicit criminal inclinations, but, as pointed out before, it is largely a question of the effect of the fight against the surroundings. This fight can manifest itself in two ways, either the invalid person has to pay for his deformity by bribery or the bodily defect may lead to isolation and loneliness calling forth thoughts of depression, defiance, and even leading to suicide. Many of the underlying factors here are psychosomatic ones, the mechanisms involved taking place on a conscious or unconscious level.

It will be recalled that Goring asserted that a subnormal intelligence was more prevalent among the English convicts than among the civilian population. For this reason he concluded that mental deficiency was a cause of crime.[20] The first extensive study in this country regarding the relation between criminal behavior and mental deficiency was made by Carl Murchison, who was unable to confirm Goring's findings. In his comparison between prisoners and soldiers he found that the first made the better score.[21] In 1928 Sutherland investigated 350 criminals and said that about 20 per cent were feeble-minded. Tulchin in an Illinois survey covering over 10,000 men and 153 women in prison concluded that they made a better score on the Army intelligence tests than the soldiers.[22] Bromberg and Thompson examined 9,958 prisoners at the Court of General Sessions in New York City and found that about 2.4 per cent were mentally deficient.[23]

Although there does not seem to be a marked connection between intelligence and crime, it must be emphasized that mental deficiency and low-grade intelligence may have a bearing upon criminal activities. On the other hand there are many criminals with superior intelligence. As a matter of fact one of the most disturbing experiences I have encountered in my work is that they have in so many cases such a high intelligence that one would think, in view of the consequences, they would try avoiding crime. However, again and again one is confronted with the sad fact that those who would be expected to know better are as much inclined to commit

20 *The English Convict*, p. 263.
21 Carl Murchison, *Criminal Intelligence*, pp. 43, 72.
22 S. H. Tulchin, *Intelligence and Crime*.
23 C. B. Thompson, "Some New Aspects of the Psychiatric Approach to Crime," *Mental Hygiene*, XX (Oct., 1936), No. 4, 533.

crime as the average intelligent person. One group of offenders comprising a particularly great number of persons with high intelligence are psychopaths. Their criminal activities may not be due, however, to the dictates of their intelligence but to their emotional conflicts, which are so dominating that they overshadow their high intelligence. It has been asserted that the feeble-minded offender is not so aggressive as the one with average intelligence, rather he is timid and passive.[24] The fact that he is easily led and does not realize that he may be caught throws him into conflict with the law. But, in my experience some of the most aggressive sexual offenders were feeble-minded.

Students of environment have tried to prove a causative relationship between social factors and crime, assuming that the causative agent of crime lies in the surroundings. Such a view has not in the least been prompted by the variety, amount, and predominant types of crime. As the Federal Bureau of Investigation has pointed out, burglaries, larcenies, and auto thefts, for instance, are most frequently perpetrated in the states comprising the Pacific Division, while robberies, aggravated assaults, and murders are highest in the states of the East South Central Division.[25]

Such an irregular distribution of crime is not surprising, if we keep in mind that the frequency of crimes as well as other social manifestations like births, diseases, marriages, and divorces are influenced by a variety of factors—the economic status, age, sex, and race of the population, its attitude in general toward law, its extent in urban and rural areas.

Related to this irregular distribution are the variations of crime during certain periods of the year. In 1941, for instance, offenses against persons were highest in the third quarter, July having the highest amount of murder, August the largest number of aggravated assaults, and September the highest number of rapes.[26]

This irregular distribution of crime is also reflected in its varying prevalence in urban and rural areas. The elements involved are influenced by the attitude and social and cultural level of the individual.

[24] E. A. Doll, "Social Adjustment of the Mentally Subnormal," *Journal of Educational Research*, 1934, pp. 36–43.
[25] Federal Bureau of Investigation, *Uniform Crime Reports*, XIII (1941), No. 4, 174.
[26] *Ibid.*, p. 166.

TABLE 2. INCIDENCE OF CERTAIN CRIMES IN URBAN AND RURAL AREAS

OFFENSE	PERCENTAGE		OFFENSE	PERCENTAGE	
	Urban	Rural		Urban	Rural
Larceny	59.7	48.0	Robbery	3.1	3.5
Burglary	21.0	26.7	Aggravated assault	3.1	6.3
Auto theft	11.9	10.7	Rape	.6	2.3
			Murder	.3	1.3
			Manslaughter	.3	1.2

So-called "poor environment" cannot be considered a sufficient explanation for criminal behavior, because a number of law-abiding citizens have lived and grown up under unfavorable conditions. A poor environment can only be regarded as causative in so far as it is combined with a certain disposition in the individual making latent criminal tendencies manifest. The personality features have to be connected with certain conditions before a maladaptation which may lead into crime occurs. This means that the largest number of criminals could, under favorable conditions, have developed into normal persons.

To what part of life then might these favorable or unfavorable conditions belong which give life a certain pattern? If we say that crimes are found in certain areas of the great cities, one might think that it was an expression of present conditions. But since crime there tends to arise when certain constellations are fulfilled, one might also think that life, no matter how variable it may be, may contain a certain criminal pattern which in one way or another is related to people's way of living. This way of living, being an expression of their attitude toward life, we might call culture, bearing always in mind that culture expresses something fundamentally of the personality. To say that crime in this country is a product of American culture, as Taft has done,[27] seems to be a simplification of the problem, because one may ask what is culture in reality? Does not culture mean the smooth surface in contrast to the genuine nature, the very progress towards a better future producing a certain pattern of life which may simply be designated as habit? If one has traveled extensively, one can see the difference in the behavior of inhabitants not only in different nations but also in different parts of the same country. All these differences and peculiarities may be

27 D. R. Taft, *Criminology*, pp. 223–41.

called culture. But even if we say that culture reflects a certain pattern of life, nevertheless, culture designates an inner property of the individual or the country.

It has been asserted that American culture is materialistic and hence furnishes a soil for antisocial activities. This same statement might be said about other nations, Sweden, for example, but crime is infrequent there. American culture is considered materialistic because the country is rich and offers unusual opportunities not available other places, and this may lead people to obtain money by every means possible. Thus, money instead of right and justice becomes the standard so that extreme competition takes place in economic and social life as well. With this competition hostility and conflicts, conscious or unconscious, are bound to arise. Success for a few and failure for some follow, and the latter may be tempted to use illegal means to maintain or obtain the standard of living they desire. In such extreme competition the individual's interests are directed more toward his immediate aim than toward the benefit of society, giving rise to an impersonal relationship among the members of society. Many people refrain from perpetrating crime because they fear their fellow countrymen would disapprove of it. If they are lonesome, they lack mutual ties and the mutual fear of the law. As one finds group loyalty, so a gang loyalty also exists. Gang members consist of those men whose antisocial activities have been approved by their entire personality, by their ego and superego.

The broken home has been thought to be a reason for the impersonalization of American social life as well as a source in producing delinquency. Investigations have endeavored to show that the broken home was an extremely contributive factor to delinquency.[28] However, Shaw and McKay pointed out that it was not so much the broken home situation in itself which was associated with the origin of delinquency, but disunity and conflict in the family.[29] Weeks found that the frequency of the broken home among juve-

[28] Juvenile Court Statistics 1927 and Juvenile Court Statistics 1934, Washington, D.C.; Children's Bureau, U.S. Department of Labor, Bulletins No. 195 (1930), p. 9 and No. 235 (1937), pp. 9–25.
[29] C. R. Shaw and H. D. McKay, Social Factors in Juvenile Delinquency, pp. 276–77, 285.

nile offenders varied with the type of offense. This had also been stressed by Reckless.[30]

In reviewing these investigations it seems that the broken home tends to act more as a risk than as a cause in delinquent behavior. The lack of proper care combined with conflicts in the family places the members in greater danger, the broken home acting as a traumatic event. Within such a family one will find poor relationships causing a child to drift into antisocial activity as an escape from family conflict and disunity. Further such a home may often be a gathering place for alcoholics and antisocial individuals, all entering in the wake of such a predicament.

Thus it appears that the family is of extreme importance in the maintenance of normal behavior. It is difficult, however, to estimate its direct influence in prompting crime. Since crime is greatly due to an instability of the social and personal situation, it is not far-fetched to assume that a stable family life will tend to raise law-abiding citizens. If a delinquent child is found in a stable family it may very well be that he is reared during insecure circumstances which he himself has, directly or indirectly, nourished by his behavior.

Bad companionship has been found to be responsible not only for the rise of a criminal career but also for its continuation, as the Gluecks have shown.[31] They found that 95 per cent of men had bad associates before being sentenced while 69 per cent in the first and 63 per cent in the second five-year period after expiration of parole had them.[32] It is easy to understand that persons incarcerated for some time are exposed to the influence of bad associates, causing them to continue their crimes. Experience has shown that many a crime has been planned in prison. At present we do not know how detrimental an effect imprisoned offenders have upon each other. Neither do we know what kind of offenders are affected by their associates or who are insusceptible to them.

What type of children are susceptible to the detrimental effect of companions? Generally speaking, offenders may be supposed to be more tense, active, and gregarious than nonoffenders, which leads

[30] C. W. Reckless, *The Etiology of Delinquent and Criminal Behavior*, pp. 23–24.
[31] Sheldon and Eleanor T. Glueck, *Later Criminal Careers*, p. 75.
[32] *Ibid.*, p. 338.

them to greater exposure to criminal behavior. In this connection it is interesting to note that Shaw seems to have discovered that carriers of delinquency may convey a pattern of delinquency from one situation to another.[33]

Among the environmental influences which have been assumed to evoke crime is alcohol. The Gluecks found that 39.4 per cent of reformatory inmates had been using liquor to excess. Other investigations tend to show higher numbers. In an examination made by Nissen in Norway it was found that out of 259 thieves only 18.2 per cent were abstainers while about 82 per cent were chronic alcoholics or intoxicated when they committed their crimes.[34] Other examinations made by him showed that the large majority abused alcohol but only a minority were alcoholics. As will be seen in Chapters VI and VIII alcohol may not basically be considered as a cause of crime.

On reviewing these investigations of heredity and environment, one cannot feel satisfied that any of the groups have made decisive contributions in establishing the causes of crime. The adherents of the environmental theory have tried to prove that certain factors concern criminals more than noncriminals. However, as far as we have seen, they have not been able to avoid bringing in hereditary factors. This does not necessarily mean that their principal view is wrong. It may only mean that their approach to the problem is wrong. This also applies to those holding a brief for hereditary elements, the nature of which, as with environmental factors, has not been wholly understood.

The question now is: What type of individuals responds to criminalistic influences and what kind remain immune to them? One cannot fail to see that a certain selection takes place. We only can understand and trace this in terms of a combination of hereditary and environmental factors. Heredity plays the part of a condition, present or even indispensable in a large number of cases. And the same follows for the mechanism of environmental influences. Thus, both elements cannot possibly act without the aid of specific causes.[35] Such specific causes may be traumatic happenings in early

[33] C. R. Shaw and others, *Brothers in Crime*, pp. 109–26.
[34] Hartvig Nissen, *Alkohol og forbrydelse*, p. 12.
[35] The reader is referred to Freud's writings on heredity and the etiology of the neurosis. See his *Collected Papers*, I, 144.

life, including disturbances in the development of biological drives, or traumatic factors in everyday life, stress and strain, disappointment in love, and so on. That a man becomes delinquent while his identical twin brother is nondelinquent may perhaps be due not so much to heredity but to the circumstance that hereditary and specific causes may replace each other quantitatively.

We see that quantitative differences produce a variety of results. For this reason it is impossible to determine whether a criminal act in a given case is due to heredity or environment or both. It is therefore wrong to say that a crime was committed because of hereditary and environmental factors. Then how much of delinquency can be attributed to heredity and how much to environment?

In evaluating both elements, one must realize that an individual's behavior, including criminal behavior, is affected by his own dynamic appraisal of the total situation. This leads to our belief that crime, like mental disease, is a result of a failure to adjust to life or a compromise of it.

Just as we say that mental disease is not caused by some "illness" but called forth as a result of a failure to adjust to life or to adjust to a pattern of living, we must apply the same view to criminal behavior.

If we therefore try to find what kind of individuals react and do not react to antisocial influences, then we must go beyond the problem of a simple causation in crime in terms of heredity and environment and see how the personality as a total structure reacts to criminalistic tendencies.

IV

FUNCTIONAL VIEW OF THE OFFENDER

W E HAVE in Chapter II maintained that crime is a product of the interaction of the person's criminalistic tendencies, his mental resistance, and the particular situation confronting him. It is a question whether or not all human acts, be they social or antisocial, are not determined by a resultant where personality and situation combine to make the act a function of a set of factors. Crime then appears to be a problem of personality, situation, time, and of geography as well. In outlining such a functional view of the criminal we will put down some stakes in a rather unmapped field.

To obtain an adequate view of a phenomenon, regardless of its kind, we must examine it in its natural surroundings—in relation to its environment. If the subject is examined outside its environment, many of its properties will be lost during the investigation, or some properties may even be added. The consequence will be an oblique picture of the examined subject.

Nowhere does this hold more true than in the exploration of crime. The fundamental concept has gradually come to the fore that the human is not an isolated being, no matter how great an individualist he is, but is connected with his environment and has to be understood on the basis of his personality and the ideas he has created in the past or present. In the new concept the individual is not an unchangeable unit, but has to be seen in relation to other persons. The human is not only a center of action, but also a center of reaction, both manifestations intimately connected with his own field.[1] From the center of action impulses run to the periphery which in turn submits impulses back to the center of reaction. An incessant reciprocal interplay takes place, calling forth an eternal contact. The center creates a unit with the surroundings. Thus the

[1] F. Heinemann, *Neue Wege der Philosophie*, p. 283. About the functional method see also K. Mannheim, *Mensch und Gesellschaft im Zeitalter des Umbaus.*

human forms a functional relation with the environment and the environment acts in a functional relation to the human.

The individual is to a large extent tied to his own field. The term field means something other than environment; it means, and this shall be stressed, a dynamic property.

In the same way that there exists no isolated human, there does not exist an isolated mind. The consistent contact the individual has with his field makes it unlikely that there is a person who lives without his field.[2] From this viewpoint many of the psychological properties of the human mind are, so to speak, effects of the field. They can be only understood in the same way as, for instance, Buddhism can be understood from a cultural-psychological viewpoint as a functional effect of the Indian nature.

The individual, being in a socio-psycho-biological field, is influenced by his own rating of the situation. He imagines a picture of the situation and arrives at an actual practical understanding of it. His practical comprehension of the situation and the integrative task combined with it one may term as the psychological field.[3]

For the offender the same situation prevails. If he has an adequate realization of the circumstances, his act is directed according to his psychological equipment and the total situation. Even if we say that the mind is behind the act, so many actions and reactions on the part of the perpetrator have taken place that in a functional sense he forms a unit with the environment. He is consciously or unconsciously bound to his surroundings in spite of being affected by his own estimate of the circumstances during which he acts. If a criminal pattern is present in his environment, and the exposure is strong enough, it may be assumed that it will affect his acts. This may take place without the perpetrator's consciously knowing it, so intermingled may his social field be with that of his personality structure.

This may be surmised from many types of cases, of which I cite two. The first case involved a holdup by several boys of a couple in a parked car. They beat and robbed the man, tied him with the slacks they had removed from the girl, whereupon three of them

2 Bronislaw Malinowski, *The Life of Savages in North-Western Melanesia*, p. 29.
3 T. M. French, "Some Psychoanalytic Applications of the Psychological Field Concept," *Psychoanalytic Quarterly*, XII (1942), No. 1, 17–32.

raped her. They then departed for another city, were arrested a few days later, and were subsequently sentenced to long-term imprisonment.

In the examination one of the boys told the following story: "I was brought up in the same neighborhood as the other boys. Two of them were my classmates and the third one I had known for about four years. We used to meet in the street and talk about all that was going on in town. A month before we robbed the couple we started to talk about robberies. I did not think there was anything wrong with it. At this time I was going to school but I lost interest in it and started staying out late at night. I did not listen to what my parents told me. The boys spoke to me about the plot and I agreed. During the holdup I did not know that the others had had intercourse with the girl. They told me I might have it too. She was on the ground, nude. Afterwards I felt it was a lousy thing to do but it was too late to think about it." Later in the examination he said that he had gone to church every Sunday up to six months before the crime.

This boy appeared to be suggestible, but had a good insight into his crime, which he now repented deeply. It seems that he was drawn into the crime without making any resistance mainly because a criminal pattern was present in the attitude of his pals.

Another boy participating in the same crime related: "We talked about a robbery and got together. I made a black jack and then the others drove to the road. In my hand I had a toy pistol. Another fellow struck the man over the head and tied him. Someone then asked me to have intercourse and I was the first on top of her." In the interview the boy was on the defensive and asserted that the others had as much to do with the crime as he had. When it was brought out that they blamed him for having struck the man and raped the girl first, he denied it.

One receives the impression that this boy was a kind of leader. The robbery only was planned, however. The rape, for which they received the greatest punishment, seemed to have more or less a suggestive character. Perhaps individually they would not have raped the girl, but being together under the influence of each other, a kind of a suggestive effect possessed them, the result of a criminalistic attitude, and the rape took place.

A third boy taking part in the same crime said: "I lay down with the girl because I saw the others do it. Really I did not want to have intercourse with her, but since the others told me to do it I did so and the girl did not resist. I did not want to do this because it was our intention only to rob and not to rape."

From his part in the crime he appeared to be an impulsive boy who had not before participated in any antisocial activity. At the close of the interview he added: "I did not know what had happened. I saw the others do it and I did the same thing."

It should be added that all these boys lived in the same area of the town where a delinquent tendency prevailed and that a criminal pattern was present in some of the boys' families.

A similar mechanism is evident in the second case. A group of boys in their teens robbed and killed a girl after one of them had had intercourse with her. They were all from the same neighborhood, some of them having lived on the border of a criminal life. Their intentions were apparently to rob the girl because they knew she had money. They tried to blame each other for the murder, but it appeared that a criminalistic pattern was present to a higher or lesser degree in all of them.

These two cases show that a delinquent pattern was predominant, but this could only have happened through the individual.

Have we now an explanation as to how criminal pattern in the environment, such as bad companionship and criminal persons in a broken home, goes hand in hand with or across the development of the personality? This problem is a crucial one because it touches our principal view of the criminal and his antisocial activities, called forth by a combination of personality and situational factors in which the individual himself figures as a function of these variables.

In trying to understand this mechanism we must first recall that criminalistic inclinations are harbored in every human. The normal human is able to control, at least within the extent of the law, his criminal tendencies and to direct them into socially approved channels, and this differentiates him from the criminal. He is also able to rate the situation accordingly while the offender arrives at a wrong conclusion. The great variety of responses to different situations is first due to the variation in quantity and traits of personality. Since each individual manifests an explicit pattern, a pattern which depends upon the outcome of how these personality features are connected, a personality is not the sum total of all these features, but the manner in which they are combined. It is this manifest pattern which renders the individual his characteristic. This being so, one may assume a close relationship between the individual's mind and his act.

Is there the same connection between a man and his act as there is between a tree and its fruit? The relationship between a personality and its act is most easily recognized in the case of a great thinker or a great artist where the product clearly reflects the personal traits of the author.[4] In persons not dedicated to an expressive art, however, it is more difficult to ascertain the connection. This difficulty is especially notable in the criminal because part of the personality usually repudiates and disowns the criminal act, not only consciously, but unconsciously. Besides, as acts in general are influenced by a general mental attitude acquired during the development of the individual, so is it with antisocial activities. The criminal pattern is seen in, so to speak, pure culture in those persons whose crimes, profit murders, for example, are approved by their whole personality.

In passing let it be said that psychoanalysis has made an important contribution in bringing to light much of the motivation in criminal behavior. It must be added that this exploration of how crime is initiated will have to include the psychosomatic aspects if a proper evaluation is to be reached. Since the human may be considered as a psycho-bio-functional organism, there is a large group of offenders whom I would class as psychosomatic.

This psychosomatic group, which has been widely overlooked, particularly in its psychological implications, embraces all kinds of physical disturbances which interfere with the normal life of the individual. Since a situation may expose an individual as a unit in physical, chemical, and psychological aspects, he may respond to his surroundings with an antisocial act, while another individual, similarly exposed, may respond with a peptic ulcer, hypertension, migraine, or an epileptic fit.

I will give a brief synopsis of some outstanding cases where bodily

4 W. Lange-Eichbaum, *Genie-Irrsinn-und Ruhm*, p. 87.

disorders encroached upon the normal development of the persons. The first one concerns a boy who had lost his eyesight in one eye as a result of a head injury. His education was retarded. He became sullen and uncooperative in school, became timid and insecure in his behavior, which resulted in several types of offenses which could beyond doubt be related to his physical disorder. Another boy suffered from stammering and poor eyesight. Both factors affected his personal relationships, made him apparently an outsider to society, causing antisocial activities. Another individual had a congenital clubfoot which considerably hampered his normal development. He tried to compensate for his hampered development by drinking, attempting to put himself in a state where he could have more courage and become more aggressive. The result was a series of crimes.

Another individual born with a clubfoot had to wear a cast until he was ten years old, after which he used an iron brace. The result was that he was teased by other boys in school. That clubfoot called forth a great deal of inferiority feelings which made him a misfit. He told me frankly that when his mother sent him to school he would hide in the woods. He became very sensitive, felt unhappy, and stayed away from school, so that eventually he fell behind. It seems that this clubfoot acted as an instrument which forced him in a direction characterized by antisocial activities. Although at the time of the offense he was earning sixty dollars a week, and thus had no reason to steal, he committed a robbery.

Finally, there is the case of a young man who was unusually tall; he was six feet six and it appeared that his height had caused him embarrassment, made him somewhat introverted, and caused him difficulty in making friends. Besides feelings of inferiority, it had probably given him an antagonistic feeling toward society, which he expressed by saying that he could not trust people.

We cannot conclude this subject dealing with offenders of this type without mentioning the physiological changes that take place in men and women at the age of forty or fifty years. There are surprisingly large numbers of offenders who start their criminal careers late in life, a start which may be more or less related to physiological changes, which give rise to feelings of being handicapped and insecure, particularly within the sexual sphere.

Besides asking what kind of humans are receptive to criminal influences one must inquire why some yield to these influences. To answer the first question it is necessary to stop for a moment and see what creates the criminal impulse. Since crime may be considered as a result of a failure to adapt to life or as a compromise of it, we must stress that every part of the personality structure which is socially adapted is more or less a learned process. No human born into the world is socially adjusted as an individual. The baby starts his life in anger,[5] no matter how difficult it is for a devoted mother to swallow such a statement. Even if we add that this anger arises as a result of frustration, it still takes place from an early moment of life. Thus, the child is born into the world maladjusted, hating certain objects, and he continues to be socially maladjusted in the first years of life. This type of maladjustment is nothing else but criminality. Investigations made by Anna Freud and Dorothy T. Burlingame at the Hampstead Nurseries in London [6] confirm this:

> Children between the ages of 1 and 2, when put together in a play pen, will bite each other, pull each other's hair and rob each other's toys, without regard for the other child's unhappiness. They are passing through a stage of development where destruction and aggression play one of the leading parts. If we observe young children at play we notice that they will destroy their toys, pull off the arms and legs of their dolls or soldiers, puncture their balls, smash whatever is breakable, and will only mind the result because complete destruction of the toy blocks further play. The more their independence and strength are growing, the more they will have to be watched so as not to create too much damage, not to hurt each other or those weaker than themselves. . . .
> In a nursery destructive and aggressive impulses are still at work in children in a manner in which they only occur in grown-up life when they are let loose for the purposes of war.
> It is one of the recognized aims of education to deal with the aggressiveness of the child's nature, i. e., in the course of the first four or five years to change the child's own attitude towards these impulses in himself. The wish to hurt people, and later the wish to destroy objects, undergoes all sorts of changes.

This development is due to physiological and psychological happenings at this period. When the baby is born he starts to breathe,

[5] M. G. Blanton, "The Behavior of the Human Infant during the First Thirty Days of Life," *Psychological Review*, XXIV (Nov., 1917), No. 6, 456–83.
[6] A. Freud and D. T. Burlingame, *Report on Hampstead*, April, 1942.

eat, urinate, and defecate. But soon all these processes become regulated; he is fed at certain times, the feeding intervals being gradually prolonged until he is weaned; and he is taught to control his bladder and bowel movement.

All these processes are accompanied by emotional disturbances, producing reactions and conflicts, reactions which may be present later in the personality structure. Conflicts related to bladder or rectum functions may call forth aggressions, compulsions, extravagances, and other features. Character traits resulting from faulty sphincter training may to a large extent be considered responsible for many antisocial activities. The stubbornness seen in so many offenders may be related to the same traits. This anal characteristic, narcissistic in its appearance and expressing a great deal of independence, is the first drive the child must be taught to obey. He must keep clean, an order which in reality gives rise to the first rule of social behavior.[7]

The child's social adaptation to his environment starts after the Oedipus complex is overcome, at about six years, and ends at puberty. The Oedipus complex is explained as the child's hostility to the parent of the same sex, which initiates in the child tendencies to feel that the parent is a seducer or a seductress, as the case may be. In the course of time the individual may succeed in repressing his antisocial drives and he may be able to lead them into socially constructive channels and thus become a normal individual. If he is unable to do this, his antisocial drives persist and he becomes a criminal.

The criminal, then, acts as a child would—if the child were permitted to. One might very well imagine what would occur if a man acted out all his wishes, fantasies, and drives. He would behave explosively, feel omnipotent, never love. He would swallow ravenously or destroy rapidly what he saw and kill with avidity. This may seem an absurd description, and yet it is only a reflection of what might happen, *mutatis mutandis,* in a criminal or what actually happens in a child's feelings.

As we will see later, the psychological structure of the personality consists of instincts, the id, from which all energy is derived, the

---

[7] Karl Abraham, *Selected Papers,* pp. 370, 393, 407. See also Ernest Jones, "Anal Erotic Character Traits," *Papers on Psychoanalysis,* pp. 680–704.

superego, and the ego, the superego being a part of the ego. It is this superego which is our authority, our conscience.

It would then appear that the criminal is a person in whom the superego is impaired or absent, though one may question whether there can be an individual without an ego with a developed superego. The function of the superego is to direct and control the person's ego and thus keep him in line with social standards. The child's superego depends on his development and social background. An alcoholic father or a prostitute mother can hàrdly provide the child with a proper setting for the development of a high-grade superego. Nor will it be satisfactorily developed if the child has been rejected by his parents. This leads one to believe that a criminal may have a superego, but it may be blocked because of some stronger drive or emotion which impairs its function.

From what has been stated it seems that much of criminal behavior is like a neurosis, and so we classify those criminals who reveal psychological mechanisms similar to those of neurotics as neurotic criminals.[8] This type of offender belongs to the reactive or symptomatic group of criminals, their crime being an expression of an inner conflict; their entrance into criminal activities may result from childhood or adolescent experiences. This type is designated as neurotic not because the mechanism is the same as that found in a neurosis, but because it comes nearer to the neurotic than any other type. It would be a mistake to think that neurotic and criminal behavior in general is the same. The neurotic is in conflict with himself because of his internal inhibitions, while the criminal has few internal inhibitions—he acts out his inclinations.

The individual's experiences from earliest childhood produce a defense mechanism in him. But this does not mean that each person develops a neurosis. It only signifies that each individual selects a certain possible defense mechanism. Which again means that each individual's ego is originally endowed with its own special disposition and tendencies. This implies that there are certain persons whose superego is influenced by their immediate environment, which if delinquent may color their superego to the extent that they accept its criminal code. To this class belong gangsters, ho-

[8] Franz Alexander and Hugo Staub, *The Criminal, the Judge and the Public*, pp. 50–53.

boes, profit murderers, and other professional criminals whose criminal acts are accepted by their ego and superego as well.

If each individual has his peculiar disposition and inclinations, may not personality characteristics and symptoms of delinquency be expressions directed toward the same aim? The correlation between the type of person and the kind of crime he commits may be analogous to the correlation between the kind of individual one is while mentally healthy and the kind of neurosis or psychosis one develops while mentally sick.

Thus, the development of a criminal's career should be studied in the life he led previous to beginning his career. An individual who is unable to adapt his behavior to the environment in the course of his development may adjust to life only through antisocial activities. Freud has described the development of psychosis, which might be applied to criminal behavior. "If we throw a crystal to the ground, it breaks . . . into fragments whose limits were already determined by the structure of the crystal although they were invisible. Psychotics are fissured and splintered structures such as these." [9] Criminal actions may be effected through the personality structure. But since the individual with his constitutional personality traits also is raised in an environment which, one might say, he inherits, an environment which is usually indistinguishable from inherited constitutional potentialities, the developmental, environmental, and social factor must be taken into account when antisocial activities arise. It is this factor which may be a clue to understanding the offender and be valuable as diagnostic or prognostic adjuvants in appraising prevention of criminal acts.

In evaluating the developmental and social factors in their bearing upon crime it is not so much the experiences as such, no matter how psychologically important they may appear, which are of importance to the perpetrator, but their meaning to him.

These factors in the social environment which may provoke crime are often called trauma, but due to the obscurity of that term, they should rather be designated as precipitating events or factors. These precipitating factors are of importance to the adjustment of the individual. To be the oldest child of ten siblings, to be born in wealth or in poverty may be a precipitating event. Birth of a

[9] *New Introductory Lectures on Psychoanalysis*, pp. 84–85.

younger sibling, a broken home situation, bodily or mental disease, overprotective parents, or strict grandparents may act as precipitating factors; and to these add such emotional and economical deprivations as death of important members of the family, financial losses, or threatened insecurity while adjusting to new situations, for example, entering a new school, job, or a new family situation.[10] What is a precipitating event for one person is not for another. There are events of this type that are, so to speak, selective. Sometimes one is unable to discover the precipitating event, so only further investigations reveal that one has taken place. At other times the event seems to be the cause, while in reality it only disturbs the equilibrium of adjustment.

In order to show the significance of such precipitating factors I cite some cases.

In the first case a fifty-year-old man was sentenced for forgery. He had no previous record. In his explanation of the forgery he said that he was unmarried and lived with his mother whom he supported. He was closely attached to her and later took upon himself the responsibility for some other members of his family, supporting a married, unemployed brother and a younger sister. He continued this burden in spite of the fact that he was sick for almost three years prior to the crime. Six months before the crime took place he was operated upon, and his convalescence being prolonged, he became unemployed. When he did obtain a new position, the salary was low and in order to support his family he forged the checks.

A thirty-year-old man was convicted of burglary in this second case. He was the tenth of 14 children, born in a Southern city. Being reared in poor surroundings, he had to start work when he was fourteen in order to assist in the support of his family. He was later married at twenty but subsequently his wife ran away, leaving him with a young child. It was difficult at this time to get work and he had to take odd jobs in a factory at night, work which made him "nervous," in order to support himself and his child. The work stopped, and he was laid off and forced to go on relief for a short

10 S. N. Clark, "Precipitating Factors in Mental Disorders," *Illinois Medical Journal*, LXI (March, 1932), 230–35; G. E. Gardner, "Precipitating Mental Conflicts in Schizophrenia," *Journal of Nervous and Mental Disease*, LXXI (May, 1930), 645–55; R. H. Hutchings, C. O. Cheney, and W. W. Wright, "Psychogenic Precipitating Causes of Schizophrenia," *State Hospital Quarterly*, XII (Nov., 1926), 3–13.

time. He could not see his way clear and one night entered a store and stole some odd things, food and clothing for himself and his daughter. For this theft he was convicted and sentenced to prison.

The third case concerns an eighteen-year-old boy whose mother died shortly after his birth and whose father, a drunkard, died when he was five years old. He was raised by his maternal grandparents whose steady quarreling created an unpleasant atmosphere in the home. Because of this unrest at home the boy was unable to do his homework and he repeatedly came to school unprepared until his teacher notified the grandparents, who punished him. Gradually he came to be punished for trifles. Little by little hostile feelings arose in the boy and when he was eleven he ran away, joining a gang of boys. He lived with another boy, and it was believed that he made some earnings as an errand boy. He was with the gang for a short while, until a public agency returned him to his grandparents.

When he was twelve years old he had an accident and had to stay away from school for a half year with the result that he was demoted. He felt very unhappy about this, developing feelings of inferiority and insecurity. However, he was of superior intelligence and later made rapid progress in school. One night he was thrown out by his grandfather because of some trifling misbehavior. In the following days he roamed around, stole a car, and a few days later was picked up by the police.

In the first case we see that there was a chain of unhappy events which separately perhaps would not be of any significance, but together served to lead him into forgery. He had to help his mother and sister, to support a brother, and he himself was sick for a long time. It might be said that the strong attachment to his mother made him somewhat immature, but on the other hand he showed much maturity and responsibility in supporting his family. And in view of his superior intelligence and his age he should have anticipated the difficulties he faced in committing the forgeries.

In the second case we see a man who, although superior in intelligence and in spite of absence of emotional conflicts, perpetrated a crime which to a large extent was prompted by the circumstances.

In the third case we have a gifted young boy reared by grandparents who did not understand him. Their quarreling upset him, and the chastisement he received for small misbehaviors aroused hostile feelings which led him to run away. He developed a great deal of insecurity and inferiority as a result of his sickness. Here, as in the other two cases, certain changes for the worse in the situation took place which became traumatic in degree or in quality. If he had criminal tendencies at the start of his life, they were certainly not diminished when he grew up under the auspices of his grandparents. Even if we grant the presence of inner conflicts we cannot disregard the special or general social situation.

In the situation is a set of factors that sensitize the individual to one direct or indirect causative factor. A certain degree of instability either in personality or in situation seems to favor or necessitate perpetration of criminal acts.

Since the human being is socially conditioned, a variety of influences are always present, whether he is a law-abiding citizen or not. Because the personality and its development vary with each individual and because each has his own peculiar reaction to social factors, the causes of crime cannot be altogether accurately determined but have to be seen in each particular case.

If a person becomes sensitized to criminal activities by, let us say, emotional or economical deprivations, a criminal act is produced only when this precipitating event has the support of the personality. We may here compare an individual becoming a criminal to a man who acquires tuberculosis. Although all humans inhale the tubercle bacillus, only some acquire tuberculosis. This is due to the fact that the body becomes sensitized to the bacterial production—it becomes allergic depending upon factors within the constitution of the individual. And so with a person who becomes a transgressor. He becomes sensitized toward committing crime by one or more precipitating events which, if he is a person with receptive personality traits, may cause an increase of his criminalistic tendencies in degree or in quality, producing a criminal act. In another individual sensitized to criminalistic influences, the precipitating factors may not find receptive traits in the personality with the result that no criminal response is produced. Saying this is no more than saying that a person in one instance under certain conditions reacts with a neurosis, in another with a psychosis, or does not react at all.

Why some yield and others do not yield to criminal influences may then be assumed due to an exposure to criminal influences intermingled with one or more precipitating events, or due to a type of reaction formation of criminalistic tendencies turning them into a manifest criminal direction, or both.[11] In both instances a mobilization of criminalistic tendencies takes place. The exposure hits certain personality traits that respond to the criminalistic stimulus in a positive way. A pattern of criminal behavior may then very well develop in the same way as an individual develops a certain pattern of behavior when exposed to a corresponding type of influence.

A quantitative replacement takes place between the personality traits and exposure. Strong criminalistic tendencies need little exposure to crime influences and vice versa.

That some commit and others do not commit criminal activities may have its root in the circumstance that the human being, including the criminal, represents a center of action and reaction, forming, in a functional sense, a unit with the surroundings. This being the case, social or antisocial concepts and standards will leave impressions on the individual which he incorporates into his personality structure, causing him under certain circumstances to succumb to criminal influences from without or within.

[11] For theories of other investigators see T. Sellin, *Culture, Conflict and Crime*, pp. 32–41. See also: E. H. Sutherland, *Principles of Criminology*, p. 9.

V

PSYCHIATRIC-PSYCHOLOGIC EXAMINATION
OF THE OFFENDER

IN EXAMINING an offender the psychiatrist is concerned with two problems, diagnosis and treatment. The basic concept in an examination is the view we have maintained of the offender and nonoffender as a *total* personality. The individual is to be considered as a socio-psycho-biological unit which can be observed, studied, and interpreted from the social, physiological, and psychological point of view. The diagnosis includes the ascertaining of how the person's mental make-up is related to his life development and his crime and the finding of the causative factors, if possible, which prompted the crime. Without such an aim, the psychiatrist will not be able when called upon to fulfill his task in giving the proper authorities his advice. Nor will he be able to probe deeper into the mind of the criminal.

Since the psychiatrist in the first place aims at an understanding of the criminal's behavior and why he acted as he did, it goes without saying that he must have a thorough knowledge of human behavior based upon psychological insight and experience. It cannot be too greatly emphasized that psychiatric practice is an art. Psychological insight can, if possible, be acquired only after long and patient experience. As a painter calls forth the peculiarities and characteristics of his subject more by intuition than previous learning, so with the psychiatrist who penetrates to the depths of the mind. A good psychiatrist, like the artist, feels with his finger tips. This may seem odd to the novice who for the first time is confronted with the criminal he is to examine. Nevertheless it has its validity, which he will experience later. The psychiatrist who believes he can become an expert merely by learning an outline for an examination of the mind, would do well to recall that the human is not a "case" which can be put into a scheme, but a living entity comprising a certain pattern of behavior characteristics.

Fortunately, there is increasing recognition of the fact that psychiatric examination of an offender is desirable if a proper disposition of his case is to be expected. Our system of probation, parole, and indeterminate sentences along with the swift development of the juvenile court show clearly the need and assistance of psychiatric knowledge.

Since each case represents an individual the psychiatric examination must take place with the view towards individualizing. Not only is it the duty of the psychiatrist to discover whether an offender is sane or not, but he must also see that society is educated to recognize normal and abnormal behavior so that the individual can be adequately taken care of. Generally, it is easy to decide a person is psychotic if he represents a disintegrated personality, but it may be difficult to determine an individual's mental make-up if his personality traits are so intermingled that they render no explicit clue as to his mental condition.[1]

Where is the border between the normal and abnormal mind? How often do we not see an individual, apparently normal, who suddenly displays criminal acts of an aberrant or quite abnormal nature, and then just as suddenly resumes his conventional character? Imagine this man as highly gifted, a man thinking along antisocial lines and clinging to his ideas although his constructive intelligence tells him that they are wrong. Is this man normal or abnormal? Or think upon an offender having violent mental conflicts which may at times threaten to split his personality, but who apparently is still able to control his mental condition by his capacity for performing organized, logical actions. Is he normal or abnormal?

It was half a century ago that a Nestor in medicine, Charcot, exclaimed: "Normal or abnormal—I dare not say where is the border!"

We may come closer to an understanding when we assume that abnormal psychological manifestations are exaggerations or distortions of normal ones, which means that abnormal mental phenomena differ from the normal in degree and not in kind. From the biological viewpoint the same mechanisms are present and they

[1] David Abrahamsen, discussion in *Archives of Neurology and Psychiatry*, XLIX (April, 1943), No. 4, 631.

have the same significance. If mental abnormality differs from normality in degree rather than in kind, then we can apply this view to the personality of the criminal in the cases where abnormality is present.

In the same way as logical thinking and social behavior has a meaning to the normal person, so also with the incoherent mind to the insane and antisocial behavior to the offender. They are all governed by the same psychological laws, varying only in degree. Thus, if we have enough knowledge of the offender's past and present history, his life situation, and his mental make-up, we are able to uncover his personality traits and arrive at an understanding of what significance these have.

The variety of personality traits and the immense number of constellations they represent make it obvious that there are hardly two individuals alike in their mental make-up. Any similarity will most likely be superficial. For this reason the psychiatrist in approaching the offender must not think that he has seen a similar case before. Such an attitude would only lead him, consciously or unconsciously, to adopt a preconceived view regarding the motivation of the crime which would perhaps be wrong. Further, a "blitz" diagnosis has no justification even if the psychiatrist is forced to hurry through an examination.

He may often be called upon to give an opinion based upon an examination performed under unfavorable conditions. No psychiatrist, nor any other physician, should render his opinion before he is satisfied that the examination is complete. Such an attitude must be maintained because the psychiatrist must not only try to explain psychological phenomena but in many cases he must also try to alleviate pathological mental conditions. If he is to alter the make-up of a patient or of an offender, it is absolutely necessary that he know the personality structure as far as it is possible.

And yet, a student of medicine is taught very little, if anything, about the technique of making a psychological examination of a patient, not to speak about performing one of an offender. In the latter case he has to teach himself. Since physicians in practically all fields of medicine have become more and more aware of the necessity of psychological examinations because of the possibility that psychological elements may be present in a disease, a procedure of examining technique has been gradually outlined.

Psychology is a science comprised of approved laws and concepts which are based upon the idea that there are certain intellectual, emotional, and behavioral characteristics of the individual that can be observed and recorded. Not all of an offender's reactions can be measured exactly but they all can be noted and written down. The order of collected data may vary, the procedure may change in some details from case to case, but a certain standard has to be followed, varying only with the experience of the psychiatrist. Thus, if he is familiar with the different parts in the examination he may be able to estimate some items without scrutinizing them meticulously, while other elements may demand careful exploration. If he is in doubt, all items will have to be checked. During the examination he takes notes on the information given by the offender and of his own observations.

Unfortunately, the extent of a psychiatric examination not only depends upon the psychiatrist himself but in a large measure upon the policy laid down by the different courts. This policy is determined by the law of the different states or by the reason for the examination. Sometimes a psychiatrist may be called upon to give his opinion after only one interview with an offender in jail. In other instances the court will give him an opportunity to observe a case over a considerable period. This is true in larger cities.

It is well for the examiner to remember that he has no right, none whatsoever, to propose any suggestions as to how an examination should be performed satisfactorily. However, if the examination was unsatisfactory because it was made under unfavorable conditions, he must point this out in his testimony. Much of the handling of such a situation depends upon the examiner's discretion and versatility. Should the court allow him to choose the place for an examination, he may propose the jail, prison, hospital, or his office, if his office is not ruled out for some reason. It is necessary that the psychiatrist be asked to perform his examination through the proper channels. At the present time the attorney for the defendant may secure a psychiatrist to examine his client, who perhaps has already been examined by the prosecutor's psychiatrist.

It will be an achievement when the psychiatrist in all court cases is appointed by the state. This would provide a qualified psychiatrist, if politics were kept out, and one would feel safer because no irrelevant factors would interfere with his decision.

Before entering into an examination it is most important to have secured and read in advance all facts available from the court record about the offender. If he has been previously in a hospital or institution, a record should be obtained, if possible. Too often the psychiatrist starts examining the offender without knowing anything about his crime, his behavior, and general attitude. I deem it essential that such information be obtained before the examination proper is begun, because it is of the utmost importance that the psychiatrist at the first interview establish an amicable and congenial atmosphere. Such an atmosphere is not possible if the examiner plunges into questions that may upset the offender, or at least make him resentful. However, if the examiner knows the salient facts in advance, he will not interrogate the offender but let him speak for himself. This pre-examination knowledge makes a preliminary interview with the offender superfluous.

The examiner must put himself on equal footing with the offender. In this way he becomes best acquainted with him and has an opportunity to gain his confidence. For this reason the psychiatrist should start his interview by talking about other subjects. Then, after a few opening sentences, he tells the offender the reason for the examination. An offender is usually suspicious of any examination, whether it is conducted by a medical doctor or a policeman. Very often murderers and other serious offenders rationalize their behavior, and they are more apt to do this if they are not told the reason for the questioning. This is particularly true after sentence has been imposed; the examiner is only able to elicit rationalizations convenient to the offender himself.

Assuming that the psychiatrist has read all the available facts, he proceeds to obtain the case history. This comprises:

I. HISTORICAL DATA

1. *Family history.* Brief statement of age and attitude of parents, number of siblings, and the structure of the family situation.
2. *Developmental history.* Behavior in childhood, school, and adolescent periods.

3. *Educational and vocational history.* Positions held, if he achieved success or was a failure, the reason for leaving or changing and so on.
4. *Social history.* Social contacts, friendships, social activities, indulgence in alcohol.
5. *Medical history.* All diseases, their treatment, and results therefrom.
6. *Sexual history.* Childhood recollections of and parental attitude to sexual life; masturbation, menstruation, premarital and marital sexual relations, marriage, children, unconscious material such as dreams.
7. *Criminal history.* Age of offender at time of first offense; type and number of crimes committed; presence or absence of criminal tendencies in family; criminal pattern.

In taking the family history, the home situation should be uncovered. It is therefore well to corroborate evidence from the offender with that of the parents. Was there harmony in the family? What type of control did the parents have over their children? What was their reaction to delinquency? Were they strict, overindulgent, or neglectful in bringing up their children? What was their attitude towards associations with church, the Boy Scouts, and kindred organizations? All these questions have their aim in ascertaining whether the parents disagreed about controlling the offender, whether criminal habits were established within the home itself, or whether the offender developed hostility towards the parents, causing an antisocial attitude.

The type of neighborhood should then be considered: was it delinquent and what was the prevailing attitude towards the law and the police? This indicates whether or not the home was a law-abiding one.

The developmental history should include a chronological survey of the schools attended; the age when the child started should be noted, and if late, record the reason. Did the child skip grades or was he kept back? Did he leave school on his own accord, misbehave in class? Was he uncooperative, negativistic, truant, and did he show tendencies toward stealing and lying? Any information about truancy should be given due consideration because many offenders start their criminal careers in this way. The truancy situation should therefore be investigated as to its start, its frequency, and in its relation to the home and school atmosphere, the possible influence of companions, and the parents' reaction. The schoolteacher is a source of information for this type of misbehavior, but the knowledge gained has to be used with insight. If the behavior in school may have some bearing upon what remedies have to be recommended, it may be necessary for the examiner to interview the schoolteacher or to employ a social worker for this specific purpose.

The educational and vocational history follows logically upon the developmental history, stressing how far the offender was able to get along with his education and later work or whether he chose a profession. The fact that he might have chosen a profession is important to uncover because it signifies a certain mental ability and endurance, which many offenders lack. It is further determined whether the offender made a success or failure in his capacities. This may, to a large extent, depend not only upon his knowledge and ability, but also upon his adaptability to the situation.

The social history should point out the offender's interests, hobbies, recreational and athletic activities, companions and his relationship to them, club life or other organized activities, cultural or political interests, religious affiliations, and so on. It is important to know whether the offender is gregarious or a "lone wolf," whether he is able to establish friendships and maintain them. Does he indulge in alcohol or in drugs? One should particularly try to determine if the offender at a certain point of his life was friendly and congenial and then either gradually or suddenly became sullen, uncooperative, lost interest in his undertakings, and became involved in antisocial activities. If so, one must attempt to discover the cause or causes. Was it the death of loved ones, losing a job, marriage with an economic burden, or a mental or economic depression?

Closely connected with such changes in life are the alterations that may take place in the mind as a result of diseases. Birth trauma, even though slight, may have caused hyperirritability or a change in personality, including mobilization of criminalistic tendencies. Accidents which may have affected the brain capacity must be recorded. X-rays, if available, or a report from the physician who treated the offender should be seen by the examiner. All reactions resulting from nursing and toilet training, as mentioned in Chapter IV, should be noted. Change of behavior after such infectious diseases as encephalitis and influenza may take place, and for this reason one should explicitly ask if there has been any prolonged fever of unknown origin or if there has been insomnia or drowsiness. This type of behavior disorders, seen mostly in children, comprising emotional irritability, overactivity, and impulsiveness, is manifested in lying, stealing, truancy, assaults, sexual offenses, and sadism, which may make one think that the case is a psychopathic one.

Altered behavior, although of another type, may even result from the occurrence of diabetes. Such a case comes vividly to mind. A forty-year-old man, who all his life had behaved well and supported his family, embezzled small funds for no good reason. Upon being examined he said that after having felt tired for the last half year, he began to take money. His memory and powers of concentration were impaired and he had only partial insight into the seriousness of his crime. He admitted he was unable to think as clearly as he could before, indicating a deterioration of his mental functioning, a finding which was confirmed by associates in his office. Examination of urine revealed sugar and the blood showed pathologically increased sugar content. Whether his diabetes was closely associated with a downfall of his mental resistance causing mobilization of criminalistic tendencies or whether it is to be considered a precipitating event per se may be debated, but the fact that his embezzlement coincided with the start of his diabetes, causing unquestionably an impairment of his mental functions would seem to lend support to the belief that there was a connection between his crime and disease.

In closing this stage of the examination, one asks the offender if he has had any venereal disease, and if he has, what sort of treatment did he receive and what was the result.

The examination of the offender's sexual life perhaps demands the greatest discretion on the part of the psychiatrist. Much carefulness in interrogation has to be exercised if the offender is to give a reliable account. If he is reluctant the examiner may first start by asking him in general terms about marriage, children, and his attitude toward them. If he responds, the interrogations may be extended to the offender's unconscious life, fantasies and dreams, and if also successful here, the examiner may ask about the offender's reaction to puberty. Finally masturbation and pregenital life such as nursing experiences, weaning, infantile masturbation, if he knows anything about it, are mentioned.

How far this part of the examination goes depends upon the case. With a sexual offender it is necessary to go into detail regarding his behavior in sexual matters, and examining him at this time may put the psychiatrist in a better position to obtain material.

If at this stage of the examination good contact has been established with the offender, the obtaining of the historical data will not in general cause difficulties. Only when the examiner approaches the criminal history may the offender feel apprehensive or defensive or even become uncooperative. If he does, it is better to avoid further questioning than try to force the issue. Important parts of the examination still remain, and it is well to maintain the good will of the offender as long as possible. Besides, nothing is gained by antagonizing him. At times the offender may lack information about familial criminality, or if he knows anything about it does not want to reveal it. The examiner should here be careful in his questioning and not immediately assume that the offender is deliberately lying. If there has been criminal activity in the family, it may, as is often the case, have been concealed from him. If the court record indicates the presence of familial crime, activities of which the offender is unaware, no information to this effect shall be given him. It only hurts his feelings, and an offender, like any other human, has his pride. If the offender is accused of stealing, the examiner should try to discover whether this was his first offense and the circumstances controlling it. Usually stealing begins in a truant childhood or adolescence and the acquisitions may be disposed of at once. On other occasions one meets the kleptomaniac whose stealing is prompted largely from unconscious motivation, perhaps the effect of a forbidden sexual act or of a criminal pattern to which he has been exposed.

In this part of the interview the offender's story is checked against the court record, and if discrepancies arise the reasons for them are uncovered. His reasons for committing the crime should be given. In cases where sexual elements are involved—exhibitionism, homosexuality—interrogations along psychoanalytical lines may be necessary. In any event, whatever the case may be, it is profitable to put down the offender's own words. They may express accurately how the crime happened and they may give a taste of the emotions involved in the crime. If necessary, the offender's statement should be corroborated by that of others who know him, friends, parents, wife.

II. EXAMINATIONAL DATA

A thorough routine physical examination should be made, indicating the general appearance of the offender, his face, physical charms, physique, manner. The experienced psychiatrist will discover the empty and silly look of a mental defective, the stiff expression of paralytic agitans, the euphoric and smiling appearance of the general paretic, the monotonous and unmovable look with drooping expression to the lips of the depressed or melancholic, the upward curling of the lips of the manic, and the distant and blank or grimacing face of the schizophrenic. One looks for scars resulting from head injuries, syphilis, or bullet wounds. The height and weight is recorded and compared, and the muscular development, which may be indicative of the offender's ability to commit a crime requiring considerable strength, is noted. Slightness of build may suggest a feeling of inferiority which prompted criminal activities (see Chapter VIII). Any developmental anomaly of the genitals, hirsutism, and irregularities in distribution of hair growth should be observed. They may be supportive evidence of possible disturbances in the sexual drive. The blood pressure range and pulse is recorded; this is particularly important with respect to older offenders or those suffering from hemorrhagic diathesis. The skeletal system should then be examined, and deformities of the skull, such as oxycephaly, dysostosis, cranio-facialis (Cruozon), size of head, and microcephalis, or bony abnormalities on other parts should be noted.

In the routine physical examination of one young fellow, I discovered a bony outgrowth on the dorsum of his hand, which also was swollen. Questioning revealed he had hurt his hand five years before and so had been unable to do his job. Unemployed for some time, he finally obtained a job as an office clerk but after a while was laid off and soon became involved in some stealing. The configuration of his hand indicated tuberculosis, which was confirmed by subsequent examination of his lungs and abdomen, the latter showing ascites. X-ray revealed tuberculosis and his case was disposed of properly.

After the physical examination comes the neurological examination. In order to be adequate a neurological examination must be done in detail. In the same way that the neurological examination cannot be a complete one without a psychiatric one, or at least without an examination of the offender's mental condition, so also a psychiatric examination requires a complete neurological examination. Since the latter is time-consuming, a psychiatrist will, under usual circumstances, be unable to do this. However, he must here use his judgment. Thus, if in the course of examination he finds the offender's speech hesitating and blurred, with omissions of one or more syllables, he may suspect dementia paralytica. If pupils are unequal, and if knee jerks are increased, absent, or weak, this confirms such a diagnosis, and a complete neurological examination with serology is necessary. It is impossible here to go into detail about how to conduct a complete neurological examination. But I refer the reader to the excellent book written by my former teacher, G. H. Monrad-Krohn, *The Clinical Examination of the Nervous System* (1938).[2] Only a few outstanding signs which the psychiatrist may encounter while examining an offender will be stressed here.

It is a good procedure to start by examining the cranial nerves, first the olfactory nerve and then the other eleven cranial nerves. Acuity of vision and field of vision (Donder's test) should be determined, and an ophthalmoscopic examination (color, border, swelling of the disc, vessels, hemorrhages) given. If testing the pupils reveals no abnormalcy, the case will hardly be of a syphilitic nature. It is not to be inferred, however, that unequal and nonreacting pupils means the offender suffers from syphilis, because in the absence of other signs and negative serology it only indicates that he has gone through a syphilitic infection which at present may not be active and may not be related to his antisocial activities. Even if Argyll-Robertson's sign—absence of light reflex and unaltered accommodation reflex—is present, it may be remembered that it can be seen sometimes in epidemic encephalitis and in tumors at the base of the cerebrum. However, it must be pointed out that Argyll-

2 Published by Paul B. Hoeber, Inc., Medical Book Department of Harper & Brothers, New York.

Robertson's sign is considered as practically conclusive evidence of syphilis of the central nervous system.

It is well known how this disease can escape detection for a long time, as the following case shows. A prisoner who had been incarcerated for several years was one day referred to me because of "nervousness." I discovered Argyll-Robertson's sign, uneven or loss of deep reflexes, loss of deep sensibility, unsteady gait, symptoms indicative of a tabes, which was later confirmed by serology. Treatment was at once administered.

While it is true that marked disturbances of the nervous system, such as exaggerated deep reflexes, tremors of the hands, and dysarthry, may be indicative of organic lesion of the central nervous system, nevertheless, these same manifestations may be seen in psychoneurotic persons or in individuals who are examined for the first time by the physician. Tremor of the eyelids may also be seen in psychoneurotics. It is therefore necessary that proper value be placed upon these findings. Hypersomnic symptoms such as drowsiness and slowness of intellectual function, hyperkinetic phenomena (due to basal ganglia envolvement), such as tremors, athetoid or choreiform movements, and myoclonias with mask face, hypokinetic phenomena (due to lesions in the substantia nigra), and disturbances of eye movements, such as nystagmus, double vision, oculogyric crises, or restricted movements upwards of the eye balls must be observed. These symptoms, particularly the last one, may be seen a long time after a slight attack of encephalitis has subsided. If these symptoms are present or if there is any story of an unexplained fever in the offender's history, the examiner should carefully try to determine if he is afflicted with encephalitis, because the disease in many cases may cause a change of the personality traits that may have a bearing upon the crime committed.

The motor system is then examined and any deformity, atrophy, hypertrophy, or involuntary movements such as tremors, tics, myoclonus, athetotic, choreatic, or similar movements, spasms, or seizures (Jacksonian or cryptogenetic) are noted. Since much of criminal behavior may have root in a poorly developed or deformed body, paresis or deformity should be looked for.

Coordination tests, such as finger-nose or knee-heel tests and Romberg's test are done.

The sensory system is examined next. There is no necessity to go into details here unless something suspicious should awake the examiner's attention. Sensation of pain, tactile sensation, and sense of temperature are tested. (Note that a decreased or lost sensation of pain on the tip of the nose and in the ulnar area of the cubital region may be an early sign of tabes incipiens.) Examination of deep sensation and of sense of position and of movements is then done, followed by examination of deep pressure pain. This last is particularly important in cases where alcoholic abuse is suspected. An increased deep pressure pain (deep hyperesthesia) of the muscles would confirm the suspicion.

Stereognostic sense may be necessary to test if manifestations of aphasia are present.

If in the course of the examination the offender states that he has suffered a disease of the nervous system of an organic type, signs of it may frequently be detected from changes of the reflexes. Since testing the reflexes is one of the most objective examinations, being independent of the offender's mood and intelligence, it is of the utmost importance to examine them. Further, the offender rarely knows how to simulate reflex changes and if he does, it is usually easy to detect. The deep reflexes, radialis, biceps, triceps, knee jerks, and ankle jerks, are tested on both sides and compared with each other. Not only should the examiner keep in mind that the absence of knee jerks is one of the three cardinal signs of tabes (the other two being Argyll-Robertson's pupils and Romberg's sign), but also that they may be absent after severe bodily exertion, as Monrad-Krohn found.[3] He should also remember that loss of ankle jerks and increased deep pressure pain may only be the signs of a polyneuritis of an alcoholic nature.

Presence of ankle clonus is usually indicative of a pyramidal lesion, but it should be borne in mind that it may be found in psychoneurotic persons. It is most important that the examiner be aware of this fact. They are differentiated in that an ankle clonus due to an organic lesion is stopped by the big toe being plantar reflected, while a clonus due to a functional disorder usually will continue in spite of the big toe being plantar reflected.

Following the deep reflexes, the superficial reflexes are tested. Of those the plantar reflex is one which is usually tested, the patho-

[3] G. H. Monrad-Krohn, *The Clinical Examination of the Nervous System*, p. 130.

logical response being most easily elicited from the lateral border of the sole. A positive Babinski's phenomenon may be elicited in persons who for some time have been under addiction to drugs. Record a normal plantar reflex downwards: plantar reflex ↓ ; and the pathological plantar reflex upwards: plantar reflex ↑ ; if no response, then record: plantar reflex o.

If there are changes in the plantar reflexes, this will be reflected in the response of the abdominal reflexes, which may also reveal signs of pyramidal lesion. In some malingering offenders, however, one may see that the abdominal reflexes are changed accordingly with a change of superficial sensibility. In that case the cremaster reflex may be of some value in determining organic or functional symptoms. Testing of corneal and pharyngeal reflexes may also have the same value. The absence of pharyngeal reflexes has been asserted to be a sign of hysteria, an assertion which may be considered doubtful.

At last, standing position is examined. Romberg's test is performed, the offender being asked to put his feet close together and to close his eyes. If he sways the test is positive. This test may be positive in psychoneurotic persons.

The gait is observed but should be evaluated together with other findings. Are the arm movements normal while walking? (Absent in pyramidal and extra-pyramidal lesions.) Is there steppage or hyper-extension of the knee? The former condition is seen in foot-drop, the latter in tabes. Does the offender drag one foot on the ground? Or does he swing it, as seen in hemiplegia, instead of lifting the leg? Is his gait staggering or propulsive, as seen in drunkenness or paralysis agitans respectively? While examining the gait one should watch for such hysterical phenomena as astasia-abasia, during which the offender, performing all kinds of sudden and co-ordinated movements, is always on the verge of falling and tries to find support.

After the neurological examination has been completed, the positive findings, if there are any, should be summarized.

III. PSYCHOLOGICAL EXAMINATION

When the psychiatrist begins the psychological examination, he may already have received an impression, though superficial, of the offender's mental make-up. He has seen his attitude and manners, seen whether he is shy or bold, alert or withdrawn, observed whether he has bitten fingernails, whether his stream of talk is coherent or irrelevant, whether he is accessible, and so on, all in all symptoms that may lead the examiner's attention in a certain direction. The following psychological examination serves to broaden and deepen his psychiatric knowledge of the offender.[4]

It should be borne in mind that an outline for the procedure of such an examination only includes suggestions that the examiner may modify or abbreviate according to the individual offender. It is rarely practicable to follow this guide systematically, but the recording and organizing of the data should be adhered to strictly.

A. General Observations
1. *Situation*. The situation or situations at the time of the interview is described; where was the offender seen, was he alone or with others, and was his behavior unusual or not.
2. *Appearance*. The personal appearance of the offender is described in general—whether he is quiet, restless, anxious, shy, lively, evasive, whether there is a particular facial expression, whether mannerisms are present, whether his clothing is careless or neat. The psychiatrist should give little emphasis to the appearance of the offender's clothing if he is seen in a hospital or a jail. However, he should also recognize offenders whose lawyers, wanting their clients to give the best impression possible, see to it that they are suitably attired.
3. *Accessibility*. The offender's attitude to the examiner—does he welcome the interview or refuse it—is remarked. His manner of speaking, whether frank or hesitating, coherent or irrelevant, circumstantial or meager, is described.
4. *Voice*. Is the voice loud, strained, or well-modulated or are there abnormalities in his speech?

B. Perception
1. *Alertness*. It should be noted whether the offender gives the examiner his attention, is dull, or is able to follow the examiner's questions. The degree of his alertness should be rated in terms of "very dull," "dull," "average alertness," "hypersensitivity."
2. *Orientation:* Time. The offender's knowledge of the date, day,

[4] It is impossible to mention by name all those authors who have served as sources for an outlining of this part of the examination. Much credit should, however, be given to Arthur B. Noyes, Adolph Meyer, Nolan D. C. Lewis, G. H. Monrad-Krohn, Karl A. Menninger, E. B. Strecher, William Malamud, Johan Scharffenberg, and others.

and year is determined. It is necessary to ask exactly these questions, because in a great number of instances, the offender may appear oriented according to his conversation while in reality he may be disoriented. Only direct questioning will detect this.

Person and place. Have the offender identify himself and let him determine where he is, naming the place.

3. *Recent memory.* The offender is asked about events in the immediate past, what he had for dinner the day before yesterday, how he arrived at the examiner's place, what new acquaintances he made.

4. *Paresthesias.* The offender is asked about his physical health, whether he has had any queer sensations of the body or how he generally feels about his physical health.

5. *Illusions.* If the offender has displayed some false perceptions, it is necessary to determine their identity. If in doubt one may ask such questions as: "Is there anybody here you have known before?" It should be noted whether the offender has heard any voices. (An illusion is a perception arising from misinterpretation of a sensation.)

6. *Hallucinations.* It may be at times most difficult for the examiner to discern hallucinations in the offender. Many offenders who have difficulty in expressing themselves may deny the presence of them, while others may speak about them. In any event considerable discretion must be used in bringing to light hallucinations and their type and character.

It is well to start by asking a question like this: "Have you at any time had any peculiar experiences that you were not aware of at the moment?" The offender may or may not give any answer. If he does not, put forth more questions. "Have you heard any noises or voices from people you did not see?" "What did they sound like or what did they say?" "Did they talk about you?" In some instances an offender accused, for instance, of murder, might, if psychotic and if in the mood, start by saying: "A voice told me to kill the man." It is most important that the psychiatrist make great effort in detecting any auditory hallucinations, because great emphasis is placed upon them when determining the presence of a psychosis.

Closely related to auditory hallucinations are visual ones. If auditory hallucinations have been brought out, one may continue: "Did you see anything bright or colored?" "Did you think they had something to tell you or did they threaten you?"

While asking about auditory and visual hallucinations one might ask: "Have you ever smelled bad odors or poisonous gases?" This type of hallucinations, olfactory ones, may have some associations with the gustatory ones. An appropriate question is: "Did you at any time feel that your food or your cigarettes or pipe had a queer taste?" If the answer is in the affirmative, then the examiner should ask: "Do you think any drugs had been put into them?" If the offender thinks so, follow with: "Who do you think placed them there?"

Finally, inquire about tactile hallucinations. "Have you at any time had any peculiar sensation throughout your body?" If he says yes, ask: "Would you know any cause for it?"

It is important to determine how long the offender has had these experiences, what his idea is as to their origin and cause, and whether he committed the crime as a result of them.

If hallucinations have been found present, one may determine whether or not there is any organic basis for them. Some visual hallucinations of hemianopic type may be due to a one-sided occipital irritation of the brain, usually due to a tumor of the occipital lobe, and complex hemianopic hallucinations may be due to a lesion in the temporal lobe of the brain. Olfactory or gustatory hallucinations may be caused by the so-called uncinate attacks, which may be indicative of a lesion such as a tumor or a scar arising from a trauma in the neighborhood of the uncinate lobe. One will find the offender subject to these attacks in a dazed condition, having a feeling of again going through some past experiences.

It should be noted that hallucinations in the usual meaning are perceptions which have no cause in any external stimulus.

C. Intellection
   1. *Thought content.* The offender is asked to give a brief summary of his previous life and of his crime. This has been done before in the preceding examination, but important information might still be elicited from further questioning.
   2. *Remote memory.* This may be ascertained from the offender's life history.
   3. *Delusions.* At this point in the examination any delusions will have been detected. If the examiner has a suspicion about them, he may continue the questioning along the following lines: "Have you had any special difficulty in obtaining companionship? Do you think people have treated you nicely or do you think that somebody is fabricating stories about you?" If the examiner is in doubt, he may go further and ask directly: "Has anybody tried to harm you or do you feel people are against you?"

At times the character of the delusions is so absurd that it is impossible to reason with the offender. On the other hand the offender's answers may seem so logical and sensible that his relatives have to be questioned in order to decide if his ideas really are of a delusional nature.

It is important to ascertain here whether the offender has conscious feelings of guilt. In persons with a neurotic make-up one may see strong guilt feelings permeating their whole personality. An appropriate question is: "Do you think you have done anything which in your opinion was seriously wrong?" Or, "Do you have a feeling of having sinned at any time?" If he answers in the affirmative, one should try to detect the nature of the "sins," so that the proper value may be placed upon them.

4. *Obsessions*. It is important to terminate obsessions in offenders because neurotic phenomena may be expressed through antisocial activities, a process in which obsessions may come into play. In ascertaining these obsessions one should ask: "Have you ever had thoughts that recur to you or have you had a feeling that the same thoughts have been going through your mind for some time?" These questions will usually bring to light any obsessional ideas the offender might have.

Closely related to obsessions are compulsions. Although the latter express actions, it may be well to ask about them at this point of the examination. An obsession may be defined as an idea that intrudes upon the person apparently without any external stimulus causing it, while a compulsion may be defined as the motor counterpart of an obsession.

If the offender suffers from obsessions, their nature and the situation that precipitates them should be described. Handwashing, dressing, door closing, and any other compulsions should be recorded. In many offenders, pyromaniacs and kleptomaniacs, for example, obsessions and compulsions go hand in hand. Sometimes it may be difficult to establish a border line between normal and abnormal behavior regarding these manifestations, because some obsessions to a certain extent exist in every person. That a man locks a door and leaves it and returns to see that it is locked may be because he is cautious. But if the same man returns again and again to assure himself that the door is locked, he is a pathological case. Varying degrees of this behavior are found in offenders. A person may have a strong tendency toward setting a fire, but if he does not do it, it is only an obsession, taking on no antisocial character. When these obsessions are transformed into action, they become antisocial.

5. *Fantasies*. It may be difficult to descry fantasies in the offender but an effort should be made because much of his wishes are contained in them. A question such as, "Do you know what you would do if you had money?" may elicit some highlights in the personality. Closely associated with fantasies are dreams which

may also be of value in determining the structure of his personality. The patient should also be queried as to whether he has nightmares.

6. *Knowledge.* By this time the psychiatrist has received an impression of the offender's intelligence and his ability to use it. Besides the information previously obtained the examiner should ask the offender about current events, history, literature, and so on.

7. *Judgment and insight.* Here the examiner should try to evaluate the offender's opinion and interpretations of matters of an objective nature, thus gaining an impression of whether or not the offender's judgment is impaired. The examiner continues then to appraise the offender's evaluation of subjective matters. Does he feel guilty? If he admits to this he has partial insight. He may not admit being sick, in which case he does not have insight. Or he may be brought to realize that there is something wrong with him, showing that he has insight into his mental condition. Estimation of intelligence should then follow.

D. Emotion

1. *Trend.* The emotional trend is noted. Sadness, depression, fear, or anxiety is recorded. At times several of these moods may seem to exist simultaneously or alternately. This should be noted. It should be added that the term emotion is used to describe both a subjective and an objective expression. The term affect may be considered a better expression for these objective experiences.

2. *Degree.* The intensity of the different trends are specified.

3. *Suitability or disharmony.* A disharmony between verbal and emotional expression may be uncovered. Such an intra-psychic ataxia is seen frequently in schizophrenia.

E. Behavior (Action)

1. *Type.* The activities spontaneously started by the examiner are recorded.

2. *Impulsivity.* Sudden or unexpected behavior is described.

3. *Range.* The circumstances under which the offender's activities are carried out are noted.

4. *Suggestibility.* The fact that the offender is particularly exposed to suggestion or is impervious to it should be noted, giving special examples.

5. *Mannerisms.* These have been seen during the general examination of the offender and may be repeated here if they are of an extreme nature.

6. *Negativism.* Here describe whether the offender manifests stubbornness or perversity and if so against whom these actions are displayed. The degree of such behavior should also be recorded.

It will be appropriate here to mention the simulation that some offenders at times display when awaiting trial or when detained in prison. They may simulate all types of symptoms indicative of either physical or mental disturbances. The character of these simulated symptoms to a large extent depends upon emotional conflicts; the stronger they are, the more acute and violent are the symptoms. Their type turns on the advantages that may be achieved by simulating either physical or mental disability.

The physical manifestations may be of motor, sensory, or visceral type. Rather simple is the situation where the offender pretends to be weak or paretic, in the arms, for instance, hoping that his case may be deferred for physical reasons. This is easy to detect by asking the offender to squeeze a dynamometer as hard as possible at even intervals. Normally the strength of the hand becomes gradually weaker and weaker, but with the simulated offender the strength is usually the same all the time, from which one may assume that he did not use his total strength. Should he claim to be paralytic in one leg, he is asked to raise it and then let it sink slowly. If he is really paralytic the leg will fall down; if he is not, it will move down slowly, as he keeps it back. If there are any sensory changes claimed by the defendant, their real nature may be brought to light when one remembers that an hysterical anesthesia does not follow the distribution of the nerve. Thus he may be anesthetic in half of the body, including loss of hearing, sight, smell, or taste on the same side, symptoms that may be extended by the examiner's suggestion. Other times the offender states that he has lost his vision or impaired it. If this is an hysterical manifestation the pupils react to light and accommodation while the visual field is centrally narrowed. Should an offender claim muteness, he is asked to write some words. He would not be able to do this if he had aphasia.

The mental disturbances of an hysterical nature that one encounters in dealing with offenders, particularly those awaiting trial, are those of the Ganser syndrome. In this syndrome the defendant starts to behave queerly, doing things that were familiar to him in an absurd and ridiculous manner, and is unable to answer simple questions correctly. He gives the approximate date, says 4 x 5 is 18 or thereabouts, replies that may show that he realizes the meaning of the question but that they are all beside the point. His whole behavior is a union of instinctive, rational, and deceiving elements, a type of double-dealing. This condition arises from a situation in which the offender unconsciously wishes to appear irresponsible, and where he becomes actually mentally sick without being aware of it. To the examiner it may look like malingering. In reality this is an hysterical phenomena prompted by a situation in which the offender is going to gain more by a mental disability than by a physical one.

The psychiatrist must have his attention directed to this syndrome so that he does not run the risk of concluding that the offender is insane. The condition will subside after a while, and then the offender himself may offer an explanation as to why he acted as he did.

Following the routine psychiatric examination it may be necessary to employ special investigatory procedures. These must be used if the material elicited is scant or considered insufficient to warrant an opinion. Poor material may be the result of the offender being uncooperative or hesitating in telling about his life story and offense. These methods may also be used if the examiner has the impression that valuable material regarding the mental make-up is still concealed.

To the first procedures belongs the free-association interview. The offender is given opportunity to put into words his emotions and preoccupations, particularly those pertaining to unconscious material, without being interrupted. By encouraging him to speak about subjects not previously uncovered in the interview, one may succeed in reaching facts not previously available.

The interview may also be eased by means of hypnosis in order to detect preconscious or unconscious trends.

Play technique is a method of obtaining an impression of the offender's attitude, behavior, and reaction to certain situations provided by play. The technique is particularly used on children, at times on adults, and has been outlined by Anna Freud, Melanie Klein, Homburger-Ericson, David M. Levy, and others.

Finger-painting and clay modeling are closely connected with this play technique. They may be used when there is a suspicion of certain unconscious trends, such as a destructive trait not previously detected.

Sodium amytal, metrozal, or other suitable drugs may be used during the interview in order to reduce or eliminate the offender's resistance. This procedure may render valuable information regarding unconscious elements in the offender's behavior. However, much skill has to be exercised in obtaining the information.

Finally, the urine is examined. The presence of albuminurie, glycosurie, or other abnormalities may indicate organic disease, and must be given due consideration in the report. Serology or other special or extra-laboratory procedures should be done in all cases deemed necessary. Among other things, it should be borne in mind that a negative Wassermann reaction in the blood does not exclude presence of a positive one in the spinal fluid. It will be an achievement when all offenders, regardless of somatic findings, are given serological tests performed by reliable laboratories. In any event these should be extended to all offenders accused of serious crimes, such as murder, rape, and robbery.

IV. PSYCHOLOGICAL TESTS

In cases where the psychiatrist is in doubt as to the offender's mental condition, an experienced psychologist can render valuable aid by means of psychological tests. The time has passed when the main function of the psychologist was to determine the intelligence quotient. Paradoxical though it may sound, the rating of the intelligence is of the least significance, and the psychiatrist will already have an impression of the offender's intelligence. If he has not, this may be due to some faulty technique or poor observation on the part of the psychiatrist. Of course, cases exist where an offender represents a border line case of mental defectiveness, which at times may be difficult to detect and determine accurately. But, as a rule, the experienced psychiatrist will discover those particular traits that reveal the true mental condition.

The strong emphasis placed on measuring the intelligence has to a large extent hampered the development of testing the total personality. While one justly should examine the psychology of the individual's thinking, one instead looked for the logic of his thinking. This occurs much to the distress of the examiner, who is essentially concerned with the person's attitude and the reason for his actions, in short, with how the individual is able to discern the essential elements in the variety of life.

Such a view prevailed also in the field of criminology—yes, it still exists. As a matter of fact, even today reports from institutions, agencies, prisons, and parole boards dealing with criminals contain mainly the rating of their intelligence. Such information is of little value. It is far more important to ascertain whether the offender suffers from paranoid ideas, delusions, or anxiety traits, which might, if only vaguely manifest and difficult to bring to light, have avoided the psychiatrist's attention, than to focus the interest on whether the offender has an I.Q. of 100 or 110. This does not mean and shall not mean that the examiner shall put aside the measurement of the intelligence. It only means that the proper value shall be placed upon the proper matter. The psychiatric examination is an examination of essentials, and therefore has to be done in keeping with such a view.

The following tests are to be performed by the psychologist, but should be known to the psychiatrist.

1. *Standardized Intelligence Tests.* The following tests are used: Bellevue Adult, Merrill-Terman, and Babcock's tests.

An estimation of the offender's intelligence is arrived at while ascertaining the amount of emotions affecting the intellectual ability. By these means discordance between the score of the intelligence test and the efficiency scores are found.

2. *Projective Personality Tests.* The following tests are used: Rorschach, Szondi, and Thematic Apperception tests.

These tests are valuable in confirming or negating the psychiatric diagnosis. Here personality traits indicating a special trend may be found. Evaluation of the different tests, particularly the Rorschach, is difficult and has not so far become objective. But they are valuable because vaguely expressed trends of the personality that may have escaped the psychiatrist's attention may be discerned. The Diagnostic Personality Test may reveal the basis for a mental retardation. If for instance the mental retardation is on a neurotic basis, the retardation may not be regarded as innate and therefore constant and stable, but a condition that may improve considerably with adequate treatment of the emotional problems of the individual.

In addition to the test mentioned above, tests for measuring such behavior traits as aggression have been constructed. One of these tests is that by Hawthorne which measures cruelty-compassion.[5] He believes that cruelty-compassion is a general trait which, possessed in a certain quantity, makes a person act in a certain direction. (The different responses can be measured on a psychometric scale.) Hawthorne believes that such a test would enable us to detect potential offenders.

Another test involves measuring the reaction to ethical standards, friendship or hatred, generosity or selfishness, altruism or egoism, honesty or deceit, truthfulness or lying. By testing these traits one may be able to detect the difference between people showing social and antisocial behavior, and also be able to detect potential transgressors. It is desirable that this type of personality traits be sought out in order to ascertain the cause of aggressive behavior. However, such tests do not go to the bottom of the problem, because while they may show that an aggressive trend is present in an individual, they do not explain why this aggressive trend is present.

In trying to establish a pattern of behavior traits characterizing people with normal or antisocial tendencies, Tolman [6] has examined first offenders and recidivists. He found that the recidivists showed a greater degree of hostility toward the father, a reserved attitude toward both parents, and an antagonism toward authority on the whole, indicating the lack of a proper relation to love objects.[7]

[5] Joseph Hawthorne, "Group Test for the Measurement of Cruelty-Compassion," *Journal of Social Psychology*, III (May, 1932), 189–211.
[6] R. S. Tolman, "Differences Between Two Groups of Adult Criminals," in *Genetic Psychological Monographs*, III (Aug., 1938), No. 20, 408.
[7] Our present knowledge of the foundation for emotions does not allow any specific conclusions. The following seems to have been established: the hypothalamus represents the center of autonomic and somatic integration of the motor expression of emotions, and emotion is characterized by sympathetic and parasympathetic excitatory and parasympathetic inhibitory discharges. It should be stressed that rage, shame rage, and fright are accompanied by a sympathetic (adrenalin) discharge and may also involve the excitation of the vago-insulin system. See Ernst Gellhorn, *Autonomic Regulations: The Significance for Physiology, Psychology and Neuropsychiatry*, pp. 202–3.

3. *Concept Formation Tests.* The following tests are used: Hanfmann-Kasanin and B.R.L. Sorting tests.

These tests reveal how the offender behaves and how he reacts to certain situations, thus giving information of the behavior pattern in him.

4. *Special Tests.* Visual, motor, and Gestalt tests are used to detect mental deviations and disturbances that may be caused by organic brain diseases.

5. *Mira Myokinetic Depression Test.* This test is used in cases of depression and is considered to have diagnostic and prognostic value, especially for the prison psychiatrist in determining possibility of suicide.

Certain tests aimed at finding out how the offender handles frustration situations are employed. They show whether his personality structure is a versatile or a rigid one. Finally, tests for educational and vocational ability and guidance, such as Brainard's test, may be used if indicated.

The scheme as outlined here may not be followed in each examination. Even so, one should always try to stress the essential points. The examination may particularly vary if it is performed on a juvenile offender. Pediatric conditions such as scarlatina, measles, mumps, and whooping cough cause character disorders as a result of pampering the child, as do convulsive conditions, developmental insufficiencies of mind, such as limited mental capacity due to mental deficiency or to an inner conflict having its root in a neurosis; further, eye and particularly ear diseases (the latter may produce paranoid trends) both interfere with the child's normal development in school, and call forth truancy or other types of misbehavior.

Due consideration should be given if the offender is a schoolgirl. Here the situation may not be so much of a problem of truancy as that of the opposite sex. As a rule one should try to learn as much as possible about the child's attitude towards sex, particularly when puberty is approaching.

Above all the child should never receive the impression that he is undergoing a psychiatric examination. If good rapport is established between the examiner and the child (transference), one should try to obtain the child's history without first asking for details. The latter may be postponed. A valuable contribution to the psychiatric examination of children, particularly regarding sexual differences, has been made by David M. Levy in his survey.[8]

No rules can be laid down for making a successful psychiatric examination. But the arrangement of and collection of data should be done as suggested here.

V. CONCLUSION OF EXAMINATION

In concluding the examination, the psychiatrist should reconstruct the life history and crime of the offender and try to arrive at a diagnosis of him, stressing briefly the following points:

1. Conditions under which the offender was born and has lived up to the time of his offense, emphasizing familial and social history, such as poverty, his position in the family (only child, twin, or tenth sibling), environment, criminal pattern, and so on.

2. Precipitating events: Here may be listed briefly those things which in the examiner's eyes may have participated in the development of the personality and finally became traumatic, acting as precipitating events prompting the crime. Such precipitating events may be bodily or mental disease, broken home situations, overprotective parents, or threatened loss of security.

3. Crime: Its type briefly described.

4. Personality structure: Outline the offender's personality structure and how he reacted to his environment and give a short summary of the etiological factors stressing *why* he committed the crime.

5. Diagnosis: (a) psychiatric; (b) characterological; (c) medical.

6. Determination of responsibility: This is decided according to the findings. If the offender is considered sane he is responsible for his act, if insane he is irresponsible. The law also disregards a crime committed by an idiot or by a child under the age of fourteen.

7. Recommendations: In giving recommendations it must first be stressed that the court has jurisdiction over the offender. The psychiatrist's position is merely an advisory one. Whether or not the court will follow it, the psychiatrist should give his advice according to his view of the case. These recommendations may in

[8] *A Method of Integrating Physical and Psychiatric Examination,* pamphlet reprinted from *American Journal of Psychiatry,* IX (July, 1929), No. 1, 121–94.

many cases not be effected because of restrictions on the part of the law; but these limitations shall not keep the psychiatrist from making recommendations. This has a double purpose. First to attract the court's attention to the case, second, to direct the court's attention to possible etiological treatment instead of a symptomatic one, if this is within the law. Thus, in a case of kleptomania, for instance, the offender should be referred to a psychiatrist with psychoanalytic experience rather than imprisoned. However, such a recommendation depends entirely upon the attitude of the court and upon the type of case. If the case concerns a child whose home situation may be said to be the main cause for delinquency, treatment regarding the environment should be referred to the social worker, while psychotherapy, if necessary, may be given. If the offender has difficulty with school, a psychologist or child psychiatrist should do the therapy.

At times the court may ask the psychiatrist to make an examination only to give the court an impression of the offender's mental condition, forcing the examiner to conduct only a superficial investigation. In that case it is impossible to follow the guide as outlined above. In another case the court may want the offender to be observed for a prolonged time, in which case the psychiatrist may use with advantage the psychiatric examination as outlined. In still other cases the court wants the offender examined between trial and sentence, as is the case in the Court of General Sessions of New York City. Here the psychiatrist may be given opportunity to see the offender several times.

It is impossible here to go into all the cases a psychiatrist may encounter. Therefore, in the next chapter we will give a classification from the functional viewpoint and, since space is limited, focus our attention on the most common personality structures of the offender.

VI

THE PSYCHOLOGY OF THE INDIVIDUAL
OFFENDER: CLASSIFICATION

THE INTIMATE relationship of the personality to criminal behavior leads us to offer some practical conclusions regarding possible classification of the offender. Since he to a large extent selects his own type of crime (see page 22), depending upon personality factors and situation, a classification must give these two constituents due consideration. The psychological conditioning and experiences to which the offender has been exposed and the personality aims which he tries to attain must necessarily involve psychopathological processes and situational characteristics in the classification. This would include those offenders who have been influenced by a criminal pattern.

It would be well if we could use those psychological and social factors as the fundamental points in the classification of the offender. However, regardless of how much of the personality is involved in the perpetration of the act and regardless of how much the social situation is entangled, there is one element that stands out, and that is the time factor—how often the act is committed. This has a bearing upon the nature of the personality and type of situation in which the offender finds himself. Whatever the offender's make-up is, one can gather from his history whether he is a momentary or a chronic offender.

Classification is always forced on nature, and hence is artificial, which is one reason why people disagree on classification. Nature does not want to be classified; it struggles against such an imposition. But in spite of the shortcomings classifications have, they are necessary. For our purpose a classification is essential not only because it may be a guide to our dealings with the offender but also because it may lead to a rational segregation and possible treatment of him.

From the viewpoint of time, we can divide offenders into: momentary or acute offenders; and chronic offenders.

I. Momentary Offenders

The momentary offender commits a crime just once or twice, only under certain circumstances. His type of crime is situational or accidental, with more or less involvement of the personality. The person may meet a certain situation and yield to an impulse which provokes his entire personality to participate vividly in an antisocial act. After he has committed the crime he may just as vividly reject and repent it, perhaps with the result that he refrains from further transgression. In either event, some unconscious desire may express itself through mistakes. In another case, the offender may be influenced by criminal patterns, such as bad companions or a poor family relationship, in which a member displays some antisocial tendencies.

We then have the three following classes of momentary offenders: (1) situational offenders; (2) accidental offenders; and (3) associational offenders. These people are not in reality criminals. We designate as criminals only those who have shown a consistent antisocial attitude and repeatedly have been transgressors of the law. We have this type in mind because it is they who make up the bulk of the criminal group.

In describing these different categories, we are here restricted to mentioning only the clear-cut types, but we may assume that transitions within these categories exist. The acute offender does not reveal any definite criminal pattern in his personality. As soon as the criminal act is executed, the person wishes it undone, his superego condemning the act.

Of the three types the first one, the situational offender, may perform a crime because an overwhelming opportunity arises, or because of a compelling situation, such as a strong feeling of injustice or a need for self-defense, or in the course of a temporary mental condition, such as a reactive depression. While a transgression is being perpetrated, the offender's impulse to act antisocially is overpowering, but as soon as this impelling force vanishes, his ego rejects the crime.

To the situational offender are ascribed those crimes committed because of opportunity. It has been said that opportunity makes the thief. Think upon the hungry fellow who passes a bakery shop and steals a loaf of bread or the poor man who finds some money that rightfully belongs to someone he knows. The temptation to keep these possessions is overwhelming. It is more an external circumstance that leads to this type of crime as is seen from the following case. A young man, after having done night work for some time, had to give up his job because of poor health. After a prolonged stay in the country, he returned to the city, but being without funds he was hungry and became desperate. He snatched a purse and was haled into court. Here the circumstances—his night work and the necessary prolonged vacation—led him into a situation where, deprived of work, he became a transgressor.

The accidental offender runs unexpectedly into difficulties with the law through mistake or chance. Careless driving or thoughtlessly throwing away a burning match may perhaps place an otherwise honest man in a predicament. In a recent case a young boy had borrowed a car allegedly belonging to another fellow and drove it through a street in the city where the policeman who actually owned it was directing traffic. The boy was immediately apprehended. He drove through this street only because he was forced to make a detour; usually he used another route.

The importance of the third type of offenders—associational—seems to have been greatly overlooked. This sort is not only influenced by his own criminalistic tendencies, no matter how weak they may appear, but also by his immediate surroundings when certain situations arise. An intoxicated man who later becomes acquainted with criminally inclined individuals may himself become a transgressor, not merely because he was intoxicated but because he fell in with people of a criminal pattern. Over and over again I have seen individuals without any criminal tendencies who from external circumstances have been forced into a criminal act which might be considered the result of association with those of a criminal pattern. One young man, who had had a few drinks, became acquainted with three sailors and took a walk in a park with them. They approached a young girl who was persuaded by one of the sailors to have sexual intercourse. Shortly afterwards the young man in question was told to kiss the girl. For some unknown reason she screamed, attracting the attention of the police. Two of the sailors fled, the third was shot to death, and the young man was caught.

II. Chronic Offenders

When an acute offender commits a second or a third crime, which may be an expression of personal maladjustment, one may then be inclined to say for the most part that a criminal pattern has started to develop in the personality. Such a pattern may become more and more deeply ingrained in the individual, so that finally a definite criminal characteristic is evolved. If that is the case, a chronic criminal is produced. This evolution occurs along different lines, depending on the various groups. These are: (1) offenders afflicted with organic or functional disorders of the body and of the brain; (2) chronic situational, accidental, and associational offenders; (3) neurotic and compulsory offenders; (4) offenders with neurotic characters; and (5) offenders with faulty development of the superego.

1. *Offenders Afflicted with Organic or Functional Disorders of the Body and of the Brain:* In this type, the personality structure is impaired by some destructive agent, toxic, degenerative, or infectious, or by some functional agent which damages the personality ego. To this category belong schizophrenics, mental defectives, epileptics, general paretics, and persons with head injuries with posttraumatic personality changes—on the whole, all those individuals whom the law does not regard as criminally responsible. In this group may also be included those offenders whom the law does regard as criminally responsible, for instance, those who commit antisocial acts because of a disease or a deformity of their body. Persons with this make-up have been described elsewhere.

Space does not allow us to consider each type here. Since one—the schizophrenics—are rather common among mentally diseased offenders, we will discuss some details of their personality and participation in crime.

In order to understand the schizophrenic, it is necessary first to describe the schizoid personality from which we assume the schizophrenic individual develops. This cannot be done better than by citing the case of a young man who was sentenced for larceny and who had a previous record of two offenses. He was a bright fellow who had been awarded a college scholarship. Though he worked hard in one way or another, his expectations were not fulfilled, and he had to start in business as a clerk.

When interviewed he spoke readily about himself and admitted that he always found himself in a dilemma in thinking and acting. The peculiarity was that in spite of his youth, he had shown already a remarkable lack of ability to adapt himself to society—and this in contrast to his high intelligence. At almost every instance in which a decision was necessary, he found himself with conflicting thoughts.

We may come to an understanding of this fellow when we consider his make-up. He reached wrong solutions because he did not have the right conception of reality and so was unable to adapt himself to his environment. His schizoid character—and his is a schizoid personality—made him unable to see reality in the right dimensions. It is such psychological traits which we find in the schizoid make-up, leading them into difficulties.

If we look further into schizoid persons, we find that they are impervious, isolated, uncertain, and often romantic. However, it has been said that their most marked trait is their autism; the individual is incapsulated in an egocentric world.[1] The contents of the autistic thoughts become incorrigible and possess for the sick person the value of reality. Thus, the autism is characterized by an unreal attitude which the imagination elicits. One of the variants of autism is daydreaming. Although Bleuler first introduced this term, "autistic," he preferred rather the term, "dereistic," by which he meant a thinking away from the subject.

Turning to the offender spoken of, the schizoid part of his personality is made up of his autistic or dereistic self-centered character. If we follow the development of a person with such a schizoid character, we will find a contradiction between his thoughts and actions. He wants to perform simultaneously the same and opposite acts. If his contradictions are marked, the result may be that he is unable to accomplish anything. If these conflicts become more pronounced, they may cause a mental split. A clue to the understanding

[1] Consult the French expressions: "Augmentation du sens de la personnalité," and "perte on sens de la réalité," K. Jaspers, *Allgemeine Psychopathologie für Studierende, Ärtze und Psychologen,* pp. 183, 185, 321.

of the make-up of such a person is his basic schizoid attitude. The roots of the evils of his personality lie in the conflicting elements in his structure.

Because of the great social implications involved, it is important to be aware of all those traits that may lead up to a schizophrenia. Since there are so many transitions between the schizoid and the schizophrenic, it is necessary to know *when* a schizoid is entering a psychosis. A breach between the schizoid's ego and his environment is one criterion. An essential trait in the schizoid constitution is a scarcity of native urges. Usually emotions and passions do not break through because of his autistic personality, but rather are locked up within him. A schizoid person will demonstrate emotional leveling in his cool manners and his lack of affectations. Such an attitude in many cases remains throughout life. However, when the distance between the ego and reality becomes greater and greater, one may talk of a schizophrenic development. For the schizoid man, the critical and disastrous moment appears when the connection between his ego and his environment is broken. That is the moment when his urges and emotions seemingly disappear, ending in schizophrenia.

It is appropriate here to mention a twenty-year-old man who two years prior to his present prison offense had performed a burglary and now was charged with a holdup. He was the youngest of three sons of a well-to-do business man. His school record was excellent, but because of his father's loss of business, he had to obtain a position which he disliked. When he was eighteen years old, he suddenly gave up his job and sat at home, saying that he did not need to work. A consultant psychiatrist advised the father that the boy had had a "nervous breakdown," and he was sent to the country. He returned two weeks later, apparently recovered. That same evening he went into a store and ran away with some articles, but was caught. He received a suspended sentence, and his concerned mother sent him to an uncle in a nearby city. He appeared at times sullen and introverted, disliked girls, and was homesick so that he was sent back to his home. At the time of his return he was carelessly dressed, for which he was criticized by his two brothers. The following night he took his father's gun, went into the streets, and held up two women. Frightened by their screaming, he threw away the gun and ran, but was apprehended after a wild chase. When I saw him, he looked unconcerned, his talk was irrelevant, and his emotions shallow. As to his offense, he always answered with a laugh that it was an "impulse." He showed a great deal of apathy, was largely preoccupied, and usually sat in a corner by himself. He denied that he had hallucinatory or delusionary ideas, although he at times was seen walking around talking and laughing to himself— a faint indication of the presence of hallucinations.

It seems that the patient's first "nervous breakdown" was apparently an approaching schizophrenic episode in which he committed the burglary and from which he later ostensibly recovered. He then went through a new phase and committed the holdup.

The psychological picture described here may show how varying a schizophrenia may appear, ranging from no striking symptoms at all to conspicuous psychotic features. A schizophrenic may in certain cases even be able to have a position and keep it (see page 156). At times he may be talkative; at other times, and this is most common, he may be silent. Such silence may be indicative of introversion, extending to autistic or dereistic smugness.

Thus, on the surface the schizophrenic may appear normal and, to some extent, lead a conventional life. Never, however, has he many friends. One may live with such a person for years without being able to say that one really knows him. His friendship seems rather superficial and simple, as does also his erotic life. His often complete coolness to sexual life, extending to utter platonism, is well known. Just as he cannot accept responsibility for his surroundings, he cannot accept his sexual responsibility, probably because his Oedipus situation has not been adequately resolved. His instinctual life may, however, be mobilized if, for instance, he should learn that his woman is in love with somebody else or if his imagination leads him to believe that there is another man. If such is the case, he is full of hatred and jealousy, which may lead to serious assaults. Because of his lack of real sexual feelings, he tries, in his imagination, to sexualize his emotions, causing a pathological compensation to take place. It may be because of this that we, in accordance with Kretschmer's view, find a disproportionately greater number of sexual perversions in schizophrenia than in any other type of mental disease. Although homosexuality is rather rare, exhibitionism and masturbation are common in schizophrenics, for which reason they get apprehended. I recall a case in which a forty-five-year-old man with a schizoid make-up, who had lead an apparently quiet life except for some drinking, was accused of exhibitionism with minors, a charge which he indignantly denied. In the discussion he involved himself in contradictions and admitted previous exhibitionistic acts, which a later check up showed to be true.

Schizophrenia is not a clearly defined disease. In a psychological sense, it may mean a certain way of meeting and dealing with experiences, or it may mean a world of an amazing totality for which we have not yet found an exact definition. It is not a disease in the more narrow sense; neither is it a group of diseases. It is characterized rather by a specific kind of alteration of thinking or feeling, and it may be considered as a form of maladaptation, in which there is an inner disharmony, an inconsistency in thought, feeling, and behavior.[2] Schizophrenia then is a disorganization of the personality, a problem in human behavior which occurs according to the stress and strain of life. We may come near the truth if we say that schizophrenia is the result of a failure to adapt to life, and it is this failure which results in crime.

This maladaptation comes to the fore when we see how the schizophrenic person thinks. When the normal man thinks upon a certain object, he attaches to it all its different qualities which come to his mind, while the schizophrenic individual focuses his thought upon the term itself, giving the term and not the object all the attention of his emotions.

This is particularly true in some types of murder cases, those which, unfortunately enough, have been designated as committed "without comprehensive motivation." I remember the killing of a girl which took place a long time ago. The murderer was at first not found, but ten years later another girl was murdered in about the same way, and a man was suspected. He finally admitted that he had killed the two girls. In court he expressed a great love for the girls but said that he had to take their lives. Laymen were rather puzzled by his statements. If we remember the make-up of a schizoid

2 See Nolan D. C. Lewis, *Research in Dementia Praecox* and *The Constitutional Factors in Dementia Praecox.*

—and his personality was basically schizoid—we know that he is able to love and hate simultaneously, in the same way as a schizophrenic person loves a rose for its beauty and hates it because of its thorns. In this case the murderer's sexual drive was adapted only to the word "love" without conveying any feelings of warmth, romance, or tenderness. This man, as with similar murderers, was filled with primitive impulses; part of the personality seemed to perform the act independently of the other functions of the person.

A man with such a make-up apparently lacks emotions because the part of his ego which is in touch with external reality is of little or no significance to him. He merely receives impressions without summing up what they mean to him, and they do not affect his inner life. It is for this reason that the factual world is without reality and is only words to him, words to which he clings instead of to facts.

Therefore he profusely employs images and symbols. His psychotic thinking reflects a regression of his instinctual drives back to the most early narcissistic episodes of his development, thereby requiring him to live in a world where he himself is the center. It is probable that it is the quality of the ego which is damaged, and this injury, whether due to organic or psychologic developmental changes, may have the same effect.

The great variety of personality changes occurring in the disease, from the normal to the obviously abnormal, makes it necessary to emphasize that schizophrenics who on the surface appear normal may suddenly commit acts which too often reveal their abnormality. The term "ambulatory schizophrenia" has been applied to this variety.[3] Such individuals may be dangerous under certain circumstances. The often unexplained, aggressive antisocial acts committed by apparently sane persons have in many cases turned out to be the acts of schizophrenics.

In dealing with schizoid and schizophrenic personalities, it should be pointed out that hysterical phenomena may be seen. If such hysterical symptoms are found in the course of schizophrenia, this does not necessarily change our principal view about this illness. Hysteria is no uncommon phenomenon in schizophrenic

[3] Gregory Zilboorg, "Ambulatory Schizophrenics, Psychiatry," *Journal of the Biology and Pathology of Interpersonal Relations,* IV (May, 1941), No. 2, 154.

disease. When supposedly hysterical patients gradually deteriorate, they are not cases of hysteria but of schizophrenia. These hysterical traits may be so pronounced that they appear to be tied up with the individual's mental make-up. It is necessary to be on the alert regarding them, because they may mislead one to diagnose hysteria when the disease is really schizophrenia.

The case of a thirty-year-old man who started his criminal career when eleven will illustrate this point. There was no criminal record in his family. He had been a truant and gradually became involved in criminal acts. In 1938 he was given a long sentence for robbery. At this time he was considered aggressive and dangerous and was a constant escape threat. In spite of his superior intelligence, he was regarded as unimprovable. Three years after he was incarcerated he attempted to hang himself in solitary and was brought to the hospital. When examined he said: "I wanted to take my life. I wanted to kill the condition in which I found myself. I could not remain in solitary, and I put something around my neck."

The examination revealed that he possessed a certain trace of self-esteem, superiority, and paranoid traits. No hallucinations were present. His thoughts were contradictory and his behavior was rather cool. It was thought that his attempted suicide was due to his desire to show off. His history showed that he always tried to be in the center of things and that he tried to assert himself. His attempted suicide betrayed a desire to escape from reality, but it was in direct opposition to his actual behavior pattern. Since early childhood his life had been full of the dramatic, including the times he had been confined in institutions. To a normal person his behavior on many occasions seemed theatrical and hysterical. Without doubt this man tried to impress on himself and others that he was something more than he really was. These psychological manifestations, to place himself in relief, to impress both himself and the world, we consider hysterical phenomena and reactions.

These hysterical phenomena are characterized by a desire to display certain emotions or ideas. Such a view is in keeping with the picture we have painted of the basic trait in this offender's personality—the self-centered protection of his ego. It seems now that his desire to impress himself and others was probably a decisive force in his subsequent development. In any event this very urge may have formed one of the starting points for his criminal career. It seems that the desire to expose himself became a guiding principle with him. The possibility of exaggeration was already present and later led him to apparent eccentric conduct. Typical is his attempt at suicide. He wants to play a role. In the light of his hysterical character and his schizoid personality, it is important to bear in mind his great self-esteem and his almost morbid feeling of superiority. These two combined made it imperative for him to feel certain of himself. Therefore he had to push ahead, simulate an attitude. This point in connection with his basically schizoid personality makes clear the intimate association between his lack of ability to adapt himself to reality and his morbid feeling of superiority.

It is easy to see that this man, thirty years old, in and out of institutions and prisons for nineteen years, was not able to adjust to society. His ever-increasing emotional instability, extending to mental derangement, made it imperative that he be recommended to a psychiatric institution.

As we have seen this from this case, symptoms of hysteria have a psychological motive more apparent than that of schizophrenia, in which normal and psychotic features exist side by side. In pure hysteria there is an alternation of normal and psychotic behavior. If the examiner suspects a schizophrenia which is well hidden, it should be remembered that a sodium amytal interview may release the patient's thoughts and emotions and reveal his true condition. Because of the aggressive behavior of schizophrenics, it is essential that their condition be recognized in order that proper care may be taken of them.

2. *Chronic Situational, Accidental, and Associational Offenders:* This type evolves naturally from the acute situational, accidental, or associational offender. We will mention only the associational type. As with the acute associational offender, the chronic one is an individual who is influenced by the criminalistic pattern of his immediate surroundings, and, hence, we may also call him a habitual criminal. Offenders of this type live in certain areas of a city where the younger ones are influenced by the older. They live from hand to mouth, and their criminal activities, which change with their opportunities and needs, are as planless as their days. One may say

that these chronic associational offenders become criminals because of their negative, rather than their positive, qualities. They are unable to resist temptations existing in their neighborhood, following more external influences than a real criminalistic inclination.

This group may be distinguished from the essentially criminal who become offenders because of a faulty development of the superego, but there are varying degrees in moving towards this latter type. In chronic associational criminals antisocial or criminal activity is often coupled with alcoholism. To this type belongs the shiftless, irresponsible, lazy, migrating, and hoboing individual who associates with men of the same caliber and who roams around the country without any plan or purpose. Prisons and institutions are filled with them. Once in a while one is released, soon to be returned. Their personality is shallow; some are demented or physically spent from the use of alcohol or from syphilitic infections; and some are in poor condition because of constant exposure to all kinds of weather. On the whole, they are a miserable lot.

3. *Neurotic and Compulsory Offenders.* We have in Chapter II touched upon neurotic offenders and stated that they were unable to disengage themselves from parental and family ties. Compulsory-obsessional offenders, who belong to the group of psychoneurotics, we should first say are to a certain extent sexually immature. Considering the mechanism of such personalities, it is probable that individuals with compulsory-obsessional neurosis, or another type of neurosis, suffer because of a failure to solve the conflicts between their drives and their egos.

Space precludes our mentioning all types of psychoneurosis. Here we will deal only with the compulsory-obsessional neurosis, since it plays an important part in instigating crimes and constitutes the underlying pathology in these compulsive or symptomatic offenses. Offenses included in this type are kleptomania, pyromania, nymphomania, dipsomania, dromomania, homicidal mania, and compulsive wandering. (The latter type is not at all distinct; the mechanism is somewhat different from that seen in a compulsive-obsessional neurosis. Compulsive wandering is seen in fugue cases, as in a depressed individual who is conditioned or sensitized to reactions of this special type. From this situation a condition emerges which is related to the conduct seen in neurotics, even in psychotics.)

The compulsory-obsessional state is a condition where fixed but irrational ideas, which the offender knows are wrong, are carried out in such a way that they interfere with normal behavior. The obsession intrudes itself upon the person apparently without any external stimulus. Compulsion is the motor counterpart of an obsession. Generally speaking, behavior impulses arise from different sources. They may originate as a result of habit, emotions, or a psychoneurosis of the compulsive-obsessional type. Bard [4] has found that experimental facts indicate that bodily responses which have in common a manifestation of rage are elicited and acted out by the more primitive parts of the brain. He found that the reactions which were conditioned by the cerebral mechanism were located in the caudal part of the hypothalamus and the most caudal and ventral parts of the corresponding segments of the thalamus.

Pyromaniacs are good examples of people afflicted with traits of a compulsory-obsessional neurosis. They usually have no motivation of revenge or any wish for material gain in setting fires. It seems that they adhere to the principle of pleasure and not of profit, and may therefore be related to certain types of sexual offenders. It then appears, as will be seen in the following case, that the offense of the pyromaniac is completely irrational.

A twenty-two-year-old man was sentenced for starting two fires on the same night. He had twice before been apprehended on the same charge. When arrested for his latest offense, he stated that he had set fire to a large garage containing several cars, and afterwards had set fire to a house where people were sleeping. He admitted that he had started four fires, succeeding only with two because it was raining. When he was asked why he did it, he answered: "It just came over me, and I started a fire." Later it turned out that he had been working in the garage he had set fire to. He denied having had an argument with his employer, and this was confirmed in a later examination. He said candidly: "When I start a fire, I continue. The night it happened, I did not know what was happening to me. I think that once I had started the fires I understood what I had done, but it was too late to do anything." Asked whether he felt an urge to do it, he answered frankly: "I get the idea and

4 Philip Bard, "The Neuro Humoral Basis of Emotional Reactions," Chapter vi in *A Handbook of General Experimental Psychology.*

I do it. I stay until the fire has started, look at it, and then I leave."

His family history showed that an uncle of his was insane. When the defendant was a little boy he stuttered. During his early childhood he became attached to his mother, who apparently overprotected him. He was evasive and reluctant to talk about his sexual life, but so much was brought out that one might surmise some abnormality of the sexual drive.

In the review of this case, no economic or revenge motive was found. The facts were that he had urges to start fires, which appeared to have taken the form of obsessions which he had to carry out. It seems that in starting fires there was an element of gratification which might be considered related to a twisted sexual drive. One could say too that his firesetting was an expression of enjoying the power of destruction or a magical power, an indication of sadism.[5] He was undoubtedly driven to the act. This driving force was an obsessional idea, revealing that he suffered from a compulsory-obsessional neurosis. In view of this condition and knowing that a compulsory act, such as setting fires or continued stealing, may occur because of a forbidden sexual act, it is doubtful whether this man had a normal sexual life. His craving and desire for starting fires was the result of an obsessional idea nourished by an undeveloped sexual drive. How compelling such a compulsory act is may be surmised from the fact that after his first incarceration, he stated that he would kill himself if he ever started another fire. This shows how far beyond his control were these firesetting urges. It is obvious that a person with such inclinations is a danger to society.

Compulsory-obsessional acts and ideas vary all the way from normal to abnormal. Those within the normal range include certain habits of eating, shaving, reading, working, or convictions which we perhaps may doubt but nevertheless like to keep. Abnormal compulsion may be seen in the person who locks a door and leaves it, then comes back to try the lock, or turns off a light and

[5] The same view regarding fire as a magical power has lately been stressed by Schachtel. He states that none of his 11 cases showed the Rorschach pattern of an obsessional neurosis, which is frequently attributed to firesetters. This is against the experience so far gained in clinical psychiatry. The only explanation seems to be that the Rorschach test, as a special test, may not be able to reflect the compulsory-obsessional trend because it is covered or because of an inadequate interpretation.

returns to see whether it is off or on. If all these acts are repeated to such an extent that they seriously interfere with a normal life, we may say that they are pathological. This becomes more evident when the acts are antisocially directed.

In interpreting what takes place unconsciously in the mind of a pyromaniac or a kleptomaniac, one may say that the desires of the id and a desire for punishment alternate, the obsessional neurosis acting as a defense against aggressive impulses. The conflict is internalized while the person's superego keeps the conflict back, with the result that he has to act out his inclinations. Deep in the unconscious is a forbidden wish such as a sexual one. Alexander and Healy [6] have described a rather clear-cut case in which the patient analyzed her feelings while she was stealing and recognized them as being analogous to or actually accompanied by sexual sensations. This may indicate the intimate relationship existing between some types of compulsory-obsessional neurosis and the sexual drive. (As in most cases, the suppression of the sexual wish seems to be related to the anal sadistic level.)

4. *Offenders with Neurotic Characters.* We will here deal with a group of offenders who, generally speaking, are often described as psychopathic personalities or by other descriptive terms. We will try to give a genetic view of them, not merely a descriptive one. In saying this, the author does not disregard the constitutional factors which may be present in such individuals. It will be seen later that offenders with neurotic characters may, regarding their appearance and their antisocial behavior, not be much different from those who have become so because of a faulty development of their superego.

A distinct trait in their conduct is aggression, which is a form of a chronic self-destruction. In acting out their aggressions, these persons wreck their own lives, creating inconvenience and trouble in their own family and causing damage to society in such a way that in many instances they have to be taken care of. They act out their aggressive tendencies which, because they are antisocial, call forth punishment from society. This type of person may act as neurotic or as a criminal. Many of them have one trait in common—they

[6] Franz Alexander and William Healy, *Roots of Crime*, p. 86.

may in one or another way succeed in life to a certain extent, but finally they fail.

It was Alexander, led by an example from Freud and Abraham, who first introduced the concept of the neurotic character. As the reader may know, the neurotic person has autoplastic symptoms while the person having a neurotic development shows alloplastic behavior. Thus the latter—the neurotic character—acts out his unconscious internal conflicts and tries to get along with this personality and also, in spite of this personality conflict, to carry out his impulses. His libidinal impulses, unconscious as they are, try to attain sexual gratification, arousing a strong guilt feeling. For this reason the individual must involve himself in behavior disorders in order to be punished. Very often one may see that such individuals have a twisted sexual life, leading one to believe that their personality condition has a touch of perversion.

We then see that the term "neurotic character" will cover a large group whose "neuroses" consist in engaging in antisocial conduct rather than in neurotic manifestations. Considering the psychodynamics underlying their acts, we will see that the underlying conflict in the neuroses or in the neurotic characters are basically the same, the struggle being between the id and the ego. One may assume that there is at an early date a separation of the ego which allows a great amount of id impulses to be expressed, and this may take place even if part of the ego is socially adjusted. This underlying conflict expresses why this neurotic character is always at odds with himself and with society and always unconsciously craves punishment. That is why he is rebellious against himself and against society. Keeping this make-up in mind, one will see that many of those individuals whom we call sexual perverts, pathological liars, gamblers, hobos, wanderers, alcoholics, narcotic addicts, swindlers, and marriage wreckers are, in fact, either neurotic characters or are closely allied to them. Only careful protection and overindulgence on the part of their loved ones keep such persons from being sent to prison. However, because of their antisocial tendencies, most of them are sooner or later incarcerated.

The following case might shed some light on such a personality. The prisoner was the youngest of six children in a well-to-do family. No delinquency was present among them. When he was seven years old he did some petty stealing and was placed in the care of some child guidance agencies and sent twice to correctional institutions. He was rather alert and made friends easily because of his agreeable conduct. Later he was involved in some theft from a store, for which there were no external reasons, and he was sent to an institution for two years. On one occasion he told his foster parent that he did not know what made him steal. In the reformatory his behavior was orderly; there was hardly an infraction of the rules. Arrangements were made for him to be paroled, and he became employed in his father's store. He seemed to get along rather well. He met a girl who turned out to be very fond of him. He married her, and was going to be in charge of the whole business, when one night he got drunk and broke into an apartment where he was found in the morning. Some friends covered up for him but he had barely escaped the police before he was apprehended for stealing a car. This violation of parole returned him to prison. His unhappy wife and family were puzzled by his conduct. He behaved very well in prison and gained his freedom once again. Under the close supervision of his family he was kept quiet for about a year. But then he broke loose, committed a burglary, and became involved in other criminal acts. The last time I saw him he was given a long sentence, while his wife and family, more puzzled than ever, waited for him.

This is only a sketchy story of this man's life. It would take too much space to give even a few details about his behavior.

This man, repeating his crime, may be designated as an active neurotic character. The alcoholic who drinks continuously or the Don Juan who seduces repeatedly are analogous types. In contrast to the attention given the active neurotic character, little study has been devoted to the passive one. In this type we find that their basic character reveals passive and dependent traits which they try to deny in aggressive behavior. Hence, the characteristics are not as clear-cut as those of the active neurotic character. Nevertheless, this type should be incorporated in a classification.[7]

An illustration of this type is found in the case of a young boy, seventeen years old, who since he was thirteen had been a runaway. He was considered bright and was raised in a good home. His father, regarded as emotionally unstable, was strict, but fond of the boy,

[7] Karl Menninger, *Man against Himself*, p. 95.

while his mother was overindulgent with him. She wanted the youngster to conduct himself as a girl, much against his wishes. In order to protect the boy, the father forbade him to go out to play with other boys in the evening. One night he did go out, stayed out too late, and did not dare to come home. In the morning he returned and was beaten by his father. He then stayed at home and the incident was apparently forgotten. Several months later he left home suddenly, stole a car, and remained away for a week. He was brought home and enrolled in a technical school which he attended for two months. But then he ran away again, became involved in some burglaries, and was sent to prison. He was soon paroled and shortly afterwards committed another burglary. I saw him when he was nineteen.

He was a tiny, good-looking fellow whom one barely could suspect of being a runaway and committing all these offenses.[8] Details must here be omitted, but he gave the impression of being a rather weak, dependent, passive individual, who used his chronic aggressions to deny his passive impulses.

Up to now we have discussed criminals with neurotic characters, including in this group those persons who are known to most psychiatrists and laymen, as well, as psychopathic personalities. Since this term has been in use for over a hundred years and seems to be incorporated in the people's vocabulary, it is probably impossible to dispense with it, and yet, I, and I think many with me, do not know of any term which has caused more harm in clouding our view of those individuals to whom it has been applied. In reality, when we speak of a psychopathic personality, in most instances we do not know what his make-up consists of. In fact, this term should be discarded. Usually, one is inclined to designate as psychopathic personalities all those persons who do not fit into our other groups.

In the course of time, the term psychopathic personality has been used to mean a certain person who because of deviations and inadequacies in his personality and in his mental make-up is neither mentally defective nor psychotic, but has a defect, especially regarding his character or emotions. We then will define a psychopath as an abnormal personality who suffers because of his aberrant char-

[8] Some information regarding a similar type of behavior is found in an article by Cyril Gerald J. Pearson, "The Chronically Aggressive Child," *Psychoanalytic Review*, XXVI (Oct., 1929), No. 4, 485–525.

acter or one who because of his abnormality disturbs society. A psychopath may, in spite of being highly gifted, show less valuable qualities. This may account for the fact that we find among offenders persons with a superior intelligence who are endowed with a capacity to accomplish criminal acts which, regarding their performance, are not only especially well done but also eccentric. In trying to describe these persons from the social and psychological viewpoints, we should keep in mind that most of them may be classified and should be classified in the near neurotic or in the neurotic character group.

These psychopaths, and we find them in every prison, are usually self-centered, aggressive, and emotionally unstable. They reveal a superior attitude and have throughout their entire life showed no inclination to be corrected. They manifest various inadequacies in their social behavior, may be directly antagonistic, or show inadequacies in the psycho-sexual field which result in deviations of their sexual drive. Special attention should be called to the sexual psychopath, where a diffuse sexual activity, including homosexuality, is present. There has been an inclination to include practically all chronic criminals in this group and even to restrict it to the antisocial. As pointed out above, many psychopathic personalities— near neurotic or neurotic characters—do not become transgressors of the law, and there are many repeated offenders who are not psychopathic personalities. The psychopath cannot express love. He shows deviations in his instinctive and emotional reactions, on the whole inadequate qualities which make him socially unfit, and in spite of the fact that many psychopaths are highly intelligent, they are unable to control their emotional strivings.

If we follow such a psychopath from his earliest childhood, we see that he has caused trouble by truancy, petty stealing, or some other type of antisocial activity. He has been unable to adapt himself to environment, and he is in episodical or continual conflict with his surroundings. D. K. Henderson has given this definition:

The term psychopathic state is the name we apply to those individuals who conform to a certain intellectual standard, sometimes high, sometimes approaching the realm of defect but yet not amounting to it, who throughout their lives or from a comparatively early stage, have exhibited disorders of conduct of an antisocial or a social nature, usually of a recurrent or episodic type, which in many instances have proved difficult to influence by methods of social, penal or mental care and treatment, and for whom we have no adequate provision of a preventative or curative nature.[9]

An understanding of the psychopathic personality may be reached when we view him as the product of dynamic psychological forces and mechanisms. These psychological forces produce in the person not only a definite symptom but lead to the building up of a certain pattern of character, including his emotions, which gives his mental make-up and conduct a certain color.

The characteristics of the psychopath are found in young people. Yes, when we speak of a psychopath, we have a young individual in mind. It is usually found that the age distribution varies from about fifteen to thirty-five or forty, the peak age being about twenty. An investigation made by Silverman showed that most psychopaths were found in the nineteen to twenty-two age group, an age instance which largely corresponds with that of most frequent criminality.[10] One would then be inclined to say that perhaps the basic trait in psychopaths is a certain emotional immaturity, which is reflected in an emotional instability. One may understand better this predominance of emotional instability when one recalls that personal maturity is not achieved as soon as sexual maturity, because the psychological development extends over a longer period of time than the sexual evolution.

What happens to the psychopathic personality? It has been found that he frequently shows intelligent superiority which, to an extent, perhaps has a bearing on a possible early sexual maturity. Emotional instability is normal in the formative period of life. In a psychopathic person the emotional instability is more pronounced. He reaches this instability earlier than the normal person and he remains in such a condition long after the normal person has reached his state of normal mental and social stability. This is the reason why the psychopathic individual is emotionally immature, impulsive, and aggressive, resembling a spoiled, incorrigible child. We may then see that his instability begins in childhood, reaches a peak in young adulthood, then drops down in the late twenties

[9] D. K. Henderson, *Psychopathic States*, p. 18.
[10] Daniel Silverman, "Clinical and Electroencephalographic Studies on Criminal Psychopaths," *Archives of Neurology and Psychiatry*, L (July, 1943), No. 1, 19–20.

and early thirties. After this the psychopathic person disappears. By that time society in most cases has caught up with him and placed him in an institution.

This may be the reason why the age groups vary in clinics and in prisons. Bromberg and Thompson found that 6.9 per cent of 10,000 prisoners examined at the Psychiatric Clinic of the Court of General Sessions were psychopaths.[11] Hartmann and Schroeder found that of 4,188 prisoners examined at the Diagnostic Depot, Illinois State Penitentiary, Joliet, 2.7 per cent of psychopaths were found in the group between fifteen and twenty-four years, 5 per cent between twenty-five and thirty-nine, and 11 per cent were forty and over.[12]

Usually the psychopaths are divided into different groups. We cannot mention here all the attempts which have been made to classify them. Such a competent investigator as Eugen Kahn went so far as to study the psychopath from the biogenetic, psychological, and philosophical viewpoints, and gives in his clinical descriptive classification 16 categories.[13] D. K. Henderson [14] classifies the psychopath according to psychobiological principles. He divides them into three groups: (1) predominantly aggressive; (2) predominantly passive or inadequate; (3) predominantly creative.

In the first group are homicides, suicides, alcoholics, drug addicts, sexual offenders, and epileptoids. His basis for the classification is their psychopathic behavior. He thereby disregards the psychopath's emotional problem. Kurt Schneider gives only a descriptive classification of the psychopath, whom he is unable to place beside the neurotic and the psychotic person. He believes that the psychopath cannot be counted among those having personality disorders. Partridge [15] wants to change the term psychopath to sociopath, but

11 Bromberg and Thompson, "The Relation of Psychosis, Mental Defective and Personality Types of Crime," *Journal of Criminology and Neurology*, XXVII (May–June, 1937), No. 1, 8.
12 "Criminology and the Age Factor," *Journal of Criminal Psychopathology*, V (Oct., 1943), No. 2, 352.
13 Eugen Kahn, *Psychopathic Personalities*.
14 Henderson, *Psychopathic States*, p. 43.
15 G. E. Partridge, "Current Conceptions of Psychopathic Personality," *American Journal of Psychiatry*, X (July, 1930), 53–99. See also: "Psychotic Reactions in the Psychopath," *American Journal of Psychiatry*, VIII (1939), 493 and "Psychopathic Personality and Personality Investigation," *American Journal of Psychiatry*, VIII (1928–29), 1053.

this is merely an evasion of the problem. Healy considers the anti-social behavior of psychopaths the most important predominant trait, supporting his assumption on the basis of constitution and diseases of childhood. Karpman [16] believes that psychopathy is a very specific mental disease which he calls anethopathy. He emphasizes that it is this group that forms the so-called habitual criminals. The conspicuous trait in their mental make-up is, according to Karpman, complete egocentricity, which also is reflected in their sexual behavior, which is narcissistic.

This survey shows how various and contradictory opinions are about psychopathic personalities. Is it possible to find an objective method by which one can determine the psychopathic personality? Where we have such a loosely organized group no effort should be spared nor any approach be overlooked in trying to discover such a method. Some noteworthy investigations have already been conducted, for example, the electroencephalographic studies. Silverman [17] examined the etiologic factors, both organic and psychogenic, which in his mind were operative in a selected group of typical psychopaths. Those persons with obvious signs of organic dysfunction of the brain, such as fractures of the skull, epileptic seizures, or other focal neurological symptoms, were excluded. Further, no attention was paid to possible psychodynamic factors, unless the clinical condition was that of a neurosis or psychosis, in which case the patient was excluded from the examination. His conclusions revealed that 80 per cent of the psychopaths had abnormal or borderline abnormal tracings on the electroencephalogram. Further examinations of the development and history of the psychopaths showed that from the psychological point of view 80 per cent had unsound factors in their childhood. The examination may imply that there exists an important organic component in the illness of the psychopath and that psychopathic behavior may be displayed in the time between infancy and early adulthood.

It may be added that one cannot avoid the impression that certain pronounced types of the psychopathic personality may show early aggressive tendencies. These may be considered precursors of the hostile psychopaths. Further, it is necessary to be aware that the

[16] Benjamin Karpman, "The Problem of the Psychopathist," *Psychiatric Quarterly,* III (1929), 495–526.
[17] Silverman, *op. cit.,* 18, 30, 31.

over-sexed or promiscuous person may in himself have a disposition for the development of a psychopathic personality. At any rate, he may be characterized by the aggressive or sexual drive which colors predominantly his whole behavior. This lends support to the belief that psychopathic persons may be seen in different types of personalities, schizoid, hypomanic, depressive, or obsessional, and they should be classified accordingly into these groups.

There are two factors in particular that may give offenders of a neurotic type a certain characteristic—their sexual drive and their addiction to alcohol or drugs. Since these two factors have a certain bearing upon criminal activities, we will discuss the sexual and alcoholic offenders. This does not imply that they are all either neurotic characters or psychopaths, although many of them are.

The sexual offender has been viewed with so much disgust that some clarifying words are necessary. One is usually inclined to think that the underlying pathology in a sexual crime is abnormal gratification of the sexual drive. This is not always so. A rape during an alcoholic spree or a sexual assault by a youthful offender may at times not have such characteristics at all. If some abnormality is present, it is revealed in the peculiarities that show up in the perpetration of the offense.

It is difficult to estimate the incidence of sexual offenses, because not all offenders are apprehended. In a psychiatric study made at the Court of General Sessions of New York by Frosch and Bromberg from the years 1932 to 1938, it was found that of 15,000 offenders, 709 were charged with sexual offenses.[18] A report of the Probation Department of the same court revealed that court crimes involving sex offenses of any kind, including bigamy, prostitution, impairing morals, and kidnapping, comprised 6.12 per cent of the total number of criminal investigations conducted by that department.[19] The Citizens Committee on the Control of Crime in New York City estimated that in New York City alone 1,891 cases of sexual offenses occurred in 1937, an increase of 51 per cent over the year 1936, while in 1938 the number was 1,888.

In 1940, 2,505 offenders were seen at the Psychiatric Clinic of the Court of General Sessions of New York City, of whom 110 were sex-

[18] Jack Frosch and Walter Bromberg, "The Sex Offender—A Psychiatric Study," *American Journal of Orthopsychiatry,* IX (Oct., 1939), No. 4, 766.
[19] Irving W. Halpern, *A Decade of Probation,* p. 52.

ual offenders. In 1941 the numbers were 2,527 and 105 respectively. It is usually considered that exhibitionism and pedophilia represent the largest number of the cases of sexual offenses.

It has been asserted that we find in the sexual criminals the greatest number of abnormal offenders. Scharffenberg examined over 600 prisoners sentenced for sexual crimes, and he found that about 30 per cent were mentally defective, which was about double the average for all prisoners.[20]

Frosch and Bromberg found that of 709 sexual offenders, 183 were maladjusted. Further, they found that only 15 per cent of the sexual offenders were recidivists. However, Apfelberg, Sugar, and Pfeffer found that 32 per cent had been charged with sexual offenses.[21]

Keeping these figures in mind, one may think that many sexual crimes are related to the offender's personality and some of them associated with their ages. It is a common experience that the greatest abnormal sexual offenders are the rather impotent, aged, or senile men who pet with children. While we see that pedophilia—an abnormal sexual inclination towards children—takes place mostly in the last decades of a man's life, statutory rape and other sexual assaults which need force are committed by young people. This is confirmed by the Citizens Committee on the Control of Crime in New York City which found that the greatest number of rape cases were among the twenty-one to twenty-five age group, while offenses other than rape occurred most frequently in the fifty-five or older group. Aschaffenburg made an examination of sexual offenders over a period of three years and he came to the conclusion that of 200, only 45 were entirely normal, and the offenses of 12 of these had been prompted by drunkenness. Ten suffered from senile dementia, 2 from dementia due to hardening of the arteries, 4 from some type of psychosis, 1 from dipsomania, and 1 from severe hysteria. Fourteen were idiots, 3 feeble-minded, and 9 epileptic. Nearly one fourth belonged in an asylum for the insane, an institution for idiots, or a home for the aged rather than in a prison. Even

[20] *The Norwegian Society of Crime*, 1935, p. 110.
[21] Apfelberg, Sugar, and Pfeffer, "A Psychiatric Study of 250 Sex Offenders from the Psychiatric Division, Bellevue Hospital, New York City and the Department of Psychiatry of the New York University College of Medicine," *American Journal of Psychiatry*, C (May, 1944), No. 1, 762–70.

the others—about 100—displayed more or less serious psychological abnormalities, especially feeble-mindedness, chronic alcoholism, or epilepsy, so that only 45 could be pronounced unquestionably normal.[22]

This examination must be compared with the investigations
previously mentioned. Apfelberg, Sugar, and Pfeffer examined 256
offenders, of whom 41 had a psychopathic personality, 87 had a
psychopathic personality with pathological sexuality, 31 were alcoholics, 21 schizoid personalities, 3 showed neurotic traits, 1 had
cerebral arteriosclerosis, 3 were senile, 1 had neurosyphilis, and 1
showed postencephalitic Parkinsonism—only 53 did not show any
abnormalities.

Although exhibitionism and pedophilia are most frequent
among the sex offenses, the most important of the perverted ones
is homosexuality. The reason for this is not only the legal implications of homosexuality but also its possible consideration as a disease.

Homosexuality is a condition where an individual prefers another one of the same sex, leading to an abnormal sexual activity
accompanied by gratification. Homosexuality may be practiced as
mutual masturbation, pederasty, inter femora, fellatio. There are
three types of homosexuality. In the first the active male plays the
part of the male in the sexual intercourse; in the second, the passive
male plays the part of the female. (The same types are reversed for
the females.) The third type is the mixed type, and perhaps the most
frequent, where a male or a female may assume both parts. One
may within certain limits say that the homosexual is an individual
who really belongs to the opposite sex. All people have originally
bisexual tendencies which are more or less developed and which in
the course of time normally deviate either in the direction of male
or female. This may indicate that a trace of homosexuality, no
matter how weak it may be, exists in every human being. It is
present in the adolescent stage, where there is a considerable
amount of undifferentiated sexuality.

It seems that homosexuality must depend upon psychological and
also, to some extent, on biological tendencies. As a matter of fact,
we must say that all types of perversions are exaggerations of the

[22] Gustav Aschaffenburg, *Crime and Its Repression*, p. 191.

different sexual inclinations in the grown-up individual which were present in childhood. In view of the presence of bisexuality, it is difficult to say how frequent homosexuality really is. One is apt to say that male homosexuality is found in only 2 per cent of the total population, but there is a general feeling that female homosexuality is more frequent. It has been generally assumed that from the psychological point of view homosexuality is closely related to the Oedipus situation. In the child occurs a rigid repression of sexual feelings, resulting in his giving up his own sex. The boy identifies himself with the mother and becomes afraid of or loves the father, while the girl does the opposite. Strong attachment to the mother or a governess may bring about the adoration and idealizing of the other sex. Normal sexual maturation may stop at an infantile stage, with the result that the individual accepts the fixation at this phase. If the person has a feminine make-up, the environment—here the mother or the governess—emphasizes his feminine attitude by raising him in female surroundings, protecting him against playing with other boys, and so on. In due course because of his pronounced female attitude, he may become attracted to boys rather than to girls, which results in overt homosexuality.

The pattern of behavior regarding the Oedipus and the castration complexes is not so rigid as was previously thought. It has been assumed that the sexual drive in children may be in abeyance.[23] Malinowski has shown that the latency stage is absent during the psychosexual development of children in some primitive cultures, such as in the Trobriand society, an assumption which he extends also to the underprivileged class of our own society.[24]

Psychological elements play a great role in homosexuality, but constitutional factors may also be present in many cases,[25] as may be seen in some male homosexuals. A typical homosexual, although *not always,* may be described thus: He is thin, has slender limbs, his cheeks are flushed, his face soft, his appearance and his manners are pleasant. Hair on the chest, axilla, and pubes is scarce. He behaves

[23] S. S. Isaacs, *Social Development in Young Children.*
[24] Bronislaw Malinowski, *Sex and Repression in Savage Society,* pp. 48–58.
[25] G. W. Henry and Hugh M. Galbraith, "Constitutional Factors in Homosexuality," *American Journal of Psychiatry,* XIII (May, 1934), No. 6, 1249–67.

like a girl, walks like a girl, smiles like a girl. He may like to cook, he may like to sew. He may even seek other girls, but this is only because his pals do, for in reality he is not attracted to them. Instead he is, without perhaps in the beginning being aware of it, attracted to boys of his own or older age. In any event, he may start to dress as a girl, perhaps take a girl's name, "marry" a man, and pose as "his wife." It is a striking characteristic of homosexuals that they often recognize each other. It is as though there is a mutual sexual attraction between them. This may perhaps be the reason why they never take into their acquaintance anyone who does not seek the same type of sexual satisfaction. Although externally they may vary a great deal, there is no doubt that in their make-up there are psychological features which bind them together. Lately, Joseph Wortis seems to have disproved the claim that there are anthropomorphic differences between the homosexual and the heterosexual individual.[26]

In the underlying mechanism of the homosexual the ego obeys the pregenital sexual impulses and prompts them to enter into his consciousness, thus accepting this abnormal sexual behavior as a natural one. But homosexual behavior must be differentiated from homosexual tendencies, which again should be differentiated from those inclinations of an unconscious nature. There is probably no normal person who does not possess some unconscious homosexual tendencies. It is for this reason that we say that latent perversion may be brought to the fore only accidentally or under such circumstances as may be found in prisons or in any place where males or females are confined to each other's company. Thus, the homosexual inclination, no matter how unconscious it is, may, when a certain situation arises, be exposed for influence and become manifest.

Have we a way to distinguish homosexual individuals from the sexually normal? Homosexual persons do not only have abnormal inclinations in psychological respects but, as it has been assumed, through the sexual hormones and therefore in biological respects. It has been thought that the sexual hormones are related in one or

[26] Joseph Wortis, "Nature, Sexuality and Effeminacy in the Male Homosexual," *American Journal of Orthopsychiatry,* X (1940), No. 3.

another way to a male or a female inclination. If this assumption is true, one would expect to find in a male homosexual the opposite amount of sexual hormones than is found in a normal person. Such an assumption may be strengthened by the belief that there exists a *hormonal* hermaphroditism in sexually immature individuals. However, even if such a hormonal hermaphroditism were present, one must doubt the ideological connection between the hormonal influences and the homosexual inclinations.

There are in the urine two hormones—the male, called testosterone (androgenic), and the female, called estrogen or folliculin. Testosterone is the masculinizing hormone and is found in the testes. Since the gonodatropic hormones in the anterior part of the pituitary gland stimulate the production of sexual hormones, one can indirectly determine the amount of this hormone in comparison with that of the folliculin hormone.

Zondek was the first who found folliculin, the female hormone, in the urine of the human, independently of sexual maturity (B. Zondek and V. Euler). The finding of the high amount of folliculin in the urine of the stallion in 24 hours, estimated to be 17 million Mouse Units, is peculiar. Zondek believes that the metabolism which leads to the formation of sexual hormones is the same in both sexes. The male hormone is first formed of unknown substances and then transformed into the female one. The fact that only the stallion excretes the folliculin in such great quantities, not the castrated horse, indicates a near relation between the male and female hormones. It is possible that a large amount of male hormones are formed, and the excess is destroyed by being transformed into female hormones which are hastily excreted through the urine.

Estrogen can be extracted from the ovary, liquor folliculi, placenta, fetal membranes, liquor amnii, adrenal cortex, and from the urine of pregnant women in large amounts. It is present in small amounts in the urine of normal adult women and in adult males.

Some different figures have been given regarding the secretion of testosterone and estrogen. Bühler has not been able to find estrogen in the urine of males over sixty, while Oesterreicher claims that the urine after this age contains only 10 Mouse Units of estrogen. Brahn has not found any difference between the urine of the normal and homosexual,[27] while Zondek [28] and Hamburger [29] claim that they have not been able to find prolan in the urine of homosexual individuals. Lately Callow and Vines have come to still other conclusions.[30] These biological investigations are difficult to perform, which makes the results uncertain. Even the conclusions of hormonal investigations may be viewed with doubt.

I recall the case of a twenty-seven-year-old homosexual man who was sentenced to two years in prison and thereafter five years custody, according to the Norwegian law for the treatment of the mentally abnormal persons who are not legally insane. He himself wished to be castrated, and since his immediate family agreed, it was decided that since castration was medically indicated, it should be done—with the consent of the Surgeon General of the Norwegian Public Health Service. The sexual hormones in the urine was determined before castration, and 55 Mouse Units prolan and 44 Mouse Units estrogen per quart of urine were present.

After the castration, the estrogen disappeared from the urine, while the prolan rose to 210 Mouse Units. A microscopic investigation of his testes showed circumscribed degenerated changes of these organs. After a short period of observation the individual was released and placed in private custody.

In another case a twenty-five-year-old individual was charged with homosexual attacks on a small boy. And in addition he had written unusually threatening anonymous letters to the boy's mother, revealing distinct sadistic leanings. The police easily deduced that he wrote the letters. He was sentenced to prison and while he was there investigations of the sexual hormones in the urine were made. In anatomical respects he was a normal male. Hormonal investigations of the urine showed, however, that the amount of prolan was more than 56 Mouse Units while the estrogen was more than 24 Mouse Units. The latter findings supported the assumption that the person in question was a homosexual one.

Limited space prevents me from dealing further with this type of investigation, but certainly the last word has not yet been said.

[27] Brahn, *Klinische Wochenschrifft*, p. 504.
[28] Bernhard Zondek, *Biologisches Zeitblatt*, CII (1933), 258.
[29] Christian Hamburger, "Studies on Gonadotropic Hormones from the Hypophysis and Chorionic Tissue," *Acta pathologica et microbiologica*, Supplementum XVII, 17.
[30] R. R. Callow and C. W. Emmens, *Biochemic Journal*, XXXII (1938), 1312.

It is well known that homosexual inclinations may be accompanied by sadistic or masochistic tendencies. These are sexual expressions of hostile impulses in which sexual gratification takes place as a result of hurting someone or being hurt. These perversions play a great part in many sexual offenses and in many cases of murder. (See Chapter VIII.)

As to the effect of alcohol, it may be estimated only when the criminal act is the direct consequence of alcoholic intoxication. One may say that intoxication from alcohol or a drug is a condition which leads the individual to perform acts in which the deliberation is either inhibited or abolished. This is shown by the fact that the highest instance of assault is found in alcoholic offenders, while in the general group crimes against property tend to be most prevalent. Such an assumption is largely confirmed in the examination made by Gray and Moore who found that the far most frequent offenses were committed by alcoholics—breaking and entering to commit larceny, armed robbery, robbery, rape and assault with intent to rape, assault with intent to rob or murder, or assault with dangerous weapons. Of the 1,086 prisoners in the examination, these six types of offenders numbered respectively 274, 148, 104, 67, 64, and 52. Of 551 nonalcoholic prisoners, the offenses were: breaking and entering to commit larceny, armed robbery, larceny, rape and assault with intent to rape, assault with intent to rob or murder, and assault with a dangerous weapon. The numbers for this group were 96, 84, 69, 27, 21, and 19.[31] The figures indicate that assault is more prevalent among alcoholics than in nonalcoholic prisoners.

The intimate connection between intoxication and crime is shown by Aschaffenburg in his famous book, *Crime and Its Repression.* He stated that most assaults occurred on Sundays, second was Monday, and third Saturday, which was pay day. Another examination analyzed the scenes of crimes. Out of 1,115 assaults, 66.5 per cent were committed in taverns, 7.7 per cent in living quarters, 8.8 per cent in the streets, 7.8 per cent in places of work, while the place was unknown in 9.2 per cent of the cases. Aschaffenburg says about this: "There can be no more distinct explanation as to the

---

[31] M. G. Gray and Merrill Moore, "Incidence and Significance of Alcoholism in the History of Criminals," *Journal of Criminal Psychopathology,* III (Oct., 1941), No. 2, 316.

immediate cause of the assaults when recalling that two thirds of all fights take place in or in front of public houses." [32]

In this connection it should be noted that Baer has obtained records from 49 penitentiaries, 50 prisons and penitentiaries for women, and 21 houses of correction and reformatories for both sexes. He found that of 30,000 prisoners in 41 male prisons, 49.9 per cent were drunkards, while of 2,796 female prisoners, 18.1 per cent were drunkards.

It is of great interest to study the family history of alcoholics. Gray and Moore examined 1,637 prisoners in the Massachusetts State Prison of whom 1,086 (66.3 per cent) were regarded as alcoholics. Of these 68.6 per cent had alcoholic relatives, 62 per cent had alcoholic parents, and 26.1 per cent had alcoholic siblings. Of the alcoholic prisoners, 34.8 per cent claimed to have been intoxicated at the time of their crime, a claim which was supported by other evidence in 22.8 per cent of the cases.[33] Halpern in his report, *A Decade of Probation*, found that in the course of ten years alcoholism was seen to be a contributing factor in 22.6 per cent of 5,755 cases investigated.[34]

Of the 928 women prisoners examined by Gray and Moore at the Massachusetts Reformatory for Women 49.4 per cent were alcoholics. What kind of conclusions can we make regarding persons sentenced because of their abuse of alcohol? The Danish judge Grundtvig wrote in 1907 an article in which he asserted that want in reality plays a minor part as a contributive factor to crimes of property while intoxication is of tremendous importance. He concludes that the abolition of alcoholism would reduce crime to such a minimum that it would not have more social interest than many other abnormalities such as color blindness, ambidexterity, and so forth. For this reason the fight against crime first of all will have to be a fight against alcoholism. Dr. Scharffenberg, a confirmed prohibitionist, maintains that 75 per cent of our crime would be eliminated if no alcohol were available.[35]

Such an opinion is too optimistic. In an extensive study by Christian Geil, *Criminal Anthropological Studies of Danish Criminals*,

[32] Gustav Aschaffenburg, *Crime and Its Repression*, p. 78.
[33] Gray and Moore, *op. cit.*, 347, 348, 349.   [34] *Op. cit.*, p. 60.
[35] Hartvig Nissen, *Alkohol og forbrydelse*, p. 21.

of 1,845 male prisoners, he found that there were a great number of crimes due to intoxication and, most often, as a result of it. There is no doubt that many individuals yield to a criminal impulse because their restraint is reduced by intoxication. He concluded, and this is an important point, that alcoholism has significance in the crimes of first offenders. However, quite different is the case of recidivists. With this type, intoxication plays a minor, if any, part in crime. In all probability they would have become recidivists without the use of alcohol.

Generally speaking, Dr. Geil may be right. However, the problem of the cause of crime cannot be answered satisfactorily unless all types are viewed together.

This leads to the consideration of the personality in the alcoholic offender. One may say that the alcoholic person is socially sensitive and one may be justified in saying that in most cases he is one who has felt a state of insecurity from his earliest childhood. Thus, it appears that he derives his insecurity from his environment which may be conducive to alcoholism.

In the course of their upbringing, alcoholics may be frustrated. This produces aggressive inclinations in which criminal leanings and abuse of alcohol are developed side by side. If this is so, one cannot fail to see that there are certain particular factors in the causation of alcoholism lending support to the belief that much of their behavior is self-punishing, self-destructive, oral demanding elements, or elements associated to the sexual sphere—on the whole, traits which may lead us to assume that, generally speaking, the alcoholic may belong to the neurotic character.[36] That this is so is seen by the fact that in some alcoholics the personality difficulties pertain to the sphere of sexual adaptation while in others the family situation is the most difficult.

One may very well assume that hate or resentment against some inadequacy of the individual himself may come to the fore as a self-destructive tendency, such as alcoholism; or as a self-destructive drive, such as a suicide; or as a criminal act. His being socially sensitive and his inadequacy make it impossible for him to live on the

[36] R. P. Knight, *The Dynamics and Treatment of Chronic Alcoholic Addiction*, Bulletin No. 1 (1937) of the Menninger Clinic, pp. 233–50; and "Psychodynamics of Chronic Alcoholism," *Journal of Nervous and Mental Disease*, LXXXVI (1937), 536–48.

same level with his surroundings, causing him to undertake an attitude of so-called security which he can do only by indulging in alcohol or by some other kind of a compensation, which may result in a crime.

In view of such a statement, alcoholism may be considered only as a symptom in a personality in the same way as criminal behavior is in most cases. Let us point out that alcoholism does not appear to play as great a part at the start of a·criminal career as it does in the career of the fully developed criminal, lending support to the belief that alcohol may not basically be regarded as a cause of crime. Following this assumption to its logical conclusion, one may say that criminalistic tendencies and alcoholic inclinations seem to develop side by side. However, it must be added that the abuse of alcohol has figured in maintaining and increasing antisocial activities. Thus, it appears that the abuse of alcohol and criminal inclinations are developed on the basis of dispositional and environmental ailments.

5. *Offenders with Faulty Development of the Superego.* These offenders are persons who perpetrate criminal acts which are primarily directed against society. They are brought up in a criminal environment which existed previously or which they themselves have promoted. They have identified themselves with antisocial activities because they do not fear punishment. They rarely show repentance for their acts, and their only regret is that they have to be incarcerated. They have an ingrained hatred against authority and society, their criminal activities being approved by their ego and superego. Their superego has been affected by their environment.

To this type belong those we consider habitual criminals, persons who have a definite criminal pattern, who commit crimes as a profession, and who have no interest in taking up a legitimate career. Such individuals are gangsters. Since they are led by their own concepts of life, which are contrary to that of the law, they organize themselves into gangs, and it is here we find criminals of the most outspoken type.

Since this group of offenders do not concur with the laws of society, they change their antisocial activities in accordance with the opportunities offered them. One could say that their crimes are an occupation. Socially, such an offender is the most dangerous individual, operating, when certain situations arise, on a large scale, as in racketeering. Those criminals are incorrigible in the most profound sense of the word. How many there are of this type is impossible to estimate. The most serious consequences of their activities are not their criminal acts but their steady engaging of other originally law-abiding individuals, who because of a less developed mental resistance against the temptation of becoming rich quickly, allow themselves to become engaged in antisocial activities. The harm done to society by this group cannot be reckoned either economically or ethically.

VII

JUVENILE AND WAR DELINQUENCY

THERE IS NO doubt that the largest number of offenders start their criminal careers in childhood and early youth. Since there is a continual interplay between a child's intellectual and emotional forces, almost all of his activity, as Lauretta Bender [1] has emphasized, has to be considered from both viewpoints. This activity includes that of an antisocial nature.

Juvenile offenders belong mainly to the momentary or acute type, but in the course of time many of them may become chronic offenders. Actually, it is from the juvenile offenders that the chronic are recruited. That we have to group many youthful offenders as either acute or chronic is only one of the limitations caused by the artificial classification to which we are necessarily restricted.

Since criminalistic tendencies are present in all humans, a child may frequently be tempted to take secretly toys, candies, and the like. At such an early age he will not, under usual circumstances, have learned sufficiently to distinguish between mine and thine. (About this development, see Chapter IV.) Such an inclination is more understandable when we remember that the child, compared with the adult, has no or few means of acquiring money. If we consider his desires, needs, and impulsiveness, it is rather surprising that he so often is able to refrain from stealing, which he does, not only because he lacks comprehension of the deed, but largely because of his fear of punishment. When he does steal, it is mostly a swift reaction to a momentary impulse. He optimistically believes that he can escape the consequences and herein lies a possible basis for his becoming an offender.

We then see that due to the personality make-up of the juvenile, theft is his usual offense. This is also reflected in the statistics of crime distribution. Larceny and burglary constituted 33.3 and 46.6 per cent respectively of offenses committed in 1941 by those under

---

[1] L. Bender, "Emotional Problems in Children," *Proceedings of the Second Institute on the Exceptional Child of the Child Research Clinic,* Oct., 1935, pp. 49–64.

twenty-one. (See pages 135–36.) For those between twenty-one and twenty-nine the numbers were 30 and 29.8 per cent respectively for the same year. In the first half of 1942 the number of larcenies was 34 per cent and burglaries 48.5 per cent of offenses committed by those under twenty-one.

From the psychological point of view these numbers are significant. As soon as the youth reaches adulthood, his type of crime changes. He grows stronger, bolder, or may have associated with other individuals with leanings to some other type of crime. This is also clearly reflected in the trend of the number of offenders from twenty-one to twenty-nine, among whom robbery and homicide are the highest, being 34.8 and 41.7 per cent respectively, while in the ages up to twenty-one the percentages are 13 and 33.[2] While forgery, requiring great skill, is the crime of the rather mature adults, statutory rape is the crime of the young offender. It is significant that rapes increased 10.5 per cent during the first half of 1942 and for the first half of 1943 exceeded the prewar average by 28.4 per cent.[3] Arson seems to be most frequently committed at or about the age of twenty-one, while auto thefts were most frequently performed by youths of eighteen.[4]

Considering the type of crime of the young offender, we see that those between the ages of sixteen and twenty-one commit petty larceny, burglary, auto theft, statutory rape—on the whole, crimes against property and crimes which require force. In the years from twenty-one to twenty-nine the type of crime changes character with robbery, criminal homicide, embezzlement, and fraud being most common. These types of crime require somewhat more deliberation. There are slight differences with respect to age between the male and female offender. The dangerous age for the latter is between eighteen and twenty-one, at which time prostitution, abortion, petty larceny, forgery, and embezzlement are commonly committed. One is inclined to think that men more often induce women to prostitution, but there is no doubt that women themselves induce others into this vice. It is peculiar to note that when a boy steals, he may hand the article to an associate of his, possibly another boy, while when a girl steals, she, and I have seen this happen

[2] Federal Bureau of Investigation, Uniform Crime Reports, I (1941), No. 4, 204.
[3] Ibid., XIV (1943), No. 1, 1.   [4] Ibid., XII (1941), No. 4, 205.

many times, often gives it to her mother. The difference here, generally speaking, may be due to a stronger attachment between the daughter and mother than between the son and either of his parents.

What does the total number of juvenile offenders indicate? They show that of 630,568 arrested offenders in 1941, 110,772, or 17.6 per cent of the total, were below the age of twenty-one. Offenders below thirty composed 46.8 per cent of the total.

If we now follow the different age groups, we see that in the years 1935–38, arrests for youths aged twenty-one, twenty-two, and twenty-three exceeded arrests for those aged nineteen, while in 1932–34 and in 1939–40 the age group nineteen predominated.[5] The report of the Police Department of New York City for the period 1937–38 reveals that there were 2,880 offenders who were sixteen years of age. Of this number 39 per cent were charged with serious offenses against property. People between sixteen and twenty-one comprise 13 per cent of the total population over fourteen years of age but constitute 20 per cent of all our offenders. This is a clear indication of the extent to which they participate in criminal activity (one and one half times their proportion of that segment of the population).[6]

Before entering on a discussion of the possible underlying causes of the great participation of adolescents in crime, it is worthwhile to emphasize that a youth of sixteen, seventeen, or eighteen is neither a child nor yet an adult. One may say that adolescence extends from the age of twelve to twenty-five for males and to twenty-one for females. This period may be divided, as Clouston has done, into: early, when certain conceptions about sexual life originate, middle, and late adolescence, when maturation is attained.

The physiological changes that take place at this stage of development have a great deal to do with the problem of youth. It is this physiological growth with which a person's motor coordination and to a large extent traits of a psychological nature are associated. Psychological elements which have root in the child's reaction

[5] Ibid., 204.
[6] Young People in the Courts of New York State, Legislative Document No. 55, 1942, p. 100.

to his environment add to the problem. Physiological growth must without a doubt have a bearing upon the social growth of the young individual. Much of juvenile crime arises not only from problems of the personality per se, but also from problems of how to conceive, to react, and to adapt to each new situation in life. Such adaptation is more difficult for the youngster than for the adult, for besides the sudden physiological growth is the instability among the organs of the various systems of the body.

And yet, generally speaking, there has not been sufficient awareness of the decisive changes that take place physiologically and psychologically in adolescents. Even physicians have often been inclined to regard adolescents as mature persons and treat them accordingly.

In dealing with youthful offenders, one finds in addition to emotional and social instability a perplexity within themselves concerning their drives and ideas. The young fellow suddenly discovers emotions and strivings which contradict themselves and produce conflicts and dissatisfactions, resulting in insecurity. This insecurity gives rise to ambivalent feelings. The individual has love and hate simultaneously for his immediate suroundings. It is natural to assume that such ambivalence may occur more frequently in adolescence than at any other time of a man's life.

In addition social obstacles may cause hardship upon the juvenile's development. The overcrowded home, the absence of recreational facilities, and the often remote possibility of acquiring contemporary acquaintances have a detrimental effect upon his social growth. Above all, the effect of a home broken either by separation, divorce, or death is perhaps a more serious matter for the adolescent than for the younger child, because such an uprooting takes place at a time when he is desperately in need of all the support he can obtain.

Further, the adolescent has reached the stage at which he is confronted by his greatest vocational problem. The sudden situation facing him in leaving school to find a job most certainly forms a new strain. It will be remembered that until the middle of 1940, the adolescent suffered more from unemployment than any other age group. During the last week of March, 1940, it has been estimated that over 2,000,000 persons in this country between fourteen and twenty-four were totally unemployed and seeking work. In addition, there were 1,000,000 youths working on relief jobs.[7]

These difficulties of a psychobiological and social nature lead to a greater instability than is felt at any other stage of a person's development. Such instability may in part lead to crime.

The plight of youth becomes more accentuated in wartime. It is impossible to go into detail, but crowded and inefficient schools, weakened enforcement of agencies, and, most of all, inadequate homes resulting from the absence of fathers in the armed services and of mothers in war work or from extensive migration are usually blamed for the rise in delinquency.

There has been a great debate as to whether or not there has been a real increase of juvenile delinquency since the United States entered the war in December, 1941. The Federal Bureau of Investigation in its report for 1942 has stated that there was an upward trend of youthful participation in crimes against property, amounting to 35.9 per cent of the total, while in the first half of 1941 the number was only 33.7 per cent.[8] A communication from the same agency (October 27, 1942) stated that 18.8 per cent of all persons arrested during the first nine months of 1942 were under twenty-one years of age, an increase of 1.5 per cent over the corresponding period for 1941. This is the first time since the Crime Tabulation Studies started in 1932 that the age eighteen has predominated in the frequency of arrests.

For the first half year of 1943 there was a general decrease for all ages eighteen and over of 26.9 per cent in the number of arrests, males and females combined. On the other hand, there was an increase in the aged seventeen group amounting to 17.7 per cent, and for all those under eighteen the combined increase of arrests totaled 13.6 per cent.[9]

In New York City it has been found that there was a 14 per cent increase in juvenile delinquency in the first six months of 1942 over the same period in 1941. The largest proportionate increase took place in the eleven-twelve-thirteen-year-old group.[10] Further, there was an increase of 20 per cent in commitments of children

[7] Ibid., p. 88.   [8] F.B.I., U.C.R., XIII (1942).   [9] Ibid., XIV (1943), No. 1, 45.
[10] Personal communication from Justice Wise Polier, Domestic Relations Court, Oct. 30, 1942.

to correctional schools of New York City in the first six months of 1942 as compared to the first six months of 1941. During the first nine months of 1942 there was an increase of 30 per cent in wayward minor cases as compared to the first nine months of 1941.[11] The State Training School for Boys at Warwick, New York, reported an increase in population of about 30 per cent.[12]

If we consider only larger cities like New York, Chicago, Boston, Philadelphia, Los Angeles, and Detroit, we find an increase in the number of juvenile offenders. The Chicago Recreation Commission reported in a survey just completed an increase of 9 per cent among juvenile delinquents. In New York, it is reported that juvenile court hearings have increased 14.7 per cent.[13]

A joint delinquency study, published in November, 1942, by the Committee on Youth and Justice of the Community Service Society, New York City, and by the Courts Committee of the Brooklyn Bureau of Charities, found that during the first ten months of that year a total of 4,080 children came to the Children's Court in the five boroughs. In addition, 2,468 new cases of delinquency and neglect were handled by the court's Bureau of Adjustment in the first nine months of 1942. These cases do not come before any judges.[14]

TABLE 3. RISE IN DELINQUENCY CASES BY BOROUGHS IN NEW YORK CITY IN THE FIRST FIVE MONTHS OF 1944 [a]

	1942 [b]	1943 [b]	1944
Manhattan	761	955	1,027
Brooklyn	752	962	1,020
Bronx	358	577	615
Queens	233	331	353
Richmond	58	72	51
Total:	2,162	2,897	3,066

a Figures issued by the Children's Division of the Domestic Relations Court of New York City, New York *Times*, June 1, 1944.
b Corresponding period for these years.

Because of the uneven distribution of the population in defense areas, it is difficult to give a certain opinion as to the validity of the

11 *Committee for the Care of Young Children in Wartime*, Oct. 28, 1942, p. 6.
12 Personal communication from Paul L. Schroeder, Nov. 4, 1942.
13 *Ibid.*   14 New York *Times*, Dec. 4, 1942.

numbers given. Charles P. Sullivan, district attorney of the borough of Queens in New York City, stated at a meeting in November, 1942, that there was a slight decrease in that year of juvenile delinquency in Queens. As a matter of fact, in the first nine months of 1942, there were two less convictions for delinquency in Queens than in the similar period for 1941.[15]

In this connection, information about juvenile offenders in England may be illuminating. In 1939 a total of 30,543 children from eight to sixteen years old were indicted and found guilty of offenses in England and in Wales. In 1942, 38,181 children were convicted, a 25 per cent increase over 1939. There has been a delinquency increase of 41 per cent in England for children under seventeen.[16]

This great increase in England's juvenile delinquency has been attributed mainly to the war. It has been estimated that of 33,000,-000 people between the ages of fourteen and sixty-four, 22,750,000, or two out of every three, are engaged in some type of war work, with women being employed in numbers approaching the men. These figures can mean only one thing—that children and adolescents from ten through eighteen or nineteen are often left without supervision either during the day or in the evening. This applies to girls, too, for illegitimacy and bigamy are common offenses. In addition to this lack of supervision, living in shelters with all types of people during air raids, the blackout with its tempting opportunities for perpetrating crimes, the closing of schools, and the lack of recreational facilities all go far in instigating children to criminal activities.[17]

English statistics show that the most prominent delinquency increase was in the age group below fourteen. The smallest increase was in the number of offenders between seventeen and twenty-one, while among those over twenty-one, there was a 12 per cent decrease in crime. Induction into the armed forces and recruiting of defense workers obviously have largely reduced the number of offenders among adults and older adolescents.

For the same reason the rate of adult crime in this country has been partly reduced. This does not hold true for women, however.

[15] *Ibid.*, Nov. 20, 1942.
[16] Communication from London, Oct. 28, 1943.
[17] Victor H. Evjen, "Delinquency and Crime," *Journal of Criminal Law and Criminology*, XXXIII (July and Aug., 1942), 136–46.

Their offenses have shown a noticeable increase. A communication from the Federal Bureau of Investigation indicates that during the first nine months of 1942, 11.3 per cent of those arrested were women. A year before the percentage for the same months was 9.2. It is interesting to see that violations among women of the Narcotic Drug Law decreased 86.8 per cent, while there was a 25.4 per cent increase in vagrancy and sex offenses, including prostitution. Other outstanding increases in offenses among women were drunkenness, 22.3 per cent, and disorderly conduct, 33.4 per cent.[18]

For the first six months of 1943 there was an increase of 18.4 per cent in offenses among women. The increase in delinquency in the first half of 1943 for girls under twenty-one years of age was 64.7 per cent over the first half of 1942. For offenses against common decency the number of arrests of girls under twenty-one increased 89.5 per cent during the first half of 1943. This category includes drunkenness, vagrancy, disorderly conduct, prostitution, and adultery.[19] Arrests of males over 21 have decreased because of their participation in the war effort, but, on the other hand, shortages of certain commodities have created opportunities for stealing and bootlegging which may to some extent counteract the decrease in crime.

As chances for employment during this war period have increased, the rise in Negro delinquency in 1942 has been much more moderate than that among whites. This is more evident when we recall that while in the years from 1930 to 1940 there was a steady decrease in the number of offenders in New York City, delinquency among Negroes increased.[20]

In explaining this fact one may assume the reason to be due to better employment opportunities for Negroes. While many of them previously had little or no chance to obtain a job, they are now working. As long as their needs are satisfied to a certain extent, their outlet for activity will be directed into useful channels.

Applying this view in a broader sense, one may say that the amount of satisfaction or deprivation in childhood and adolescence, together with the strong physiological development, influences the

[18] Communication from the Federal Bureau of Investigation, Oct. 27, 1942.
[19] F.B.I., *U.C.R.*, XIV (1943), No. 2, 45–46.
[20] Max Winsor, "Delinquency in Wartime," *American Journal of Orthopsychiatry*, XIII (July, 1943), No. 3, 511.

juvenile's psychological, physiological, and social stability, the result of which may decide his ability to adjust to society.

A better understanding of the juvenile's situation in relation to his environment may be reached when we follow the development of his instinctual drive. One of the instinctual drives manifested in the child is the drive to catch or grasp—the psychic equivalent of which is a wish to dominate or to possess (the oral-sadistic phase). If this instinctual development is disturbed, which may happen if the child has been denied adequate nursing or has been abruptly weaned, hostile and aggressive feelings may result because he feels deprived, cheated, or suspicious.[21] Or if breast feeding has been continued longer than usual, the baby becomes spoiled and acts spitefully when weaned, as though he does not want to give up a right.[22] The child clings to its habit as a drowning man to a raft. Following such a viewpoint, it has been assumed that kleptomania may have its root in this period of the child's development.[23]

We must now ask what, if any, are the reasons why some individuals have enough of inhibitory mechanisms to refrain from transgressions while others lack these prohibitory functions? Part of the answer to this problem necessitates mentioning the fundamental drives which are essential to life, and out of which the ego first evolves. In describing the personality structure we must use the concepts introduced by Freud. Even if they may appear strange to some, these concepts have opened a channel to the study of the personality and have contributed more to an intelligent grasp of it and mental illness than any other method of psychology.

We must first point out that instincts or drives are innate, automatically acting tendencies which appear as energy and which try to express themselves in the individual. Those instincts are originally asocial. Recall that in the first years of his development the child has been trained, or to be more accurate, forced, to keep clean.

[21] L. K. Frank, "Cultural Cohesion and Individual Distortion," Psychiatry, II (Feb., 1935), 21–22.

[22] David Levy, "Fingersucking and Accessory Movements in Early Infancy," American Journal of Psychiatry, VII (1927–28), 881–918. A. T. Childers and B. M. Hamil, "Emotional Problems in Children as Related to Duration of Breast Feeding in Infancy," American Journal of Orthopsychiatry, II (1932), 134–42.

[23] Franz Alexander, "The Castration Complex in the Formation of Character," Journal of Psychoanalysis, IV (1923), 11–42; "Concerning the Genesis of Castration Complex," Psychoanalytic Review, XXII (1935), 49–52.

Instead of becoming angry or hateful he has had to learn and accept the rules of those who are stronger than he. He has in short had to learn the significance of "do" and "don't."

But hand in hand with this type of evolution another development, in which the child starts to teach himself, takes place. By this self-teaching he transforms a part of the reservoir of his instincts in order to more or less conform to the rules of his environment. On the basis of his experiences with the outside world a part of his instincts develops which is called "I," or as we refer to it, the "ego." The ego is largely conscious, and represents the thinking, feeling, and knowing personality.[24]

Thus, a part of our drives serves the ego, but other drives are still left in the reservoir and they try to weaken the ego, perhaps by bringing total destruction to it through assault, murder, or incest. That reservoir is known as the "id." It is unconscious, contains primitive, animal-like, unorganized amoral drives, and is the source of emotions. This id must be checked if the ego with its elaborated defenses is not to be destroyed. Apparently for this reason the ego must have help, and thus it constructs a new defense between itself and the id. This defense takes over and incorporates into itself the social demands of the environment and of the parents or guardians who are charged with the child's upbringing. From now on this part hampers the instinctual drives. Whereas previously the parents told the child to keep clean, now this new defense assumes the burden. What was before an external pressure now becomes a pressure from within. This part of the ego we call the superego.[25] The original outward conflict between parent and child has been transformed into an inward conflict between two parts of the same child, his ego and superego.

It is this superego which is our judge and our conscience. It is our authority, always present, always asserting itself, saying, "Thou shall not." The superego censures not only criminal activities but also mere thoughts or intentions of them, giving rise, consciously or unconsciously, to a sense of guilt. The superego is inexorable, primitive as the id itself, and largely unconscious.

If we now give an arrangement of the psychological structure of

[24] Ives Hendrick, *Facts and Theories of Psychoanalysis*, pp. 141–51.
[25] Sigmund Freud, *The Ego and the Id*, pp. 9–18.

the personality, we have first the primitive reservoir of instincts, the id, surrounded by the ego, which is in steady contact with the id and reality as well. All energy derives from the id. The superego, being a part of the ego, is also in contact with the id. The superego controls the ego, and does not yield to the id more than it is permitted to by the moral code. It then appears that the ego is the only part which acts between the outside world and the personality, and is therefore the only conscious part of the personality.

Should a person's ego and superego be done away with, he would become impulsive, disorganized, and psychotic. If the superego should be impaired or destroyed, all inhibitions would disappear, and the result would be an antisocial individual, a criminal.

We think that this is what takes place in varying degrees in a large number of criminals. The instinctual drives have to be domesticated. This occurs when they are sifted through the ego and superego. In a certain number of persons, however, tension, instead of harmony, arises between the ego and superego. The ego fights to regain its independence and tries to follow the antisocial impulses of the id, and thus perhaps elicits overt antisocial activities. In the child between four and six years of age incestuous unconscious feelings associated with resentment, fear, and hatred are present. If this merging of the ego and superego is unsuccessful, a regression to these earlier drives more or less takes place. This regression may be considered responsible for a great number of mental diseases, from neuroses to psychoses, and in many cases it may be related to criminal behavior.

In treating antisocial juveniles the psychiatrist will in one way or another encounter some element, either an intolerable school situation for a truant child or a cultural or religious conflict, which makes it imperative for the psychiatrist to have an open eye for the essential factor in the picture. If one tries to treat the truant child without knowing his school situation, or an adolescent without knowing his social background and without being able to evaluate these factors, he will barely succeed in reaching a workable solution for such individuals.

There recently has been a great increase in juvenile delinquency, but many people are under the impression that it did not as a whole exist before. However, since a certain amount of crime has always existed, the present increase is no more than would be expected considering the amount of instability in society today.

What is said here about the handling of the juvenile offender may also be applied to the acute one. Only some essential points must be stressed. The youngster who for the first time in his life has become a transgressor will, if his offense is not of a serious nature, be given probation in most states, which means that he will be under supervision for as much as three years, depending on the court's decision. If the psychiatric examination reveals no deviation or abnormalities in his mental make-up and the whole affair appears to be a situational or an accidental offense, it would be wise to see in what kind of activities the boy participates and if he has proper outlets for his needs and desires. However, if the examination shows that the offense is an associational one, then the offender's companions should be scrutinized and his parents or relatives be advised that he should be kept away from them. Investigations in the school or place of employment should be made so that the possibility of a social maladjustment might be ruled out.

It is necessary, even with a first-time offender, to keep in mind that he has in himself inclinations which might develop into chronic ones. A boy who has had a tendency to lie, steal, or be truant since he was six or seven years of age requires entirely different methods of handling. In such a case one should look for personal maladjustment stemming from precipitating events, such as deprivations, lack of love, broken home, drunken father, sibling rivalry, hate against home or authority, disease, and deviations in sexual life. If the offender is an adolescent who has left school and found employment, one would look into, besides family and developmental history, the background of his occupation and the endurance which he displayed in his work. An early social maladjustment may reveal itself through changing jobs or losing friends—symptoms which may have root in one or another type of psychological deviation. Psychoanalytically oriented psychotherapy or psychoanalysis would be the proper treatment for such a case.

It is beyond the scope of this book to try to go into all the remedies which have been proposed for the solution of juvenile delinquency. But the treatment of juvenile delinquency is a community problem, and its solution should devolve upon the community itself. Let the constructive forces and agencies of the community be unified and extended. The basis for such a plan is that mental and socially maladjusted young people and delinquent youths are in need of the same care, attention, and the same outlets as their non-delinquent brothers. Yes, as a matter of fact, their desires are in greater need of satisfaction because their personality structures cause them to react to situations in quite different ways than the normal. They require nourishing food, adequate clothing, leisure time, medical care, proper schools, church activities, and, above all, a proper home.

External activities have been stressed in all discussions about the treatment of juvenile delinquency, while one has been inclined to forget the perhaps most important ingredient of the child's total situation—his home.

There is no doubt in my mind that it is in the home that the child receives his first impression of social conduct. Here he notes the behavior of the father towards the mother and vice versa, the conduct of the siblings, and the teaching of what is right and wrong. If parents knew how easily impressions invade the mind of the child, how easily children imitate, and how easily they react towards unusual or odd behavior on the part of their parents, they would be more circumspect in their conduct and would probably be more careful as to how they teach their offspring.

True education of the child consists in training. We must train children, just as we do animals, from the earliest possible moment in order to make them fit for society. To be sure, who is to train them? The parents, naturally. But if the parents are unfit who is going to replace them?

This is a crucial problem in the prevention of all types of social maladjustment. There exist those parents who do not have the ability to educate their children. After one session with a child I have often had to speak with the mother or the father. The child was in many cases maladjusted, but this maladjustment could never be eliminated if the attitude in the home were not radically changed.

To my mind comes the case of a bright, twelve-year-old boy. Up to half a year before he began treatment, he had behaved well. At that time he started stealing at home, lost interest in school, and used headaches and other excuses for not attending. His parents were much distressed when the principal advised them of their son's changed behavior. A family council was held, and it was thought that the boy should have more friends, but nothing came of this. Time passed, and he continued to receive bad marks in school, so that he was brought to me for treatment. His story, which was corroborated by the mother, revealed that he was bored with tedious studying all day long under the supervision of his ambitious mother. It kept him from participating in any outdoor activities and from enjoying the company of other boys. The boy in himself was shy and timid and grew still more so under the overprotection of the mother, thus becoming more maladjusted than before. No doubt a new psychological attitude started to develop in the boy, with resentment against his mother and home, a resentment which led to a loss of interest in school and some stealing of money which enabled him to buy candies. Fortunately, however, the vicious circle was broken.

In another case a young boy had a sister with whom he did not get along. The parents did not realize their rivalry, and the boy started to be absent from school, to lie, and to steal. He was older than his sister and until she was born had received all the consideration of his parents. However, after his sister's arrival, they did not pay so much attention to him. He eventually began to misbehave, and his despairing parents could not account for it. When the child was sent to a foster home, his behavior and attitude changed overnight. He was happy, took an active interest in his studies, and became well adjusted to life—to his parents' surprise.

We all may make mistakes, but those mistakes which others suffer for we can hardly condone. And yet, instances in which innocent children suffer for the errors and faults of their parents are so numerous that I can hardly stress enough the fact that very much of social and personal maladjustment, except among mentally abnormal children, has its root to a large extent in an inadequate home. We know, of course, that poor economic and social conditions, overcrowding, and hapless external situations exist in many homes, but on the other side, there are people who have been able to raise law-abiding citizens in spite of their abject poverty. They were able to train their children and train them well. Since there are more poor than rich people, it is chiefly poor children who come to juvenile courts or to correctional institutions. However, as Judge Jonah J. Goldstein of the Court of General Sessions of New York City has said, "with the rich, governesses often take the place of probation officers, and military schools substitute for correctional institutions." [26]

That it is an abnormal home situation which may be a starting point for antisocial activities is shown by the fact that even in peacetime such inadequate home conditions are known to be the major cause of juvenile delinquency in Britain.[27]

Thus, while we are going into the different remedies for a proper handling of juvenile offenders, it must always be kept in mind that the home is one of the most important instruments in an adequate upbringing and adjustment of the individual in society.

Experience has shown that reformatories are usually poor places for the treatment of juvenile delinquents, because of the obvious fact that several hundred of them are gathered together in intimate contact. This has been one of the greatest disadvantages for all such institutions. The Gluecks reported that of 510 individuals who left the Massachusetts Reformatory during 1911–1922, 80 per cent continued in criminal activities for as long as five to fifteen years after their release. This does not mean that society can abolish reformatories, because there are those offenders who must of necessity be incarcerated so that society may be protected, even if it is apparent that the method has its shortcomings.

Even the procedure of probation has not yielded the good results that were expected. It has been estimated that probation was unsuccessful in modifying the behavior of between 50 and 80 per cent of boys. (The latter figure is given by the Gluecks.) This has been amplified by Dr. Thompson in a study in which he stated that a repetition of a criminal act originates from a certain automatic behavior pattern or setup in the individual who reacts when an adequate stimulus is present.[28] However, one must ask what hap-

[26] J. J. Goldstein, "The Church, the Child, and Crime," speech delivered at Christ Church on Jan. 5, 1944.
[27] Communication from London, Aug. 17, 1943.
[28] C. B. Thompson, "A Psychiatric Study of Recidivists," *American Journal of Psychiatry*, XCIV (Nov., 1939), No. 3, 591–604.

pens if stimulus is removed through constructive probation treatment? Will not success be achieved in many cases, as is seen in the Probation Department of the Court of General Sessions?

Child guidance or behavior clinics were assumed to be one of the cornerstones upon which the rehabilitation of the young offender might be built. In spite of the painstaking efforts made by the different clinics in this country as well as in Europe, the results are not what it was hoped they would be. There are different reasons for this. One is that it is very difficult to call forth a change in the juvenile's social situation when he is treated in a psychiatric clinic because of the few means available. One may surmise that the clinic itself is so far removed from the juvenile's actual situation that little can be done in respect to it. While the individual's personal situation has been stressed, the social one has been put in the background. The treatment following upon psychiatric and psychological examinations should include some attempt to solve the social situation of the offender. (For treatment of the potential offender in psychiatric clinics, see Chapter X.)

A scheme for the treatment of the juvenile offender must be based on the premise that he is a member or a part of a group, the activity of which is reflected in his behavior. A sufficiently strong exposure to a criminal pattern present in that group may possibly affect the juvenile's conduct. As we pointed out in Chapter III, the offender forms in a functional sense a unity with his environment, being consciously or unconsciously tied to it. The member exists, as it were, by virtue of necessity in the group. Then in treating an offender, we must extend the treatment to the group.

A plan for combating juvenile delinquency must necessarily consist of the following four parts: (1) diagnosis and treatment of maladjusted and antisocial children and juvenile offenders; (2) community activities; (3) educational measures; (4) correctional methods.

1. *Diagnosis and Treatment of Maladjusted and Antisocial Children and Juvenile Offenders.* We have shown before that there are a certain number of juveniles who manifest some mental abnormalities and that they must be diagnosed and treated accordingly. On the other hand, there are those who show only some slight mental

deviations who also must be diagnosed. The first group may include those so seriously abnormal—mentally defective or psychotic—that they have to be confined to institutions in order that society may be protected and they themselves treated. If an adequate handling of juvenile offenders with mental abnormalities is to be accomplished, intimate study and diagnosis is necessary. Reasonable facilities must therefore be made available. (See the plan proposed in Chapter X.) Child guidance and psychiatric clinics must be located at central points, be permanently in use, and be readily available to render such service as the general program of the local community may require.

It is impossible to go into detail here, but it should be pointed out that in New York City there are about eight child guidance units in the school system and only one psychologist to every 46,000 children in the public schools. That being the case, a child who needs psychiatric care must wait months in order to have an appointment. In many cases a single interview lasting only a short while is possible, and in most cases there is time only for diagnosis and none for treatment.[29] Those mentally disturbed children under twelve years of age who it is thought will recover receive long-term treatment free only at the Rockland State Hospital. Care of mentally defective children in New York City is limited to two state institutions—Wassaic and Letchworth. These places are inadequate for the treatment of any large number.

The number of child guidance units in the city should probably be greatly increased. It is not farfetched to believe that a similar lack of facilities prevails in the rest of the country, leading one to assume that adequate measures are also needed there. It is gratifying to know that New York City has planned four new child guidance clinics.

New York City has tried to provide facilities for the diagnosis and treatment of maladjusted children and juvenile delinquents in the Psychiatric Division of Bellevue Hospital, and the state has provided the Psychiatric and Neurological Institutes in the city, but there are still a great number of children who are in need of psychiatric care. Since much of mental and social maladjustment

[29] *Committee for the Care of Young Children in Wartime*, Oct. 28, 1942, pp. 4–5.

has root in the personality, it is a pity that society has so far provided insufficient means for the treatment of them, although experience has shown that many of these juveniles can be successfully treated, but only under the best available conditions.

Maladjustment and antisocial behavior may to a large extent be difficult for the private physician to treat when diagnostic and therapeutic measures in a new environment are indicated. Many times, therefore, it is necessary to remove juvenile offenders who are neurotic, depressed, or on the borderline of mental abnormality from an environment to which their previous conduct was closely allied to other surroundings, which can provide understanding, diagnosis, and treatment. Such an environment requires collaboration and planning among psychiatrists, psychologists, child analysts, and social workers. This may be difficult to execute, but it would probably lead to better results than heretofore obtained. There are only a few such institutions in this country. One is the Southard School in Topeka, Kansas, which is closely connected with the Menninger Clinic. Recently a plan was put into effect which provided that a child guidance unit be mobilized to study and treat delinquency in a limited area of New York City. The results of this study should be illuminating.

2. *Community Activities.* Prevention of crime is very much a question of community action, but only an action based upon cooperation of the various people in the surrounding neighborhoods and small localities. It is impossible to outline a plan as to how each community should proceed, but the needs of each community must be decided upon only after a careful study of the existing facilities. An overall planning agency in each community should first be established in order to advise the courts and all social agencies, including schools, churches, clubs, and business organizations, of the possibility of extending or strengthening their services to the young people or to the family. Such a planning agency should see its first duty in calling people's attention to the nature of the problem of crime in that area, so that the community would have to face and solve this problem to the extent of its ability. The second range of its activity would comprise making specific recommendations—the extension of recreational activities and of guidance facilities and urging affiliation with churches and clubs. As

with air raid wardens, one might establish "anticrime wardens," one or more to a block.[30]

3. *Educational Measures.* All cases of crime more or less involve social factors, the personality lurking in the background. Educational measures must necessarily take the form of a re-education in order to bring about a rehabilitation of the juvenile offender. To change a person's attitude, adaptability, and aims, such a re-education must go hand in hand with a modifying of the personality. Here the psychiatrist, the psychologist, and the teacher will have to outline a course of action.[31] But this re-education cannot take place if proper attention is not called to the social elements. In this program the "Big Brothers and Big Sisters" would play a great part. As a matter of fact, I cannot have enough praise for those who are a big brother or big sister to the juvenile offender. They make a great personal sacrifice in their effort to save those unhappy individuals who have taken the wrong track. The many good results obtained by certain private agencies, such as the Jewish Board of Guardians of New York City, must, in my opinion, be attributed as much to their system of Big Brothers and Big Sisters as to the psychological and social treatment they offer. This is a system where an offender is provided with a person of balanced personality who has been given some training and who acts as his or her close companion and adviser in all walks of life.

4. *Correctional Methods.* In a certain number of cases the criminal pattern is so ingrained in the offender that it is necessary to send him to a vocational or industrial school for education and correction. This should only be undertaken after all other alternatives have failed. If the training school is to be in accordance with its purpose, there should be a vivid connection between its program and the situation in the community from which the offender is recruited. This is to a large extent utilized in the Borstal System in England. One of the weaknesses of practically all reformatories here and abroad is the lack of provision for personal influence on the offender. In the Borstal System, education and vocational and physical training are directed to enable the individual to compete with the members of society. Prior to his release contacts are made

[30] *Federal Probation*, p. 38.
[31] M. L. Reymert, "Prevention of Juvenile Delinquency," *Journal of Exceptional Children*, VI (May, 1940), No. 7, 300–3.

with the offender's community in order to establish his future. After release treatment of the offender or the new born citizen, as we might call him, is extended to the parole or after-care period, in which his re-education continues.[32]

One is inclined to think that one of the reasons for juveniles and adults committing crimes may be that they are immature. This term may mean many things. There is, however, one thing that it does not mean, and that is *why* the person cannot react adequately. The term immaturity, hazy as it is, is used for all classifications and descriptions of the offender. Behind this word are hidden traits and symptoms such as fears, inhibitions, and timidity, which may be a part of or constitute a mental condition. The term may also conceal aggression, rebellion, stupidity, feelings of inferiority, and hundreds of other symptoms which, all in all, may participate in or lead to immaturity. Therefore, before a diagnosis of "immaturity" is decided upon, one should scrutinize all the character traits in the offender and ascertain what makes him behave as he does and why he does not have an understanding of the situation. All with the provision that there is no mental deficiency present. It has often been said that maturity is a matter of training. True as this may be, it is also a matter of circumstances, of emotional involvement, of psychogenic reactions, of enduring situations, and, above all, of rating the situation.

This whole problem regarding the adaptability of a person to a new environment may include other correctional measures which we will take up in Chapter X.

[32] William Healy and Benedict S. Alper, *Criminal Youth and the Borstal System,* p. 236.

VIII

THE PSYCHIATRIC-PSYCHOLOGIC
BACKGROUND OF MURDER

AS POINTED OUT before, many antisocial acts may be attributed largely to inner forces beyond the awareness of the perpetrator. Perhaps in no other type of crime is this more true than
in a crime of such devastating dimensions as homicide, whose motivation may be disguised in such a manner that only a probing
deep into the mind can reveal it. The understanding and judging
of the personality behind the murderer presents enormous difficulties, since we do not have an adequate basis for measuring the normal mind, let alone the abnormal one.

Even more baffling becomes the problem when we see the large
number of homicides committed annually in the United States.
The Federal Bureau of Investigation [1] set the total number of
murderers in 1938 at 7,500, of whom 6,600 were apprehended. Of
these 6,600, 3,900 were indicted, of whom 1,750 were found not
guilty, 1,600 were found guilty, and 550 were found guilty on
grounds other than homicide. In 1940 and 1941 the numbers for
the whole country were estimated respectively at 7,540 and 7,562. [2]
The latest report available, covering a period from January 1 to
June 30, 1942, and including a population of 48,531,025, gives the
number of murderers at 2,725, [3] indicating that in the additional
half a year and counting the total population the number of criminal homicides would remain substantially the same. The incidence
of murder is so high that 1.7 offenses occur every two hours, while
20.7 take place every day. [4]

The large number of homicides committed here becomes more
significant when compared with that of other countries. While the
homicidal rate of the United States in 1941 was 5.5 per 100,000 of

[1] Federal Bureau of Investigation, *Uniform Crime Reports*, IX (1938), No. 4 and X
(1939), No. 1.
[2] *Ibid.*, XII (1941), No. 4, 168.　　　　[3] *Ibid.*, XIII (1942), No. 1, 7.
[4] *Ibid.*, XII (1941), No. 4, 168.

population,[5] that of England was only 0.5 in 1922 and 0.6 in 1923.[6] In 1941 there were 268 homicides in New York City and 228 in Chicago, 3.8 and 6.2 homicides per 100,000, respectively.[7] The rate in cities of other countries for the period 1907 to 1911 was as follows: London, .9, Berlin, 2.0, Paris, 3.5, and Copenhagen, .45.[8] Only one country, Italy, seems to have a homicide rate approaching that which exists in the United States.[9]

In judging these numbers of homicides, one must bear in mind that international statistics may not always be comparable, because each country may have a different basis for determining a homicide. Also, it must be remembered that statistics of homicidal deaths based on death certificates do not necessarily correspond with judicial statistics, because an actual homicide may not be similar to a homicide in law.

Nevertheless, it seems that the trend toward homicide is more pronounced here than in other countries. This makes it necessary to investigate first, in passing, whether there are any general factors related to the psychiatric-psychologic aspect of the problem which are contributory causes of this prevalence of homicide.

The general background of murder will be more or less characterized by those factors that cause crime in general. Murder has psychological root in the person's aggressions related to attack and defense. These are expressions of his fight for survival or may be due to an erotic drive, no matter how distorted or concealed it may be. These aggressions prompt him to assert himself, and thus competition arises. Even if the competition becomes sharp, either within primitive tribes or within a highly developed society, the individual will steadily try to find new means to assert himself against the environment. These means take not only an economic character but also a social one. Such competition is in all probability a potent contributive factor in causing crime, including murder. (For general discussion, see Chapter III.)

American life has developed a certain pattern, which is due partly to the people and partly to the country itself. In the early days of the country's history, the ever-expanding frontiers had to

[5] *Ibid.*, 172.   [6] F. L. Hoffman, *The Homicide Problem*, p. 2.
[7] F.B.I., *U.C.R.*, XII (1941), No. 4, 185–88.
[8] Hoffman, *The Homicide Problem*, p. 25.   [9] *Ibid.*, p. 79.

be defended. This necessitated having a gun at hand at all times, a habit which is somewhat prevalent today, and which is reflected in the many homicides by firearms. In the years 1910 to 1912, 62.1 per cent, and in 1920, 71.8 per cent of all murders were committed by firearms.[10] In the year 1923, only 10.4 per cent of all homicides in England and 17 per cent of all homicides in Australia were committed by firearms.

Another factor which may have contributed to the prevalance of homicide in America is the rapid development of the country, with the great rise of industry and agriculture, the steady influx of immigrants, and the migration of the population to newly opened territory. As was the case in other parts of the world where an industrial and agricultural expansion took place, people had difficulty in becoming adjusted to the new form of life. Their emotions were centered around their immediate objects rather than directed for the use of an organized society.[11] Thus, frictions and conflicts arose, which under the strain of life brought forth antisocial activities, including homicide.

In this connection it may be appropriate to compare the homicidal situation in this country with that in Australia. Except for a greater wealth of natural resources, a more advanced development, and a more cosmopolitan population in this country, the social conditions of both countries are largely the same, since both were pioneering countries. Nevertheless, the rate in Australia was 1.6 per 100,000 in 1923, while in America it was, as stated previously, 5.5 per 100,000 in 1941.[12]

A comparison of the rate of homicide in this country with that of Japan shows a puzzling condition. In the year 1922, the rate in Japan was 0.8 per 100,000.[13] One reason for this low rate may be the fact that homicides are not reported accurately. Another and more telling reason is the old Japanese tradition of committing suicide by hara-kiri. The peculiar custom that a man, for instance, has a right to ask his sister to kill herself if he deems this necessary on account of his honor, and that she will carry out his request even against her will conveys the impression that the Japanese possess an inclination towards self-destruction.

[10] *Ibid.*, p. 24.   [11] *Ibid.*, p. 4.   [12] *Ibid.*, p. 2.
[13] *Ibid.*, p. 2.

How the number of homicides vary in the different parts of this country may give a hint as to their underlying causes. The number of homicides seems to be highest in the East South Central section, where in 1941 it was 31.19 per 100,000 population in cities between 100,000 and 250,000, and at its lowest, 11.7 per 100,000, in cities between 25,000 and 50,000. In the Middle Atlantic States (New York, New Jersey, Pennsylvania) the number varies between 1.28 and 3.28 per 100,000.[14] The East North Central area has a rate varying from 1.80 to 5.81, the Mountain States, .67 to 11.06, and the Pacific area, 1.34 and 3.82, all per 100,000 population. The high number of homicides in the East South Central section is also reflected in the considerable amount of aggravated assaults and robberies that occur in this region. Hooton's investigations, questionable as they may appear, show that first degree murder is most frequent in Kentucky, while second degree murder is most common in Tennessee, Kentucky, and North Carolina.[15]

The prevalence of homicide in the South can only be understood when we stop for a moment and think of the historical background of the Southern states.

First, up to the period including the Civil War, Southern society was to a large extent dependent upon its relation to slavery. Violence and threat of violence were commonly expressed in daily life, among slaves themselves as well as between master and slave, so that one might say there developed a pattern of violence and individual disregard of the law.

Secondly, the years after the war were filled with tension, chaos, and disorder, thus increasing the sources of aggressions, and with the end of Reconstruction the white elements that had resorted most openly to violence and murder as instruments of policy were put into control.

Thirdly, since this same period the people of the South have been socially and economically frustrated, which, in addition to their Negro problem, has apparently left its mark upon their attitude and given rise to aggressions.

One phenomenon that may have increased the number of homi-

[14] F.B.I., U.C.R., XII (1941), No. 7, 182.
[15] E. A. Hooton, The American Criminal, I, 35. For general discussion of Hooton's investigations see Chapter III.

cides in the South is lynching. There is an apparent relation between the homicide rate and lynching. In the period 1885–1923, the number of persons lynched was 4,487, of whom 1,038 were whites, and 3,449 were Negroes.[16] However, in April, 1944, Dr. Frank P. Graham, president of the University of North Carolina, stated that lynching of Negroes had decreased from 57 in 1920 to 5 in 1941 and that there were fewer still today.

If we look into the actual psychologic background of lynching, we find that the action of the crowd is motivated by the common aim that has to be fulfilled. This goal may originate from hate felt for the culprit or affection felt for the victim, both resulting in a desire for retaliation and revenge. Since emotional reactions are easily roused, even an accidental circumstance may be sufficient to release pent-up feelings and thus cause lynching. The people forming a lynching party are dominated by a common purpose. Their individuality disappears, while their responsibility decreases, with the result that they lose self-control and act impulsively.[17]

Traces of manifest retaliation are still found in Corsica where revenge is accomplished by the immediate family or clan. While revenge in such a case is usually a planned act, lynching often follows as a result of some provocation made in the heat of passion. Here an element of mass-suggestion and mass-psychosis occurs. The thought of revenge is harbored with violence in "the animal" of the human.

Since a great percentage of murders in the South are committed by Negroes, there is a tendency to attribute the prevalence of homicide there to this large group. A study of 200 murderers revealed that 34 per cent of them were Negroes.[18] The annual report for 1941 of the Federal Bureau of Investigation showed even a higher percentage. Of 6,628 criminal homicides, 3,288 were committed by white men while 3,130 were committed by Negroes.[19] Since Negroes constitute about 10 per cent of the total population, their participation in homicide is greatly out of proportion to their numbers.

[16] Hoffman, *The Homicide Problem,* p. 78.
[17] David Abrahamsen, "Mass-Psychosis and Its Effects," *Journal of Nervous and Mental Disease,* XCIII (Jan., 1941), No. 1, 63–72.
[18] J. H. Cassity, "Personality Study of 200 Murderers," *Journal of Criminal Psychopathology,* II (1942), No. 3, 297.
[19] F.B.I., *U.C.R.,* XIII (1941), No. 4, 209.

However, one will also find among them a high rate of other criminal offenses. In 1941, 2,591 defendants charged with various offenses were admitted to the Psychiatric Clinic, Court of General Sessions, New York City, of whom 1,065, or 41 per cent were Negroes.[20]

The high disproportionate rate of homicide among Negroes seems to be but a reflection of the criminality found in general among them. This may be a contributive factor to the higher number of murders occurring in the South. The prevalence of criminality among Negroes is perhaps an expression of the unfortunate environment in which they are raised and lack of competitive spirit, as well as a result of discrimination against them. Discouragement and frustration at being unable to gain a foothold within a society mastered by the whites may lead the Negro to turn to unlawful activities.

While the general background of murder varies within the country, the law is clear in determining what constitutes homicide.

The law defines murder as the unlawful killing, with malice aforethought, expressed or implied, of a human being by a person of sound mind and memory and discretion. The law says further that murder perpetrated by means of poison, lying in wait, torture, or by any other kind of willful, deliberate, and premeditated killing is murder of the first degree, and that manslaughter is the unlawful killing of a human being without malice, either voluntary upon a sudden quarrel or in heat of passion, or involuntary in the commission of an unlawful act not amounting to a felony.

Sometimes it is difficult to decide whether or not a homicide was planned. My experience is that a person who has committed a homicide usually will deny it was planned. A criterion for determining this phase of the case is whether or not the murder was committed in secrecy. One committed in secrecy frequently demonstrates that it had been planned and is therefore to be considered as murder of the first degree.

The penal codes of the states of the United States make three basic distinctions in law regarding homicide: (1) Excusable homicide: Committed by accident or misfortune or in the heat of passion or upon combat on sufficient provocation, when no advantage was

[20] Personal communication, Oct., 1942.

taken or no dangerous weapon used, or if the killing was not done in a cruel manner. (2) Justifiable homicide: Committed by a public official or by a person acting by his consent as his aide or assistant; committed in defense of habitation or property, in the lawful suppression of riot or in the lawful preservation of peace; committed by accident or through misfortune, under threats or menace sufficient to show there were reasonable causes to believe the person's life would be endangered. (3) Felonious homicide: Committed willfully under such circumstances as to consider it punishable.

The last and most important point in reference to our considerations is that the law disregards a crime committed by an insane person, or by an idiot, or by a child under the age of fourteen years. The insanity issue may be raised in the time between the indictment and the sentencing of the offender. The statutes in the penal codes of all the states provide that an insane person cannot be tried, incarcerated, punished, or executed.

One would assume that there is a clear distinction between a sane and an insane person. Nevertheless, in one of our states the following case is on record: A low-grade, feeble-minded boy, who previously had been an inmate of a state school for mental defectives, had, together with an older boy, raped and killed a girl. He was put under observation in a mental hospital, and three physicians rendered an opinion to the effect that the boy was mentally defective and incapable of distinguishing between right and wrong. The jury, however, gave more credence to the police officers who had arrested him, and who testified that the boy was of normal mentality. The boy was convicted, sentenced to death, and executed.[21]

There is no reason why we should not examine a murderer even if the recommendations of such examination should not be followed, disappointing as this might be. On the contrary, since life is a continuous process of trial and error, we must constantly try to demonstrate that without an appreciation of the quality of the psychological features and the personality pattern, we will be unable to fathom the man behind the act and to correct his behavior. The murderer has his own personality just as any other individual. Indeed, if a detailed investigation is necessary for each offender, it

[21] For further details see Winfred Overholser, *Psychiatry and the Law—Cooperators or Antagonists?*, p. 10.

is all the more important in the case of a murderer in view of the enormity of his crime.

In such an individual observation we shall try to ascertain the motivation of the murderer. From a broad viewpoint, it will be found that the force which compels a person to commit homicide is frustration in sexual, economic, or social strivings, the murder being instigated by rational and irrational motives.

Where only rational motives are apparently present, such as a desire to obtain money or a wish to get rid of a person, irrational motives can hardly or never be ruled out. This is shown by the fact that the murderer is so completely dominated by his inner forces that apparently no means is too foul for achieving his goal. The following case comes to my mind.

A twenty-five-year-old man who had impregnated a girl, planned to kill her. He met her in an isolated place. While having intercourse with her, he hit her in the face with a stone, then threw her down a steep cliff to her death. The manner in which he killed her showed his desperate desire to get rid of her and expressed the inadequacy in his mental make-up and the unconscious forces which drove him to killing.

It is questionable whether an apparently senseless or purposeless murder is not in reality incited by strong, although unconscious, motives. If we could study the personality thoroughly enough we would be able to trace these types of motives in the largest part of cases. The unconscious motive, which is by far the driving force in a homicide, usually remaining unknown to the culprit, is one of the reasons why he is unable to give an explicit explanation for his act. The public is surprised, the judge baffled, but justice has to be meted out on the perpetrator.

This strong unconscious motivation in homicide is perhaps best described by Dostoyevsky in his masterpiece, *Crime and Punishment,* where a need of self-punishment called forth by a strong unconscious sense of guilt is the main motive. It is beyond doubt that Dostoyevsky has touched upon a common trait in the hearts of humans—a sense of guilt—in his haunting story.

As the reader will recall, a poor student, Raskolnikow, murders his landlady, who is a pawnbroker, and her invalid daughter. Raskolnikow has a clear intelligence and has ingratiated himself with them. This seems to show that he is not a daydreamer but a realistic man who tries to secure his existence. However, beneath the surface he is emotionally instable and imagines that he is a superman who has a right to kill the two, in his eyes, worthless women and take their money. He plays with these thoughts and little by little becomes preoccupied with them until he at last deems it necessary that a murder has to be committed. When he finally kills them he does not take any precautions against detection.

After the murder he returns home and goes to sleep. When he awakes the next day he carelessly throws away the purse which he has stolen. A few days afterwards he behaves peculiarly, unconsciously trying to attract attention to his feelings of guilt. Taken to the police station on a triviality, he mentions the murder, thereby betraying himself. In this act he tries to link his person with the murder. Later he revisits the scene of the homicide and the police become suspicious of him. Since, however, the police are not alert enough, he confesses the murder after a fashion, and they grow more suspicious. A few days later he unburdens himself to one of his women acquaintances. So strong are his feelings of guilt that he believes another man has overheard this confession and fears now that this person will betray him. In this fear he roams around the city and enters a bar where he unexpectedly encounters the same person, his fancied accuser. In this instance we see how Raskolnikow, by sighting the man whom he thinks would denounce him, tries to be punished. Finally he makes a complete confession of the murder and is sent to Siberia. He goes readily and willingly, thus being punished and relieved of his sense of guilt. Led into its extreme consequences one may think that the reason for such self-punishment is self-pity or love of the object, introjected into the ego and nurtured by a strong sense of guilt.

The novel is an explicit contribution in explaining a severe neurosis in which unconscious guilt produces a desire for self-punishment. This in due time leads Raskolnikow to perpetrate a crime through which he can be punished. Dostoyevsky has with a master stroke shown a profound insight into the mechanism and the deep-seated unconscious motivation for crime.[22]

[22] *Crime and Punishment* can be understood only in the light of Dostoyevsky's own life. He showed a great need for punishment, which made his life miserable; he was

Homicide committed even in a psychosis, no matter how motiveless it seems, may have been brought about by unconscious elements. In a case I saw some time ago a man suffering from schizophrenia murdered his wife, to whom he had been married for 15 years. When he was a child his mother left him and his father for another man. In school he was teased about being "motherless," and he withdrew and became seclusive. At fifteen he had a love affair, but the girl rebuffed him, although (he said) he "realized she loved him." He became depressed, thought of suicide, and felt deserted by everyone. His father took him out to the country where he gradually recovered. Later he went through high school and entered a university but had to leave because of financial difficulties. His father secured a job for him, but he felt he was in the "wrong place" and was going to quit. Then the girl who was to be his wife became interested in him, with the result that he remained in his position. Because of the break in his university studies, he could no longer attend his former club, of which he had been an ardent member. He became sullen and impervious, and often stayed in bed for days at a time, drinking only water because his thoughts had to be "pure." At other times he was overactive reading books about religion and philosophy. Although he became less and less sociable, he was able to keep his position, but finally he requested and obtained a leave of absence. Relations with his wife had meanwhile become strained. She left him but returned when he threatened to commit suicide. He apparently recovered and resumed working, but he grew more and more suspicious that she was going to leave him again. He became more restless and seclusive than before, "everything went dark," and one evening he shot and killed her.

The main point here, beside the identification of his wife with his mother, is that the psychosis seems to be a kind of a preparatory stage to annihilating the victim, a point which also has been emphasized by Dr. Philip R. Lehrman in another case.[23]

A homicidal act has not one but several motives, although only

---

steadily humiliated, for ten years was kept in an insecure state through his unwarranted gambling, and as a climax, was sent to Siberia as a revolutionary, although he in his heart was a true conservative adherent of the Orthodox Church. This unconscious need for punishment without doubt had root in his strong sense of guilt concerning his father, whom he had for a long time felt a strong desire to kill.

23 P. R. Lehrman, "Some Unconscious Determinants in Homicide," *Psychiatric Quarterly*, XIII (Oct., 1939), No. 4, 605 ff.

one may be conscious.[24] The following case will illustrate this. A couple had been engaged for a long time; the engagement was terminated by the girl, who jilted the man in favor of his business partner. The jilted man, of an extremely miserly nature, attributed the recent decline in their business to his partner's lack of interest, arising from his preoccupation with the girl. He schemed revenge. Finally he killed both his partner and the girl. It was assumed that jealousy was the only motive for these murders. But the revelation that the murderer had previously accused his partner of having lost interest in the business shows that his miserly attitude was a decisive factor in this tragedy. This miserliness was a basic constituent in his personality that colored his whole life and nurtured his jealousy. On a deeper level, both the jealousy and the miserliness were related to infantile experiences which determined the irrational and self-destructive reaction of murder.

We may here stress that certain inner conflicts, frustration, and repeated disappointments are among the inner forces that may call forth an abnormal attitude or elicit an abnormal drive which may tend to steer the individual in an antisocial direction.

Such criminal tendencies are more easily elicited when abnormalities are originally present in the person's make-up. Criminal activities and mental pathologies are like two plants that derive their nutrition from the same soil. The frequency of gross mental abnormalities in criminals supports this analogy. Drs. Healy and Bronner found in comparing a small group of delinquent children with their nondelinquent siblings that 91 per cent of the delinquents and only 13 per cent of the nondelinquents had deep emotional disturbances.[25] Drs. Bromberg and Thompson examined 10,000 prisoners at the Psychiatric Clinic, Court of General Sessions, New York City, and found that 10.8 per cent showed gross mental abnormalities; 2.4 per cent were mentally defective, 1.5 per cent

---

[24] David Abrahamsen, "Den psykiatrisk-psykologiske bakgrunn for et barnedrap begått av en vanför," in *Frihet Sannhet; Festskrift til Johann Scharffenberg*, pp. 404-19.

[25] William Healy and A. F. Bronner, *New Lights on Delinquency and Its Treatment*, p. 122. One might be apt to doubt these findings in view of the fact that in cases previously known as delinquent, emotional disturbances would be more predominant than in nondelinquent cases. One would therefore think that Healy's findings could not be generalized. However, if similar studies were made and confirmed Healy's findings, they would be of decisive value in determining the prevalence of abnormalcy in delinquent behavior.

were psychotics, and 6.9 per cent were psychopathic cases.[26]

Somewhat similar statistics apply to murderers. A study of 200 murderers by Cassity showed that 3 per cent were mentally defective, while 2.25 per cent were psychotics, committed to institutions for criminally insane.[27] These figures might convey the impression that the rest of the murderers, about 94 per cent, had normal personalities or at least did not show demonstrably abnormal traits. It should be noted, however, that the prisoners did not receive a prolonged psychiatric-psychologic examination because of the short time available. This, together with the difficulty of detecting possible abnormal traits, may account for the apparently low rate of abnormality discovered. Further, since 38 per cent of the murderers were previous offenders, which in itself might indicate some mental deviations, and 50 per cent were intoxicated when they committed their crimes,[28] and a part of these would also show abnormal traits, it is reasonable to assume that by thorough examination one would be able to ascertain a much greater prevalence of traits having a pathologic quality.

This is a point of paramount importance. Even if the individual is not considered insane in the legal sense, the discovery of pathologic features in his personality indicates an underlying pathological process. The criterion of a murderer's "sanity" or "insanity" should be based not only upon the murderer or the act in itself, but also upon the connection between the murderer and his act, that is, upon the relationship between his mind and the accomplished act.

As pointed out before in Chapter II, when an individual commits a crime, it is usually done in a manner corresponding to his mental attitude. This leads to the question of whether there are the same dynamic connections between a murderer and his act as between any other offender and his type of crime. We have in Chapter IV pointed out in general the difficulty in ascertaining such an intimate connection, a difficulty we also encounter in a homicide. It must be borne in mind that it is not enough to say that the connection between the murdered and the murderer is

[26] Walter Bromberg and C. B. Thompson, "The Relation of Psychosis, Mental Defect and Personality Types to Crime," *Journal of Criminal Law and Criminology*, XXVIII (May–June, 1937), No. 1, 9.
[27] Cassity, *op. cit.*, 296.   [28] *Ibid.*, 297.

clear when he has confessed and the corpse is discovered. It is equally important to obtain the story that leads up to the fatal act, to bring to light the manner in which the homicide was carried out, and to trace the murderer's behavior before, during, and after his act. These facts, if brought out, will reveal in many cases the deeper and more intimate relationship. What has to be determined in the cases where a psychosis is not obvious, is the relation between the individual's make-up and his act. This relationship may be a decisive criterion in judging whether or not the man has an abnormal mind.

Thus, in cases where a murderer appears normal, one must inquire whether previous to, at, or following the time that the crime was committed his emotions, thoughts, and will were deviated from the normal line to such an extent that they were of a pathologic quality. If they were, then one must ask whether the presence of these characteristics was the main force which caused the murder.

The following case shows how a man seemingly without abnormal traits may become a murderer. A forty-two-year-old man killed his wife with an axe. The immediate circumstance leading up to the murder was this: his wife, after having received the largest part of his salary, asked him to give her the rest of it; he gave her the money, turned around, seized an axe, and then killed her.

A superficial examination might lead one to the belief that the man killed his wife merely because he was driven into a sudden rage over money. His history, however, revealed the following facts:

They were both born and raised in the same community. Her home environment was one of constant bickering, quarreling, and disagreements. He was a factory worker and she was intellectually his superior. They had to marry because she had become pregnant. At first they lived near the factory where he worked, but she was restless and could not remain in one place for long, so they moved about. She objected to his visiting his parents, and scolded him continually. When he was home, he had to take care of their four children, while she went visiting her family. When her relatives were out of work, they lived in his house for many months. Her sister-in-law stayed with them for a long time. Later another sister with three children came to live with them. The house was overcrowded and life became intolerable for him and the children. A condition of "war of nerves," so to speak, existed.

Two years before the murder he heard that his wife was associating with another man, but he could not prove the truth of this. In any event, the relations between them became steadily worse. She took all the money he earned, complained that everything he did was wrong, made him the scapegoat for each out-of-the-way thing that occurred in the home, and thus increased his uncertainty and feelings of inferiority.

In the last months before the murder his earnings were slight, and in order to support his family he worked in a factory at night and drove a car in the daytime. He was exhausted when he came home. One day his wife started her usual nagging, accusing him of not supporting her and the children. When she finally asked for the rest of his money, he gave it to her, and then killed her. The murder is to be considered not as sudden irrational act, but as a result of long accumulated bitterness and passive rebellion of masochistic coloring.

The judge in the case, recognizing this fact, stated that the man did not act from a criminal will in the usual sense, but from a greatly harassed and tortured mind. For this reason the murderer was regarded with leniency and received a short sentence.

From the psychiatric point of view, however, it is too naive to say that this man was tortured to the breaking point so that he committed murder. This is only a part of the story. The fact that murder seemed the only solution to his troubles indicates a basic inadequacy in his personality which was shown over a long period in his inability to live with his wife or to break away from her. The judge's statement is not clear to the experienced psychiatrist who would ask what "a criminal will in the *usual* sense" is.

There is no such scientific entity as "a criminal will." I doubt whether individuals exist who perpetrate criminal acts without having experienced some kind of inner conflict more or less connected with some development of hate in childhood resulting in feelings of guilt and anxiety or in a self-punishing mechanism such as that seen in the above case.[29] It is by uncovering the unconscious

[29] See Hugo Staub, "A Runaway from Home," *Psychoanalytic Quarterly*, XII (1943), No. 1, 2.

that we are able to trace the motives of antisocial activities. When a man kills a person it is not farfetched to say that he killed him a long time before he actually commits the homicide. The same protracted development also takes place in suicide, as Dr. Karl A. Menninger has pointed out.[30]

The cases mentioned above may show how difficult it is to decide whether a person is to be considered "legally sane" or not. It is safe to say that unconscious elements play an overwhelming part in homicide, and if uncovered, they will provide us with material enabling us to establish the dynamic connection between the killer's mind and his homicide. As the individual manifests his actual and potential traits in a certain pattern, so this very pattern is reflected in the homicide committed. The murder is characterized by the acting person. Though circumstance and situation may give the murder a certain color, nevertheless the motivation which brought it about lends it a certain character which makes it possible to a large extent not only to classify the killer but also to distinguish between the different types of homicide. Adhering to the principle that some homicides are the result of inner conflict caused by some hate directed against a person in childhood calling forth guilt feelings and self-punishment or through another type of mechanism, we may consider them to be symptomatic or secondary or reactive, while other types of homicide appear to be primarily directed against society. We are justified in differentiating this type of crime in symptomatic and manifest homicide. Let it be added that there are homicides in which different basic elements enter. A homicide may, for instance, be committed because of jealousy, followed by robbery, during an alcoholic spree.

A. The symptomatic murder can be classified under the following headings: (1) murder due to a distorted erotic drive, which can be divided into (a) jealousy murder, and (b) murder in the course of a sexual offense; and (2) murder due to the aggressive drive, which can be divided into (a) alcoholic murder, (b) surrogate (substitute) murder, (c) murder due to physical inferiority.

B. The manifest (essential) murder can be classified as (a) profit murder and (b) murder from motives unknown.

[30] *Man against Himself*, p. 22.

A. Symptomatic Murder

1. *Murder due to a Distorted Erotic Drive:* (a) Jealousy murder. It is a fairly well established fact that jealousy is a strong force in driving an individual to murder. Generally speaking, the background is frustrated love caused by a triangular situation. The psychological mechanism behind such an act is that the person's self-esteem and prestige is injured. The individual believes not only that he possesses the partner but also that he has a right to possess her, and this makes him jealous. By killing the partner his self-esteem is restored.

Often a man's love for his mother may hamper or prevent satisfactory union between him and his wife. The man shows more attention to his mother than to his wife, which creates a feeling of jealousy in the latter that may lead to homicide. The reverse situation, in which a woman kills her daughter-in-law, also occurs. This type of crime is an expression of hatred and jealousy having its roots in the childhood Oedipus conflict of the woman.[31]

The varying direction of homicidal jealousy may often give a hint as to the underlying personality conflict. A young person in love with a young partner will kill the subject of his love, whereas an older one will frequently kill the rival. In the latter case there may be a sexual inadequacy or impotence of which the individual is only vaguely conscious.

Somewhat different is the situation where strong mother attachment is present. A widely known case is the following. A fifty-year-old highly intellectual teacher with a strong attachment for his mother killed an eighteen-year-old girl and afterwards made an unsuccessful attempt at suicide. Later he admitted he had completely identified the girl with his mother. The motivating force of the murder was probably jealousy, which in itself caused him to believe that he possessed the girl. Coupled with this was an unconscious feeling that she should always belong to him, in the same way as his mother had always been attached to him. When the man discovered the girl had a boy friend, he feared he was going to lose her, which to him, in a psychological sense, meant losing his mother.

---

[31] Alexander and Staub have described such a case where the infantile Oedipus situation plays the fatal part in *The Criminal, the Judge and the Public,* pp. 190–206.

Several cases of murder as expressions of jealousy have been characterized by the thoroughness with which the victim is killed. Stab upon stab may follow, even after the victim is dead. Such total destruction may even extend to all that symbolizes the victim. In the case mentioned above, the murderer not only killed the girl, but destroyed her photograph, piercing the eyes and slashing the face.

(b) Murder in the course of a sexual offense. Sexual elements play a larger part in homicide than is generally realized. Murder in the course of rape or a homosexual act, is not infrequent, although not as common as murder during a holdup or robbery. I will mention only one case, the homicide committed by Richard Loeb and Nathan Leopold in 1924. The case is particularly significant, because for the first time in the history of medical jurisprudence the court paved the way for a completely scientific investigation of the mental conditions of the murderers. Only the outstanding facts are given here. (For a more detailed history see *Clarence Darrow's Plea in Defense of Loeb and Leopold.*)

Richard Loeb's family was well-to-do and was recognized as being of high intelligence. His father's first cousin developed a definite insanity at eighteen years of age and was committed to the Elgin State Hospital. While Richard's grandfather was quite abusive to his children and beat them severely, his father was lenient to him. His mother died early in his life and Richard was raised very strictly by a governess. She exerted a great influence over him, so in order to get by, he started to lie, by which means he escaped detection and punishment. Later he admitted that upon her leaving when he was fifteen years of age, he "broke loose." Due to her rigid discipline and supervision he was far ahead in school and was later the youngest graduate of the University of Michigan. They became very attached to each other. She effeminized him and kept him ignorant as to sexual life. At a very early age he began his criminal activities. He stole money, "picked up" things in stores whenever the opportunity presented itself, taking them even if he did not need them. Later he filched liquor from a relative, began to steal cars, and also set fire to some shacks. He developed a moral callousness, became "hard-boiled" and egocentric. During his childhood and early adolescence, he had a vivid imagination, thinking he would be a great man. Mostly, he imagined himself in jail and as the greatest criminal of the century.

The family of Nathan Leopold was also well-to-do. His grandfather was an intellectually alert man. On his father's side there were two cases of insanity of the paranoid type. His mother died of a kidney disease, and Nathan was therefore raised by three consecutive governesses. When he was five years old he had a vivid fantasy, imagining himself a king and a slave. He identified himself with the king, but he usually preferred to play the role of the slave. He made rapid progress in school. In the fifth grade he became interested in ornithology and later, with another young fellow, wrote a pamphlet on the subject. At sixteen he entered the University of Michigan, where he studied psychology, ornithology, and various languages—German, French, Russian, Greek, Latin, Spanish, and Sanskrit. Turning to his sexual life, we find that he was never attracted to women, that a woman never satisfied him, that he worshipped his mother, his aunt, and the Madonna. This caused a dislike of girls. He never had a true love affair. Above all, he had definite ideas or imaginations of a king-slave constellation.

The two met. If one is fatalistic, one can say that their meeting was not by chance. Nevertheless, it was their undoing. They fitted each other as a key in a lock. Loeb, being apparently the stronger, took the lead. A warm friendship developed. It may be assumed that this friendship was basically a sexual one. In this connection it must be recalled that sexual elements, unconscious and unnoticed though they may be, may exist even in the finest friendship between persons of the same sex. In this case, with their peculiar upbringing, intellectual endowment, repression of sexual feelings, and vivid fantasies, the basis was established for an intimate friendship.

Leopold regarded Loeb as more intelligent and offered him his friendship so that in the course of time it became impossible for Leopold to live without Loeb. Soon he was so affectionately drawn to him that he became his slave. Although Leopold thought at first that Loeb was not good-looking, he later became his ideal, and Leopold fitted him into his slave-king fantasy, which was in nature a blind worship.

In November, 1923, Loeb planned with the aid of Leopold to return to Ann Arbor to rob his fraternity house. They succeeded in the robbery and drove back to Chicago without being detected.

After the robbery, a series of quarrels which threatened their friendship occurred. It was suggested that the relationship be dissolved. However, since both gained by it, they agreed to bury the hatchet and continued the friendship under certain restrictions. Loeb was to have complete domination over Leopold, and whenever Loeb used the phrase "for Robert's sake," Leopold was to yield to Loeb's demands.

In November, 1923, they planned to kidnap a boy, but the plan was not carried out. The following May, they intended to kidnap Loeb's father or his younger brother, but this also was not done. On the day of the murder, they hired a car and drove around in the vicinity of their homes looking for a suitable victim. First they picked up a small boy, but let him go without injury. Then they picked up another boy, Robert Frank, and hitting him over the head, killed him. They undressed the boy from the waist down and in the evening placed him in a drain. Later they wrote the child's parents that he would be returned if they paid $10,000 ransom.

Several days later the body was found. Nearby lay a pair of eye glasses which were traced to Leopold. Both were arrested but denied any connection with the case. However, after a few days, Loeb's chauffeur discredited their alibis, and they thereupon confessed. Leopold told in his confession that his participation in the crime was an expression of friendship for his companion in the latter's desire to commit a homicide. Leopold was frightened during the killing, but Loeb was detached and amused. Leopold denied having any emotion of remorse for the crime, being without feeling of having done anything wrong. Nor did Loeb show any emotional reaction to the murder. He admitted that previous to the murder he had been subject to spells of depression and had frequently contemplated suicide.

Leopold can be considered as a highly gifted, selfish, narcissistic person who during his childhood and adolescence developed feelings of insecurity. For this reason he was sensitive to other people's opinions. In order to overcome this sensitiveness, he repressed his feelings, which, in turn, tended to develop his intellectual faculties. Thus, although apparently cold and aloof, he had emotions, his make-up therefore being similar to that of a schizoid person. Since he did not find any outlet for his emotions, he sought intellectual interests at which he excelled and among many things studied rare languages. His mental activity drove him constantly at high speed. Never fatigued, he always had to accomplish something. As a result of his intellectual growth his ego developed and with it a definite pattern of a philosophy whose hightest aim was to achieve things to his own advantage.

He experienced vivid imaginations of a sexual nature, but one may question whether these imaginations were dreams. His sexual fantasies and desires were so powerful that his sexual drive became twisted, leading to strong homoerotic tendencies. This assumption is strengthened by his own words about Loeb: "I almost completely identified myself with him," thus admitting his strong love for him. There is here a psychological identification. This indicates that there was a firm love relationship between them, which is also proved by their reported sexual relations with each other in the presence of a fraternity brother. Further proof may be seen in his frank admission that he went into the crime as part of his friendship with Loeb, and finally, in the fact that they undressed the boy from the waist down. Since the murder took place about five o'clock in the afternoon and they did not bury him until late that evening, at which time the body was stiff, the possibility cannot be ruled out that some sexual acts took place after the murder.

Loeb was found to be intellectual, narcissistic, and cool. His personality was marked by the strict upbringing under his governess, by the strong attachment to her, and by feelings of inferiority. He developed the habit of lying and escaping all responsibility, and apparently did not experience any feeling of guilt. Because of this attachment and his strict upbringing, combined with a feminized personality, his psycho-sexual development not only seemed to have stopped at an infantile state but also took an abnormal deviation. To a certain extent, he apparently became sexually impotent, for which reason he boasted of having many affairs with girls. This abnormal sexual development could hardly be satisfied by usual homosexual methods, and his distorted sexual drive had to find another outlet.

In the course of time he developed a great resistance to the precepts of his governess and his father, and as a reaction against the restrictions imposed on him he started a criminal career. His inner conflict against his abnormal drives and the conflict with Leopold made him depressed. He felt that he ought to commit suicide, but evidently contented himself with a psychic killing of himself. Thus, one can say that the plan to kill the boy and the murder itself were expressions of his desire to commit suicide. In a Freudian interpretation, simultaneous with killing the boy physically he killed himself psychically. It seems that, by killing the boy, he committed unconsciously an indirect suicide. Deep in his mind he might have felt that he ought to commit suicide, but unable to do this, he killed the boy, expecting death for himself as a penalty for the crime.[32]

Thus, the murder on his part represents a disguised suicide. But he himself expected to be punished with death. This only expresses the predominant current of self-punishment in him, originating as a result of unresolved strong feelings of guilt. That he needed a great deal of self-punishment is evidenced by the fact that even as a young boy he imagined himself in jail; further, after his confession of the murder, he went apparently with joy into the prison cell and felt gratified in being deprived of his liberty, so precious to the normal human being. Leopold also behaved in this manner.

In view of their strong homoerotic tendencies and the desire for self-punishment, it seems rather strange that during the trial the murder was called a "senseless, useless, purposeless, motiveless act." It is more probable that the homicide was committed because of their abnormal ingrained erotic drive giving origin to strong wish of self-punishment caused by a strong sense of guilt, all components representing a load that compelled them into a road of criminal activity that climaxed in the murder. It is rather that the definite abnormal sexual inclination of the two was instrumental in giving their whole life a pathologic pattern, by which their emotional life was deviated to such an extent from normal behavior that their personalities developed traits of pathologic quality.

Taking into consideration the dynamic connection between the murderers' make-up and their act, one is apt to assume that the act

[32] Indirect suicide, as seen throughout human history, may very well take such a form. In the seventeenth and eighteenth centuries there was an epidemic of indirect suicides in Norway and Denmark. Depressed people committed murder so that they themselves might be put to death.

was a product of two morbid minds. If we follow this assumption to its logical conclusion we will tend to believe that the killers might have been considered to have had abnormal minds but they did not suffer from mental disorders. The main point was that they were considered dangerous to society, an aim which was fulfilled by their imprisonment.

In conclusion, it may be noted that except for profit murder, a homicide committed by two partners of the same sex, generally involves, to a greater or lesser extent, sexual components.

2. *Murder due to the Aggressive Drive:* (a) Alcoholic murder. There is no doubt that alcohol plays an important role in a large number of assaults. Sheldon and Eleanor Glueck found that 39.4 per cent of men in reformatories had used alcohol to excess.[33] In Norway it was found that 90 per cent of those who committed assaults were alcoholics, and 80 per cent of the total were intoxicated at the time of the assault. Of those accused of negligent manslaughter, 92 per cent were found to be intoxicated. Of those who committed murder, 60 per cent were intoxicated.[34] In a study of 200 murders, Cassity found that alcohol as a precipitating factor was present in approximately 50 per cent of the total cases.[35]

Alcohol as a contributive factor in a murder may be viewed from two angles, the perpetrator's attitude toward alcohol in general and his attitude at the time he committed the homicide. The fact that a murderer is intoxicated does not mean that the homicide is senseless. An alcoholic may show the same pattern of behavior at the time of his homicide as in previous sprees, the only difference being that in the latter case his behavior was not so extreme. Alcoholic intoxication may be not only a contributive factor but even a causative factor in homicide, as shown in the following case. A twenty-year-old boy who was inebriated was brandishing a knife before his friend who was likewise drunk. The boy lurched forward and by accident struck the friend between the upper vertebrae (atlas and occiput), cutting the spinal cord and causing immediate death. Had he been sober, in all probability no crime would have been committed.

It must be stressed that the importance of alcohol as contributive

[33] *Five Hundred Criminal Careers*, p. 86.
[34] Hartvig Nissen, *Alkohol og forbrydelse*, p. 20.   [35] Cassity, *op. cit.*, 297.

or causative factors in first-time murderers and recidivists differs. A first-time homicide may be attributed to alcohol if it is found that the perpetrator was intoxicated. Quite different is the situation with recidivists. Individuals with a previous criminal career who commit homicide on an alcoholic spree may have murdered without being intoxicated.

(b) Surrogate (substitute) murder. A surrogate murder is defined as murder of a person who serves as a substitute for the individual originally intended to be killed. The homicide may at first appear to be an ordinary one committed in the course of an assault or some other offense. If sufficient psychological examination is possible, however, a connection of dynamic character may be discovered between the murderer and the originally intended victim. An illustration of this class of murder is the case of a taxi driver who murdered a passenger because of the latter's resemblance to his father whom he hated.[36] Since the wish to kill his father was impossible of fulfillment, he found a substitute. Similar mechanisms may be seen in many neurotic murders. It is safe to say that careful psychologic examinations would reveal that surrogate murders occur more frequently than is generally realized.

(c) Murder due to physical inferiority. It is an old axiom that a healthy mind can exist only in a healthy body. Conversely, a diseased or deformed body may in the course of time affect an individual's behavior and result in criminal activity. In *The Iliad* Homer described a hunchback, Tersites, who because of his malformation and monstrosity became repulsive, and so tried to assert himself by deceit and fraudulence. Unique in classical literature is Shakespeare's description of Richard III whose hideous crimes, Shakespeare explained, were perpetrated in revenge for his being an ugly misfit. Shakespeare's conception of how a cripple's mental attitude can be affected by his bodily deformity is revealing:

> But I, that am not shap'd for sportive tricks,
> Nor made to court an amorous looking-glass;
> I, that am rudely stamp'd, and want love's majesty
> To strut before a wanton ambling nymph;
> I, that am curtail'd of this fair proportion,
> Cheated of feature by dissembling nature,

[36] Gregory Zilboorg, "Some Sidelights on Psychology of Murder," *Journal of Nervous and Mental Disease*, LXXXI (April, 1935), 442.

Deform'd, unfinish'd, sent before my time
Into this breathing world, scarce half made up,
And that so lamely and unfashionable
That dogs bark at me, as I halt by them;
Why, I, in this weak piping time of peace,
Have no delight to pass away the time,
Unless to see my shadow in the sun
And descant on mine own deformity:
And therefore, since I cannot prove a lover,
To entertain these fair well-spoken days,
I am determined to prove a villain,
And hate the idle pleasures of these days.
Plots have I laid, inductions dangerous,
By drunken prophecies, libels, and dreams,
To set my brother Clarence and the king
In deadly hate the one against the other . . .

ACT I, SCENE I

We may say that each bodily disease or bodily defect may tend to produce a change in the mental attitude of a person. This inclination may disappear when the disease vanishes, but it may also develop further, particularly in the case where the disease leads to physical inferiority.

Of special interest are those homicides which occur as a result of a physical disease or deformity of the body. The dynamic connection between the homicide and the acting person may be difficult to trace because of the complex picture made by the elements involved, but the ascertaining of such a connection is eased if the perpetrator becomes consciously aware that his mental attitude is changed by his body disease or defect.[37] The degrees in which a person apprehends that he is different from his fellows, if he is at all conscious of it, vary all the way from the most vaguely comprehended to full realization. It is important to stress that his awareness of his mental make-up and subsequent feelings of inferiority are largely due to environmental factors.

[37] In an examination of about 2,000 boys and 1,000 girls with inferiority feelings, it was found that physical, mental, and social conditions of objective inferiority did not per se give rise to inferiority attitudes. However, another finding was that higher intelligence tended to be associated with inferiority attitudes. Luton Ackerson, "Inferiority Attitudes and Their Correlations among Children Examined in a Behavior Clinic," *Journal of Genetic Psychology*, 1943, p. 85.

A changed mental attitude resulting from a bodily disease or deformity may prompt criminal activities, even though a bodily deformity may, in cases where institutionalizing is necessary, actually prevent the individual from becoming a criminal.[38]

Whether or not a cripple turns to criminal acts may depend upon the degree of his bodily deformity. He is particularly inclined to commit sexual crimes, because he cannot readily secure a suitable partner for his sexual needs, and if he does, he may be involved in difficulties which can be traced indirectly to his bodily deformity.

I cite here the murder of a newborn baby in which the crippled condition of the murderer forms the psychiatric-psychologic background of the homicide.

It is the case of a fifty-year-old man who was a typical chondrodystrophic dwarf, three feet, two inches in height, with arms and legs extremely shortened, and a seemingly normally developed torso. Except for an elder brother who was similarly deformed, there was no previously known case of dwarfs in his family. Nor was there any criminality, alcoholism, mental deficiency, or insanity in the family history. But before his parents' marriage, his mother had a son out of wedlock who died at twenty-three. This illegitimate boy caused friction in the family.

The dwarf himself grew up on a small farm with his parents. Later he started school but did not show great interest in it. As his comrades grew steadily taller, while his own growth was stunted, he had to play with younger boys and this made him resentful, so he rather shunned the companionship of others. When he finished school, he worked on a farm and continued to be a "lone wolf." On the rare occasions that he went dancing, he did not enjoy it. In short, he became somewhat antisocial.

One autumn a new housemaid came to the farm. They became sexually intimate, which finally resulted in her pregnancy. Both wanted to marry and have the child but feared that it might be born with the father's deformities. When the time of birth approached she wanted a midwife, but he refused this saying he could handle the delivery himself. That evening she gave birth to a girl. He strangulated the infant, wrapped it in paper, left it under their

[38] David Abrahamsen, *op. cit.*, p. 404. See also Friedrich Stumpfl, *Studien über Vererbung und Endstehung geistiger Storungen*, p. 44.

bed all night, and buried it the following day behind the barn. A few days afterwards they were both arrested, confessed the murder, and later the body was found.

The psychiatric examination did not produce any particular findings. His mood was dark, as would be expected. There was no sign of paranoid ideas, delusions, or hallucinations.

Here was a dwarf who on account of his disability was unable to keep pace with his comrades and to find suitable friends, which provoked feelings of inferiority. For this reason he remained at home with his dreams; this was substantiated at the trial by his teacher. That he was a dreamer is not surprising. His tendency to daydream had root in his unfulfilled wishes and fantasies which originated from the idea that he was different from other people because of his bodily defect. He wished to be like other people, but they did not accept him because of his deformity, so he withdrew into himself. The consciousness of his deformity gradually pervaded his whole mentality, invaded the sphere of his thinking, feeling, and willing faculties, and affected his moral attitude.

In this mental state he met the housemaid and a friendship arose. Their fear that the child would perhaps be deformed like the father put them in a mood from which they could not free themselves. These feelings were accentuated by her being ashamed of having people know that she had relations with a dwarf. He on his side feared having a child born as himself. In the same way as he hated himself, he was filled with hatred against the child. He therefore killed it. Thus, the homicide of the child is in fact a killing of himself. A direct line, as it were, leads from his being a cripple to his developing an antisocial attitude climaxed by the murder. The factors show how intimately interwoven his bodily defect was with the homicide.

That was the view taken by the court. In pronouncing sentence, the judge regarded the situation as so extraordinary that he could not mete out the usual punishment prescribed by law. The murderer's bodily deformity and the motivation was in the court's opinion so mitigating that a lenient sentence was imposed.

This is in keeping with our view. Where an obvious bodily defect is present in a murderer, one will usually find an immediate relation between him and his act. Such a man will not readily speak about himself, but, once induced to do so, he will reveal to what extent his deformity has influenced his mind and produced a deviation from sound judgment, forming a basis for the dynamic connection between him and the homicide.

B. Manifest (Essential) Murder

Crimes of this sort are committed primarily against society. The murderers come from that bracket of society which identifies itself with crime in general and homicide in particular. In this group are included two types. (a) Profit murder. Persons who commit this type of murder act in accordance with their special concept of life and of the rules of society. This concept is developed as a result of their murder being approved by their whole personality—by their ego and superego as well. The motive of personal gain is obviously present, as is seen in the murder rings. The mechanism is simple and hardly needs further elaboration.

(b) Murder from motives unknown. To this class belong homicides in which the murderer is undetected or the murder is surrounded by such a complex of factors that the motivation cannot be determined. It would perhaps be more correct to call this class "murder with unrecognized motives."

From the medical and criminological point of view it is imperative that every person accused of murder or any other serious crime be examined psychiatrically before trial by a qualified psychiatrist appointed by the state.

The details as to how this examination is done are mentioned in Chapter V. Its purpose is to find the predominating features in the personality structure which enable one to explain the dynamics of the personality, the course of events, and whether or not the person is psychotic. One must also keep in mind the projections, phobias, and compulsions which arise as a disguise in the criminal's defense reactions against the aggressions. Psychiatrists are sometimes apt to be accused of "sentimentality" in regard to criminals, because they do not make moral discriminations. For example, some murderers behave in a peculiarly callous and unfeeling manner. To the public this makes the crime more heinous. But the psychiatrist sees this as a characteristic way of handling anxiety. The following cases illustrate the point. In one case a man killed his mother, put her body into a suitcase, and then went to a movie with his girl friend. In another, a man, after having killed his girl friend by throwing her down a steep cliff, went to a stadium and played football.

These murderers continued their activities as if nothing had happened, and when they were eventually caught and questioned, the lay examiner was puzzled and horrified by their apparent indifference. The psychiatrist recognizes such behavior as a pathological means of relieving unconscious tension.

This psychological technique of finding relief from feelings of guilt by repudiating responsibility for the criminal act is commonly seen in convicted murderers serving a life sentence, in whom the conscious motive for concealment and self-preservation does not play as large a part as it does before they were apprehended. On the surface they appear to be no different from the other inmates, but actually they live in the past with all their past hopes and wishes. Their inner life may take the form of reality so that psychically they continue to live as they did before the crime. By this rationalization, which approaches a self-deception, they cling to their past, and are thereby able to ease their mind in the discomfort of incarceration. Such prisoners frequently offer the examiner transparent rationalizations concerning their motives and acts which are more in the nature of self-deceptions than conscious, self-protective deception.[39]

This is particularly true when the murderer does not know the reason for the examination.[40] It is, therefore, important that he be informed in advance of the reason for the examination and that the examiner endeavor to become acquainted with and gain the confidence of the murderer through conversations on other subjects prior to any discussion of the homicide. A murderer, like any other offender, will usually be on guard and suspicious of the intrusion on the part of the examiner. In any event the examiner must use insight based on scientific study in observing and recording the intellectual, emotional, and behavior pattern characteristic of the murderer.

What practical conclusions can we draw, if and when we are

[39] Andreas Bjerre, *The Psychology of Murder*, p. 73.
[40] U. Bumke, *Handwörterbuch der Kriminologie und anderen strafrechtlichen Hilfswissenschaften*, p. 200.

able to detect the motivation for homicide? If we know the forces that drive a man to murder, we can, provided the case is suitable for deep psychological therapy and the circumstances are favorable, help him to grasp his own situation, make him understand his own personality structure, and enable him to find acceptable, socially constructive channels for his primitive aggressions, thus making possible his re-education. We may possibly succeed in discovering these forces in individuals before a homicide or other type of crime is committed. If we know that certain inner conflicts and frustrations cause lifelong suffering which may culminate in a crime such as homicide, there is a great chance to detect and prevent potential crimes.

A way to find those potential murderers would be to establish clinics in which all antisocial persons would be examined and receive treatment. (See Chapter X.) The task is great, but considering the number of homicides committed every year causing unspeakable suffering to the persons involved and producing serious damage to society, it would in view of saved lives and saved happiness be more than worth the expenses.

IX

THE PSYCHIATRIST AND THE
CRIMINAL LAW

THE ORIGIN and development of criminal law can readily be understood when we remember that society must be protected so that its members can work and create a foundation for an orderly life. Compliance with the law has to be maintained regardless of what the individual thinks of it. But his opinion does not always coincide with that of the law. The reason for this may be that the law not only metes out punishment to the individual but also operates without regard to the interests of the persons it may affect.

It may seem strange that the law itself has become more or less commonly accepted, but this is an order of nature which humans themselves have produced. History has repeatedly shown that there have been conflicts between that which the law considered ethical and that which humans individually regarded as ethical. However, despite any disparity between the individual's ethical concept and that of the law, the law has always tried to find an ethical basis for its existence, with the result that the order of the law has become partly an order of ethics.

This basis is the product of years of experience and evaluations, while that of the individual is the result of his thinking and feeling during his lifetime. These two different forces have each claimed that they possess the right ethical concept of life, and it is this point which is the center of the conflict.

The law is largely concerned with the manner in which one individual behaves towards another, and the psychiatrist is primarily interested in human behavior, which necessarily involves the relationships among persons. Thus, psychiatry and the law have had to come in touch with one another, though this has been accomplished only recently.

We cannot go into detail as to how this development occurred.

It must only be noted that psychiatry in the last decades has directly, or perhaps more indirectly, influenced the evolution of criminal law so much that today we cannot conceive of their being separated. If we think that much of criminal behavior is of a pathologic nature, or at least behavior which in one way or another may be related to the personality make-up, then criminal law cannot disregard this fact, because in keeping with its spirit the law should always consider those new concepts of life continually being brought forth. Needless to say the law too often has been rather tardy in revising its rules when confronted with new scientific evidence. However, it must be remembered that the law exists for the purpose of maintaining the established order. It is easy to criticize a judge who metes out a punishment which might be regarded as unwarranted. In passing such a judgment, one so easily forgets that the judge is bound by the law and must render his decision and pronounce sentence in accordance with the rules governing the particular case, otherwise he would be derelict in his duty.

And yet, at times there have been judges who have expressed opinions that ran counter to the existing law. This happened in the case of Daniel McNaghten, who was tried in 1843. A principle was laid down in this case that had a great bearing on British and American criminal jurisprudence. Daniel McNaghten suffered from the delusion that Sir Robert Peel was one of those who wanted to kill him. One day in attempting to assassinate Peel, he shot and killed Peel's secretary. He was charged with murder but was acquitted by the jury on grounds of insanity. The case caused a great sensation. The House of Lords formulated five questions for the fifteen judges of England, which concerned the proposing of a concise test for criminal responsibility in cases of delusional and ordinary insanity.

In response to the questions the Lord Chief Justice, Tindal, in 1843 proposed a test for criminal irresponsibility in cases of ordinary insanity. He said: "To establish a defense on the ground of insanity, it must be clearly proved, that at the time of the act, the accused was laboring under such a defect of reasoning as not to know the nature and quality of his act, or, if he did, that he did not know that what he was doing was wrong." In explaining what was meant by "wrong," he said that if the accused was conscious that the act was one that he ought not to do, and if it was at the same time contrary to the law of the land, it would be punishable.[1]

Regarding the delusions it was said: "If the accused labors under partial delusions only and is not in other respects insane . . . he must be considered in the same situation as to responsibility as if the facts with respect to which the delusion exists were real." [2] It was in this way that the concept of legal insanity was formed. In principle it had been present in the writings of Sir Matthew Hale (1609–76) and Blackstone had said: "If a man in his own memory commits a capital offense, and before arraignment for it becomes mad, he ought not to be arraigned, because he is not able to plead to it with the advice and caution that he ought. And if, after he has pleaded, the prisoner becomes mad, he shall not be tried; for how can he make his defense." [3]

In the next few years an attempt was made to establish the rule of "Irresistible Impulse" as an excuse for crime, but such an attempt was defeated in England. In America the law in the beginning followed the principles laid down in the English cases. Francis Wharton in his book, *A Treatise on the Criminal Law of the United States* (1846), Isaac Ray in his *A Treatise on the Medical Jurisprudence of Insanity* (1838), and other writers of the time were concerned mostly with the English law.

The first important case on insanity in America was *Commonwealth v. Rogers* in 1844, in which the judge in his instructions repeated the rule of McNaghten's case and also held for the rule of "Irresistible Impulse." The next outstanding case was *State v. Spencer* in 1846, in which the rule of McNaghten's case was also accepted but the rule of "Irresistible Impulse" was disregarded. Up to about 1900 the courts of the different states adhered either to the rule of *Commonwealth v. Rogers,* the "Right and Wrong Test" plus "Irresistible Impulse" or the rule of *State v. Spencer,* which was the "Right and Wrong Test" alone.

The fixed and rigid view of criminal law regarding insanity in the criminal can only be understood when seen against its historical background. What does this history tell us?

[1] Regina v. Oxford, 9 C. & P. 525, 173 Eng. L. & Eq. R. 941 (1840); Offord's Case, 5 C. & P. 168, 172 Eng. L. & Eq. R. 924 (1831).
[2] H. Weihofen, *Insanity as a Defense in Criminal Law,* pp. 28–29.
[3] *The American Students' Blackstone,* IV, 24.

For centuries the testimony of physicians has been used in criminal prosecutions. The evidence of expert medical witnesses was utilized as early as the sixteenth century, probably as early as the fourteenth century. At any rate, in the famous law of Emperor Charles V, *Constitutio Criminalis Carolina* (1532), the assistance of a physician was demanded in cases involving homicide, poisoning, manslaughter, infanticide, and—what is of great interest to us —in the question of whether or not an offender was insane. It is noteworthy that the physician was called to give his testimony as *amicus curiae*. He was respected and he did not take any sides. Later, probably in the eighteenth century when the power of the jury increased, the court itself ceased to request an expert, so that he had to be called upon by the parties in the case, resulting in his diminished importance. The survival of such a custom is seen today in many states where the right of a party to call upon an expert in a case exists by statute or under the common law.[4]

There is no doubt that this change in the expert's position in the court affected the value of his testimony. This was to a large extent due to the fact that he had to speak in terms of the law rather than in medical terms.

One does not need to use one's fantasy to see what kind of constellations were called forth by the various tests of insanity which have been employed through the ages. It is needless to discuss the "wild beast" test, "the child of fourteen" test, or the test of "partial insanity," which was taken over from the classical medicine of Hippocrates and Galen.[5] The latter test has been in effect in spite of the fact that medicine has given clear evidence that the human mind is a whole and not a partial unit. Such a happening is only a single link in a long chain of discrepancies.

And yet basically there is little difference between the goal of law and of psychiatry. The law is primarily interested in the well-being of society by giving security to the individual, while psychiatry is concerned with the mental welfare of humans.

That the law has been keenly interested in mentally sick persons is a matter of fact. Yes, the law gives actual rules as to how mentally diseased individuals shall be treated, handled, and protected. Not

4 Winfred Overholser, *Psychiatry and the Law—Cooperators or Antagonists?*, p. 7.
5 Gregory Zilboorg, "Misconceptions of Legal Insanity," *American Journal of Orthopsychiatry*, IX (July, 1939), No. 3, 549.

only does the law commit a mentally sick person to an institution if he is unable to take care of himself, but it also sees that he is committed without having his constitutional rights infringed. The court even gives full protection in order to prevent the mentally sick person from being exploited by other persons. In the case of commitments, the judge follows the advice of the psychiatrist, although he adheres to certain precautions of a formal nature. There are, of course, those occasions where a judge will have to have new testimony, but all this is done in order to protect the individual.

Thus we see that when the law deals with a mentally sick person it takes every precaution to give him adequate consideration and protection. However, considering what medical science today knows of human nature, there is a deplorable discrepancy between the view of the criminal law and that of psychiatry concerning these offenders.

Since the question of insanity is of importance as a defense in criminal trials, it is essential to determine *at which time* the offender became insane. It is equally important to recognize what kind of effect the insanity has had on the defender, because many states in the Union have certain tests to determine the defendant's insanity. The psychiatrist should be aware of the legal aspects of insanity as a defense under existing law. To be sure, the psychiatrist when called into court is an expert only, but he will do well to have at least some cognizance of the law's attitude with respect to an offender's capacity to commit a crime and his responsibility therefor.

In the field of legal psychiatry, there have, practically speaking, been only two distinctions as to the offender's mental state, that of being sane or insane. With a few exceptions, the law has not accepted the borderline cases—persons mentally abnormal without being insane in the legal sense—which psychiatry has recognized as existing. And courts of one state do not accept any tests of insanity because they believe all criminal cases depend upon the circumstances.

Let us see how the insanity of an offender affects his criminal responsibility for the crime. We will consider the consequences of insanity in the following four different situations: (1) the consequences of insanity at the time when the criminal act was committed; (2) the consequences of insanity after the committed crime and before the time of trial; (3) the consequences of insanity during trial; (4) the consequences of insanity after trial and during the completion of sentence.

It is clear that in the first situation the problem of insanity has a bearing upon the criminal responsibility of the defendant. If he was insane at the time of the commission of the act, he is not criminally responsible.

One would think that all forms of insanity have been recognized by the courts as a defense against criminal responsibility, but this is not so. Considering mental functioning only, insanity may be classified as intellectual, perceptional, emotional, or volitional. Some courts have, for instance, been disinclined to accept volitional insanity as a defense for criminal acts. Only when this type of insanity has been accompanied or followed by some sort of intellectual insanity has it been held that the individual in question suffered from an "Irresistible Impulse." The same has occurred where a case of emotional insanity has been found. It should be added that if a person is able to distinguish between right and wrong, emotional insanity, or what we would call in psychiatric language a strong emotion filled with anger, jealousy, or hate, would not excuse him from being responsible for his crime.

It is interesting to see that intellectual insanity was that variety which was first accepted by the criminal law. This is the test for insanity called the "Right and Wrong Test."

Finally, there are those cases where during an epileptic fit or an attack of delirium tremens some type of automatic behavior or loss of memory may take place, and criminal acts may be committed. These conditions, if they are extensive, may cloud the mind of the perpetrator and then diminish or eliminate the ability of the person to distinguish right from wrong. If that is the result, then there is no criminal responsibility.

How does the law in the different states handle a person who has committed a crime while suffering from a delusion—a case of the perceptional type? In *Commonwealth v. Rogers* the Court of Massachusetts said that "if a crime is committed because of a delusion, the committing person is to be judged, so far as criminal responsibility is concerned, just as if the fact in his delusion he believed to be true, were true." [6] Thus, the court accepted the delusion as a cause of the insanity and considered the person not responsible for his criminal act. Other courts, in Alabama, for instance, do not follow this line. It is interesting to note that Mississippi courts use the "Right and Wrong Test" when delusional insanity is pleaded.

In determining criminal responsibility of an accused person some states use the "Irresistible Impulse" test. By this they mean an impulse which is induced by some mental condition which affects the person's will, and while he is able to understand the consequences and wrongness of his criminal act, he is unable to resist the impulse. Even if such a test is used, not all courts agree that this irresistible impulse establishes an excuse for a crime. If that is the case, the court employs the "Right and Wrong Test" before a decision is made. This is the test which most courts use.[7]

1. *The Consequences of Insanity at the Time When the Criminal Act Was Committed.* It has been an old unwritten law that a person who at the time of his crime was insane cannot be punished or be considered criminally responsible for an act. This, however, is not always so. In a case in one of our states, the court asserted that there are forms of mental deficiency or derangement which will not excuse the perpetrator of a crime. If the mental derangement shall excuse the crime, it must be of such an extent that the offender was unable to form a criminal intent. In contrast to this verdict there stands out an opinion expressed by an Illinois court in the case of *People v. Marquer* where it was held that if the mentality of a person is of such a subnormal character as to render him incapable of distinguishing between right and wrong, it undoubtedly constitutes a legitimate defense.[8]

2. *The Consequences of Insanity after the Committed Crime and before the Time of Trial.* Under common law and by statute in several jurisdictions, an insane person cannot be tried, sentenced, or executed. If during the criminal procedure the defendant shows signs of insanity, the court will have to consider this problem before further proceedings take place. How this rule is to be acted upon is a matter of discussion. The situation may arise where a person might be tried even while insane and the question then brought

6 7 Metc. 500 (Mass.), 41 Am. Dec. 458 (1844).

7 Weihofen, *op. cit.*, pp. 14–17.   8 344 Ill. 261, 176 N.E. 314 (1931).

up is how to remedy the situation. If the defendant has been convicted and if later evidence is produced to show that he was insane during the trial, courts have recognized the right of the defendant to move for a new trial. In Michigan, a writ of habeas corpus may be obtained by the defendant or by another person in his behalf. In other jurisdictions again, an application for a writ of error coram nobis is proper.[9] Generally speaking, the law has been aware of the mental fitness of the defendant on trial.

3. *The Consequences of Insanity during Trial.* In this situation the trial is interrupted until the problem of sanity has been taken up and the person has been judged sane or insane.

4. *The Consequences of Insanity after Trial and during the Completion of Sentence.* If an individual was sane at the time of the criminal act and at the trial and at the time he was sentenced, and then claims to have become insane during his incarceration, he is absolutely not entitled to a new trial to determine his present condition. The criterion is whether or not the defendant at the time of the psychiatric examination realized thoroughly the nature of the trial against him, its goal, and the implication of the punishment. If the question of sanity arises in the case of a person who is tried under a death penalty, a psychiatric examination of the defendant is made if the court is in doubt as to the person's mental condition.

The insanity tests mentioned here are generally applied in most jurisdictions in America, but there are a few states which adhere to other rules. Such is the case with New Hampshire. There a rule was introduced saying that if a man was insane, the act was to be considered as the product of a morbid mind. The ruling had its origin in *Boardman v. Woodman,* in which Mr. Justice Doe,[10] dissenting, said "the whole difficulty is that the courts have undertaken to declare that to be a law which is a matter of fact." In New Hampshire there is no legal test for irresponsibility by reason of insanity. Whether the accused suffers from a mental disease is in each case a question of fact for the jury to decide, and if it decides that he does suffer from a disease, it further determines whether or not the disease was of such a character or degree as to take away the capacity to form or entertain criminal intent.[11]

[9] Hawie v. State, 121 Mo. 197, 83 So. 158 (1919).   [10] 47 N.H. 120 (1866).
[11] State v. Pike, 49 N.H. 399 (1870); State v. Jones, 50 N.H. 369 (1871).

New Hampshire is not the only state which does not accept the "Right and Wrong Test" for criminal responsibility, and there are other states which do not completely accept the rule laid down in the McNaghten case. California for one does not accept the rule regarding delusional insanity,[12] and Rhode Island has never passed a law upon the test for legal insanity as a defense of crime.[13] It should be noted that the Federal courts have accepted the "Right and Wrong Test" but are apt to stress its moral rather than its legal meaning.

It is difficult to explain in detail how the interpretation of the tests regarding insanity is made in the different jurisdictions, because the judges are inclined to use their own discretion as to what wording is best fitted to convey to the jury the meaning of the tests. The resulting variations add to the perplexity connected with the laws regarding insanity, but the meaning of the law is basically unchanged.

When a psychiatrist testifies in court, he is faced with the conception—or misconception—of "legal insanity." As it appears to the lawyer, to the psychiatrist, and to the layman as well, the term is asserted to be a specific condition, the meaning of which is taken for granted and the purpose of which is supposed to be understood by the parties involved.

If we scrutinize thoroughly the questions asked by the court— did the defendant know the nature and quality of the act, and if he did not, did he know what he was doing was wrong—we will see that the law circles around the word "know." By the concept of "know" the psychiatrist today means something different than what the law basically holds for. Understanding involves the ability to use knowledge and reasoning, whereby a person can discriminate the essentials of the matter. Our psychological knowledge of today makes understanding a much more complex process than the law hundreds of years ago implied in the word "know."

Beside this, there are other difficulties of a practical nature. First, the expert who is called into the court testifies only for one party, and it is therefore unfortunately assumed that he testifies against the other one. The Supreme Court of Delaware said, with respect to

12 People v. French, 12 Cal. (2d) 720, 87 P (2d) 1014 (1939); People v. Troche, 206 Cal. 35, 273 Pac. 767 (1928).   13 Weihofen, *op. cit.*, p. 15.

a statute by which an expert was appointed by the court, that when he took the stand he became a witness of a party, "thus implying that such a thing as a neutral witness is impossible and unthinkable." [14]

The distressing fact is that the courts when they have called upon an expert have not always required *qualified* experts. Today there is nothing to prevent practically every licensed physician in America from testifying as an expert on any condition, mental and bodily as well. The damage done to the defendant, to the court, to society, and to the profession is too obvious to mention. Fortunately, many states have passed laws empowering the courts to appoint experts in criminal cases. We shall briefly discuss the procedure in the state of New York.

Up to September, 1939, persons charged with felonies were examined by a lunacy commission if there was any doubt about their mental condition. This commission consisted of a physician, a lawyer, and a layman, but the physician was not required to have any psychiatric knowledge until 1936, when this defect was remedied. The qualified psychiatrists are certified by a board—the Board of Psychiatric Examiners—which demands that the psychiatrist shall have had at least five years actual practice devoted to the care and treatment of persons suffering from nervous or mental diseases or defects, of which two years shall have been spent in an institution having at least 50 patients suffering from mental diseases or defects, or shall have had three years experience in a clinic approved by the Board dealing with the diagnosis and care of mental disorders. Their competency is certified by two duly qualified psychiatrists. The Board further requires that the expert shall have had at least 800 hours experience in an out-patient clinic. Those who are charged with criminal offenses must be examined psychiatrically by experienced psychiatrists who are employed in public hospitals, and the psychiatrist must report on the defendant's sanity at the time when he saw him. The psychiatrists do not necessarily have to report on the defendant's mental condition at the time of the commission of the crime. One part of the law provides that when the court has a reasonable basis for believing that a person charged with a felony is in a state of idiocy, imbecility, or insanity which makes

14 Overholser, *op. cit.*, p. 9.

him incapable of understanding the proceedings or of making his defense, or if the defendant pleads insanity, the court may order the defendant to be examined to determine his sanity. In some cases the court may release the defendant either on bail or on probation when the qualified psychiatrist finds him unharmful to public peace and safety, although he is incapable of understanding the charge against him. If, however, he is no longer in such a state of insanity as to be unable to understand the charge, the court shall require that the defendant be brought again into custody and the proceedings against him resumed. It should be added that if a defendant is found mentally defective or psychotic, the judge will commit him to the proper institution.[15]

The law then makes a clear distinction between insane and sane offenders. However, with borderline cases, those who are mentally abnormal without being legally insane, the law has made little or no progress.

Since we have maintained that much of criminal behavior is closely related to some type of pathology in the personality make-up, one will see that it is important for the law to consider the clinical manifestations that involve the state of the offender's mind. The incidence of the recognizable types of mental diseases or defects leads us to the conclusion that some of the individuals accused of criminal acts must be considered mentally abnormal. It is estimated that about 300,000 persons are confined in mental hospitals having an admission rate of about 75,000 annually. From this rate we may assume that there are today about 1,000,000 boys and girls in our schools, homes, and factories who in the course of their lives will become mental patients. And we may also assume that out of every hundred men, women, and children, one will during his lifetime be arrested and sentenced. Statistics reveal that about 11 per cent of offenders show gross mental abnormalities. I think I am justified in saying that this percentage is too small (see page 158), and investigations made by Overholser would seem to bear me out.[16] The large number of offenders who are not recognized either by courts or by prison authorities as mentally abnormal are for the

---

[15] B. Apfelberg, "Experiences with the New Criminal Code in New York State," *American Journal of Psychiatry*, XCVIII (Nov., 1941), 415–21.
[16] Winfred Overholser, *Psychiatry and Crime*, p. 5.

most part those who have been sentenced without having been psychiatrically examined.

In this connection we should mention the Briggs Law in Massachusetts, which went into effect in September, 1921, and has since been slightly amended. The act provides that whenever a person is indicted for a capital offense or whenever a person is known to have been indicted for any offense more than once or to have been previously convicted of a felony, he is to be reported to the State Department of Mental Diseases. The Department appoints two psychiatrists to examine the defendant and report on his mental condition. This report is available to the court, the district attorney, the counsel for the defense, and, under a recent amendment, to the probation officer.[17]

A similar law was enacted in Michigan in 1939. This legislation has been without doubt the most effective step taken toward solving the problem of expert psychiatric testimony in criminal cases. It should be noted that the Briggs Law provides that certain classes of offenders are to be examined before trial by the State Department of Mental Diseases. If it is recommended that the defendant be committed for observation, the court so disposes. If a psychosis is present, the court arranges for the commitment of the offender to a mental institution until his recovery. In case no mental illness is present, the jury accepts the findings of the impartial experts. Dr. Overholser found that during the first fourteen years that this law operated, 5,159 defendants were examined. Of these 69 were reported to be insane, 169 were considered as requiring observation in a mental hospital, 432 were reported as mentally defective, and 100 were diagnosed as presenting other mental abnormalities, such as borderline intelligence, epilepsy, drug addiction, or psychotic personalities. Dr. Overholser concludes with the following words: "770 or 14.9% were found to be frankly or suggestively abnormal mentally." [18]

With only a few exceptions the states continue to recognize criminal responsibility in individuals who are mentally abnormal without being insane. For instance, the New York courts have held that

[17] General Laws, Chap. 123, Sec. 100A; Chap. 105, Acts of 1929, Mass.
[18] Winfred Overholser, "Some Possible Contributions of Psychiatry to a More Effective Administration of the Criminal Law," *Canadian Bar Review*, Nov., 1939, 645–61.

"feebleness of mind or will, even though not so extreme as to justify a finding that the defendant is irresponsible, may properly be considered . . . and thus may be effective to reduce the grade of the offense." [19] Only California, Illinois, Michigan, and Minnesota have passed laws providing for the commitment of sexual aggressive offenders to hospitals rather than undertaking criminal procedures against them. [20]

In Illinois the Psychopathic Sexual Criminal Law has recently been enacted. This provides for the indeterminate commitment of persons indicted for crimes when they are found by qualified psychiatrists to be suffering from a mental disorder and not insane or feebleminded. The mental disorder, combined with criminal propensities to commit sex offenses, must have existed for a period of not less than one year. [21]

Perhaps the greatest difficulty in passing a law which would take care of the psychopath arises from the definition of the term itself. It is interesting to see that Minnesota's law has tried to cover this term from the psychiatric viewpoint. "The term 'psychopathic personality' means the existence in any person of such conditions of emotional instability or impulsiveness of behavior, or lack of customary standards of good judgment, or failure to appreciate the consequences of his acts, or a combination of any such conditions, as to render such person irresponsible for his conduct with respect to sexual matters and thereby dangerous to other persons." [22]

The state of Michigan has recognized a condition of insanity termed criminal sexual insanity. The statute states: "any person who is suffering from a mental disorder and is not insane or feebleminded, which mental disorder has existed for a period of not less than one year and is coupled with criminal propensities to the commission of sex offenses is hereby declared to be a sexual psychopathic person." [23]

Thus the statutes furnish a basis for a proper disposition of such cases. They provide that any person who is found in the original

[19] People v. Moran, 249 N.Y. 179.
[20] D. A. Thom, "Irresponsibility of Juvenile Delinquents," *American Journal of Psychiatry*, XCIX (Nov., 1942), 330–37.
[21] Smith-Hurd, *Ill. Annot. Stat.*, Chap. 38, Criminal Code, Div. XVI (1938).
[22] Thom, *op. cit.*, 330–37.
[23] *Mich. Stat. Annot.*, XXV, XXVIII, 967 (2), (3), (4), (5), (6), and (7), (1942).

hearing to be a criminal sexual psychopathic person, and such finding having become final, may thereafter be tried upon the offense with which he originally stood charged in the committing court at the time of the filing of the original petition.

Since 1942 Michigan has provided particularly for the sexual psychopath, but except for this group does not make any distinction with regard to the mentally abnormal persons who are not legally insane in the sense of the law.

In the other states there is at present little or no correlation between the view of the criminal law and the view of the psychiatrist on the sexual offender. In the penal code of the state of New York, sexual offenses such as exhibitionism, sexual intercourse between adults in the presence of children, masturbation of boys' genitals, and even gambling are included in the class designated as "impairing the morals of a minor." There is, however, no law like the one in Michigan concerning sexual psychopaths. In the city of New York there is a provision that all convicted sexual offenders must be psychiatrically examined and observed before being released from any of the city's institutions. It would seem time that a law similar to the Michigan enactment be passed.

One will see that the Briggs Law in Massachusetts and the law in Michigan dispose of a great number of cases of persons who because of their mental conditions are unable to undergo a trial. The number of "dogfights" in the courts has thus been reduced.

It is important to note that the law tries to apply itself to many offenders who are mentally abnormal but not legally insane. Yet, society is still in a predicament as to the treatment of such persons. I recall the case of a thirty-year-old offender who had been admitted to various state hospitals eight times, the first time when he was about fifteen years old. Each time he perpetrated a criminal act, he was observed at the state mental hospital where he was kept for some time. However, on two occasions he escaped, the last escape occurring after he had been in the hospital for six years. Before I saw him he had been observed in a Midwestern hospital where he was considered to be a psychopath. Although at this time he had had at least 14 years of particular maladjustment, he was permitted to take up his life in the community and live there in poor circumstances until, four years later, he committed another offense. This only reflected his confused personality make-up. He was observed in a hospital and was concluded to be a psychopath with some deviations in his make-up, but he did not show a psychosis. Anyone reviewing his life would doubt from his previous history whether this man was sane. In any event, without knowing any details of his make-up, one would be justified in saying that since he was kept and observed in seven different state hospitals from his fifteenth year, he was psychotic, which the psychiatric examination showed him to be.

It seems that in most states there is considerable weakness in the tests used to determine insanity. The lay jury has difficulty in comprehending the medical knowledge which concerns the defendant when he pleads irresponsibility for a crime because of insanity. One would think that we now have a great deal more knowledge about a psychosis or, to speak in legal words, insanity, than we had years ago. In as much as we recognize a psychosis as an illness, one might be inclined to say that the only adequate way to solve the question of insanity is to give the jury proper instructions. One may compare the situation of a jury deciding whether a person is sane or insane with that of twelve of our neighbors deciding whether we are ill and what kind of treatment is necessary. If one of us is really sick, we do not call for our good friend; we summon a physician whom we think is an expert and let him decide what our sickness is and what the treatment should be. In like manner, psychiatric experts should be used in the courts to pass on questions of insanity.

It would seem advisable to have the American Psychiatric Association appoint psychiatrists who are experienced in psychiatric criminology. The court could choose from that list two or three psychiatrists to examine the defendant and to give the jury their findings as to his mental condition at the time of the crime. This service should be paid for by the state. The court should then instruct the jury that the findings of the psychiatrists are impartial evidence upon the question of whether or not the defendant was insane at the time the crime took place. As it is now, one expert may give one opinion while another may give a contradictory one, with the result that the jury is puzzled and is forced to draw its own conclusions as to whether or not the defendant is insane. Thus the jury is the expert.

In this procedure, experts would examine the defendant, utilize all data about him, and put this before the court in a psychiatric-psychological study of the defendant. (This was the procedure in Norway.) When the psychiatric report had been put before the court, the opinion of the psychiatrists could be maintained. Of course, these psychiatrists would be subject to cross-examination, but this should be limited to the material which they had submitted in their official reports. However, this procedure would not exclude the possibility of the counsel's calling in other expert witnesses to advance a different view of the defendant.

If such a procedure could be followed in the criminal courts, the knowledge that medical science has today of mental illnesses would be utilized advantageously in the interests of the true administration of justice.[24]

24 W. Hubert Smith has proposed that the court should appoint expert referees from authorized lists in which the qualifications of the expert are beyond doubt. These referees would then have the power of acting as an "auditing" committee, whereby all medical data concerning the case could be properly considered and put before the court in a detailed scientific report. Such a committee could act as an advisory body not only to the jury but to the judge and counsels themselves. "Scientific Proof and the Relations of Law and Medicine," *Boston University Law Review*, XXIII (April, 1943), 143–82.

X

TREATMENT AND RESEARCH

WHATEVER type of treatment we want to give the offenders, we must keep in mind that there are many of them whose mental conditions may be suggestive of some abnormality. Since we do not have accurate means of determining their exact condition, they may remain undetected. It should be stressed in these cases that all abnormal psychological phenomena are exaggerations or deviations from the normal, and they can be ascertained only by an examination of the offenders' make-ups. If we do not remember that these abnormal mental phenomena are distinguished from the normal only with regard to degree, not to type, we will not start at the right point in treating the offenders. Since the offender commits his crime as an expression of a certain maladjustment, the psychiatrist may in a large number of instances be able to relieve this maladaptation, and thus psychiatry will then be to maladjustment what public health is to medicine.

It is this personal and social maladjustment which causes instabilities in the personality as well as the social situation, bringing about an unbalance of the equilibrium between criminal inclinations and the mental resistance of the offender. However odd antisocial behavior seems to the normal individual, to the offender himself it has no abnormal significance. Because normal and abnormal behavior have the same basis, society must be educated to differentiate between the two. If we know the abnormal mind of an offender we may be able to redirect him to a normal state.

The concept that the abnormal mind differs from the normal mind only in degree has a direct and indirect bearing upon our treatment of the offender. Such a view means that the treatment shall be a positive one. This is an idea based not only upon mere emotional viewpoints but is also in accord with our previous statement, that we deal with a human being. Every man, even an incorrigible one, may have in himself a nucleus of some good traits, of some good feelings, of some good intentions which may be brought to the fore, developed, and promoted and upon which his future may be built. I admit at once that there are those who are beyond correction, but this shall not keep us from trying to help those who in our opinion might be improved through treatment. I admit also that this is a difficult task and that there will be many disappointments, but we shall continue to believe that human nature is basically good. It is this good nature that we assume is present in the wrong doer when we think we can rehabilitate him.

As for the incorrigibles, we have institutions in which they can be taken care of. If we think these individuals need constitutional treatment either in an institution or in a prison, we may with justice say that they are maladjusted and unable to adapt to society, at least for the time being. This does not imply that all or some of them are mentally sick, no matter what label we attach to them. It only means that they are socially ill.

If the treatment of an offender, juvenile or adult, involves taking him out of his group, one must remember that he feels secure in this environment, has companions, and leads a life which has the ethical consent of that group. When removing him from these surroundings one must make him a part of another group which he accepts.

It is too often forgotten that the chronic offender has been living in a distinct pattern from which he shall have to break away. If this is to be successful, he will have to take up vocational and social activities in a new life, for which reason his new group must be ready to offer rewards. The offender evaluated the advantages of belonging to his old group, so he will have to be stimulated to work in the new one and estimate the advantages present in it. This means that we shall direct our attention not only to the offender himself, but also to the attitudes, estimations, and values of his group, all of which give him the actual moral basis for his antisocial career. If the offenders were reared outside criminal surroundings, they would, in all probability, have become socially adjusted individuals, provided no personal maladjustment was present. They had the bad luck to grow up and adjust to the criminal part of their environment.

Psychiatric and psychological studies and social investigations of a great number of chronic offenders have shown that their lives are loaded with a number of psychological, developmental, and environmental alterations on which punishment and incarceration have little or no effect. On the contrary, in many cases, as in those with neurotic character disorders and in instances where antisocial acts have been committed largely because of guilt feelings, punishment is one of the aims more or less unconsciously striven for. If such an offender is incarcerated, his need for punishment is satisfied for the time being. Upon his release, a new sense of guilt may arise, resulting in further criminal activity and in a new incarceration. On the other hand, there are those who suffer either from a neurosis, a near neurosis, or from a neurotic character disorder, who because of strong guilt feelings or because of some other type of mechanism have to act out their antisocial inclinations, which makes them socially defective, for which reason society has to take care of them.

This problem is a crucial one. We will see how it may be dealt with and what kind of difficulties we encounter in using our present tools.

Treatment of Chronic Offenders

1. *Offenders Afflicted with Organic or Functional Disorders of the Body and of the Brain.* With this first group of chronic offenders, including schizophrenics, epileptics, and mental defectives, the procedure for handling them is clear if they are insane or mentally defective according to the law. However, the cases where these are persons mentally abnormal without being legally insane are of serious concern to the psychiatrist, the judge, the probation officers, and all other authorities who will have to deal with them. The case of a man who was sentenced from three and a half to four years in the Michigan penitentiary for attempted rape of a negress will demonstrate this. He was kept out of society as long as the law permitted. The prison psychiatrist stated that his release would be definitely dangerous to society: "He is not frankly psychotic, not committable to an institution for the insane, but he is definitely assaultive and potentially homicidal." Because his term of punishment expired and he was not in the sense of the law insane, he could

not be held any longer by the prison authorities, and hence he was released. Within two weeks he had murdered three people.[1]

Such cases are too numerous to be mentioned in detail. As will be understood, it is a question of whether such persons are able to get along in society. Further light may be shed on this problem when we think upon those individuals who according to psychometric tests are not mentally defective and, for this reason, not being legally insane, cannot be taken care of properly, in spite of the fact that they are socially defective. I remember one instance where a man who had been kept in an institution for mental defectives throughout his childhood later led a disorganized life full of antisocial activities. Psychometric tests indicated an I.Q. of borderline intelligence, but in view of his personality make-up and his antisocial activities I raised the question whether this man would at all be able to adjust to society. He would be a source of steady trouble, and it was imperative that he be given adequate care. The judge, according to the law, sentenced him to prison, but when he is released, he will certainly start his criminal activities again.

On the other hand, there are those individuals who are found to be mentally defective by psychometric tests who are not really socially defective. In fact, they are able to adjust themselves socially. The case of a twenty-five-year-old man comes to my mind. He was mentally defective, but up to the time of his prison offense, which was a minor one, he had been able to make a good adjustment, so good that even his friends, neighbors, and employers gave him the best recommendations. One may readily doubt whether such a man, even though he was mentally defective and for this reason committable, should be institutionalized. The fact that some mentally defective people are able to adjust may indicate that the psychometric tests cannot fully reflect the intellectual behavior and ability of the individual to get along in society. There is apparently something wrong in deciding the whole question of whether or not a man is mentally defective by a psychometric test only.

In view, then, of the insufficiency of information gathered from psychometric and psychological tests, one may think that there are nonintellectual as well as intellectual factors which may determine

[1] Associated Press dispatch, April 3, 1942; J. B. Waite, *The Prevention of Repeated Crime*, p. 32.

the behavior of a person. These nonintellectual factors would therefore have to be tested if one is to obtain a proper appreciation of the person's endowment. Testing of both intellective or nonintellective factors would certainly be a better determinant of those who were able to make a good social adjustment.

An approach to such determination has already been made by Wechsler with his Bellevue Adult Scale and by Doll with his Social Maturity Scale. In the near future one will certainly hear more about such tests applied to the handling of mentally abnormal offenders.

An important reason for having adequate psychological tests is that in many cases training of mental or borderline defectives may within certain limits develop their ability in certain trades, as mechanics, craftsmen, and the like, thereby making them more socially adaptable.

2. *Chronic Situational, Accidental, and Associational Offenders.* It has been customary to put all chronic situational, accidental, and associational offenders in prison when they had to be taken out of society because they could not be put on probation. Whether or not this type of offender could be rehabilitated by putting him to work, on a closed farm, for instance, is debatable, but an attempt should be made. They comprise a great manpower potential which might be utilized if facilities could be developed.

3. *Neurotic and Compulsory Offenders.* To speak about the neurotic and compulsory offenders in detail is impossible here. The ideal approach in treating an offender with neurotic traits is first to make a psychiatric study in order to understand his behavior and the motivation which prompted his antisocial acts. Then either psychoanalysis or analytically oriented psychotherapy, according to the symptoms and personality make-up, should be begun. Depending upon the case, the psychotherapy, whatever form it takes, may be supportive or uncovering. Most cases of neurotic manifestations seen in people in general and in offenders in particular represent what we call a mixed neurosis.

An important type of the psychoneuroses is compulsory-obsessional neurosis which is the affliction of such offenders as kleptomaniacs and pyromaniacs. As mentioned before, the treatment is either prolonged psychoanalysis or analytically oriented psychotherapy, which are the only ways, if any, that may lead to a recovery. Such treatment is difficult and may be supported by occupational and recreational therapy. In addition, a regular program for the patient's life should be outlined, aiming at increasing his various interests so that the system of compulsory-obsessional ideas which he has built up may be broken as far as possible. For this reason such a person should avoid entering difficult situations, such as those that would arise if he took part in social activities on a large scale. The management of such patients demands great patience and manifest friendliness.

4. *Offenders with Neurotic Characters.* The offenders with neurotic characters represent perhaps the most difficult problem to the psychiatrist and prison authorities. There is hardly another group in which therapy and prognosis is of so much significance. Punishment is without success, except that incarceration protects society against such offenders. So far, therefore, incarceration is symptomatic treatment. A great many of these offenders act anti-socially because of a sense of guilt which makes them feel, more or less unconsciously, that they have to be punished. However, in many others unconscious conflicts of a different nature are present. This has made one think that psychoanalysis should be of great help. Again, however, the nature of the individual case is the important consideration.

If the treatment of offenders with neurotic character disorders, or psychopathic personalities as they are also called, is so difficult, one may consider the possibility of whether or not a training program in an institution which has its aim in repairing their character defects might be considered. This could only be accomplished by keeping them under a continued disciplined regime in a friendly way. The main point in handling such psychopaths is to treat them firmly but at the same time let them know that they are not rejected. The trouble with psychopaths has always been their ability to utilize and to exploit their environment, which has sooner or later brought them into open conflict with their surroundings and with the law. Society has failed, both abroad and in this country, in incarcerating psychopaths in prisons where little understanding of their personality problems exists. This view still prevails, and when prison authorities see a man who is labeled "psychopath," they at once believe that he is completely incorrigible and has to be treated accordingly. Only the Federal prisons, headed by the capable director, James V. Bennett, and a few state prisons are exceptions to this method of treating psychopaths and similar offenders.

Training in an institution whose authorities have due consideration for the individual capacity of the offenders will in the course of time hardly fail to bring results. The offenders will, provided no mental defect or organic brain lesion is present, have a chance to mature and to adjust socially when they reach about forty-five. Such training, in addition to some type of psychotherapy when indicated will then be a question of re-education.

The treatment for homosexuality or any other type of perversion is either psychoanalysis or psychotherapy. The outcome of the treatment may to a large extent depend upon the patient's desire to get well. The outlook for a pervert is better when his distorted drive is related to a neurosis or is a part of a neurotic character, because he seeks help, which he would not do if he were not suffering from a neurosis or a neurotic character disorder. If the perversion is not connected with any neurosis or with any other defect of a neurotic character, the patient does not seek help because the pleasure he receives from his perversion is too pronounced. Some homosexuals, like other offenders, have an unconscious desire to be punished due to guilt feelings, which makes them avoid psychoanalysis so that they can be imprisoned.[2]

Although homosexuality may possibly be considered a disease, no law has up to now accepted such a view. Because psychotherapy is lacking in most prisons, there is little or no possibility for a real readjustment of homosexual offenders. Further, it is only in certain cases that punishment of homosexuals by incarceration should be indicated. For the large number of homosexuals, incarceration has no abstaining effect. The rather severe punishment to which homosexuals are subjected, in comparison with the short sentences given to other sexual offenders who have committed more severe acts, is out of order in an organized society. It is not unusual to see sexual offenders who impair the morals of minors given shorter sentences than homosexuals, although the former are considered more dan-

[2] E. Bergler, "Suppositions about the Mechanism of Criminosis," *Journal of Criminal Psychopathology*, V (Oct., 1943), No. 2, 239.

gerous to the security of society than homosexuals, because it is in their group that we find many murderers. The time will come when one may look with different eyes upon those persons suffering from homosexuality.

The problem of the sexual offender versus the law is too large to be dealt with here. One point should be taken up, however, the tendency on the part of the law to make sexual intercourse with girls under a certain age a felony regardless of the circumstances. The age of consent in the United States varies as it does in Scandinavia. It is unscientific to specify an arbitrary age limit for consent to sexual intercourse. The law should heed biological views and set the age according to the sexual maturity of the individual rather than at a specified chronological age. As far as I know, no country has yet applied this biological view to the law.

A girl under eighteen may be sexually mature and aggressive, but in spite of this, sexual relations with her are punishable by law in some states. Another girl may be over eighteen and be infantile, and may have sexual intercourse, but the law would not punish the man. In a case in Norway, where the age of consent is sixteen, the counsel for the defendant succeeded in having the jury bring in a verdict of "not guilty" by establishing that although the girl was under sixteen, she was so developed that she was no longer a child. This interpretation was, of course, without legal foundation.

It is in such cases that one would do well to take the girls under care rather than punish the man who has committed, as the law defines it, statutory rape. It is known that women of eighteen years and more have sexual relations with boys under eighteen, but such relations are never called to the attention of the legal authorities nor are such women punished. Offenders who have perpetrated statutory rape, which in all probability was committed with the consent of the girl or in many cases induced by her, should not be punished. After a girl has started her menses, she is no longer a child. She is entering sexual adulthood with sexual desires no less pronounced than those in boys of even an older age.[3] Statutory rape as it is interpreted here and abroad must be considered a relic of medievalism.

[3] Johan Scharffenberg, pamphlet containing his discussion before The Norwegian Association of Criminology, Oslo, 1935, pp. 112-13.

Another problem is prostitution. As was said before, prostitutes should if possible be given a psychiatric examination. A large group of them are mental or borderline defectives, and they should be cared for from the time when they first show signs of being inclined towards prostitution. If necessary, they should be kept in places far away from temptations up to the time they are twenty-five years old. They should be taught useful work, discipline, and regularity, but at the same time also have recreational activities which might very well be a means of developing their sense of responsibility. On Sprogo Island the Danes have established a home for mentally defective and borderline mentally defective prostitutes where they are taught regular habits. After the girls have been there for some time, they are moved to a less strict institution which emphasizes home life. Then they are provided with employment in the country with a guardian who can help them in all their work. The results from these Danish institutions seem to be very favorable. It has been estimated that 80 per cent of the girls have been able to get along without reverting to their previous inclinations, and half of them have been married.[4]

As it was pointed out regarding the personality of alcoholics, they are socially sensitive and do not feel that they comprise a congenial part of society. In some cases their personal difficulties may have root in the sphere of sexual adaptation; in other cases the family or social situation causes the difficulties. If this is so, then the best prevention lies in securing an adequate development of social and sexual adaptation and in avoiding any increase of insecurity. As the ordinary offender has to be removed from his delinquent group, so the alcoholic offender must also find a new social group if he is going to succeed and make an adjustment. Because the alcoholic offender is insecure, a solution to his problem will probably not be reached until there is first a basic change in the institutions of our social order aiming at a more definite security for the individual. Then the cause in each individual case can be treated.

This means that psychoanalysis, including psychotherapy, for the alcoholic offender is indicated. Once in a while one sees alcoholics cured as a result of a long determined stay away from alcohol. Some of these individuals come out of the cure with changed attitudes and become ascetics or fanatics. In any event, in most offenders

4 H. Evensen, *Prostituerte*, p. 299.

suffering from alcoholism, psychoanalysis is essential. One will readily see that imprisonment hardly cures alcoholics. If psychotherapy can be given during the incarceration, it should be continued while the person is on parole. As a matter of fact, psychoanalysis, including psychotherapy where that is warranted, should be the treatment if an alcoholic offender is put on probation. Giving him probation without psychotherapy will in most cases lead to more alcoholism and probably more offenses, even if his probation is given upon the condition that he stay away from alcohol. It cannot be stressed too much that alcohol when abused represents a danger to society in general and to the offender in particular.

In conclusion, let it be stressed that all therapy used in combating mental disorders shall be made available to the offender. Hypnoanalysis and the various types of shock therapy—electronarcosis, as introduced by Dr. George N. Thompson, narcosynthesis, lobotomy, the latter introduced by Dr. Walter Freeman—used on noncriminals should also be extended to the offender whenever this is indicated.

The Outlook

Now that we have reviewed the treatment of the different types of offenders, let us consider their potential danger to society. It is not surprising that one criterion for treating the offender is *how* dangerous is he to society. Such a view is not new. It was mentioned at the first meeting (1888) of the International Association of Criminal Law, at which it was maintained that punishment, although one of the most important means in eradicating crime, was not the only means, and for this reason had to be adapted to the different types of offenders. The aim of this new idea was to fight the principle of retaliation and the demand for a conscious special prevention of crime.

This revolutionary view in the criminal law, which had its starting point in the new scientific concept of crime, produced repercussions in penal codes throughout Europe and later in America. It was asserted that the protection of society from crime was not to be considered in the light of greater or smaller crimes but in respect to the degree of how *dangerous* the offender was. The criterion according to which an offender shall be sentenced shall therefore be: how dangerous is he? With this in mind, one will have to inflict strong penalties on habitual and dangerous offenders and lesser ones on the great number of occasional and less dangerous offenders. The more harmful offenders will thereby be restricted from committing new crimes, while the less dangerous will be enabled to return to society. The reason for classifying offenders according to their degree of danger to society arises partly from their ingrained criminalistic tendencies and partly from the external conditions under which their offenses are committed.

If we are going to retain this criterion, the old system of inflicting punishment in proportion to the moral faults of the human must be eliminated. A judge is hardly able to measure the moral errors of a man, since he is quite unable to acquaint himself with the offender's background, family life, economic and social condition, and the many circumstances leading up to the crime. Only in cases where the judge has a full probation report and has had a psychiatric examination made of the offender can he properly evaluate the offender's situation in relation to the law.

From this one would think that the old system with definite sentences should be replaced by incarceration or isolation for an indefinite time. The ideas which were found in Ferri's proposals of 1921 did not mention punishment. There is no doubt that with the advance of knowledge in psychiatry and in penology, the soil is being prepared for a total change of the treatment of the offender.

How shall we know which offender is dangerous? We can decide this by gathering all available material about him and making a psychiatric examination, thereby forming an opinion as to his make-up, endowment, ability, adaptability, and the prospect of his future in society. In many cases a psychiatric examination is a prerequisite if the correct mental status of the defendant is to be determined.

What kind of offenders should be given a psychiatric examination? With a few exceptions, there are at present no rules regarding such a proceeding. As we have pointed out in the previous chapter, the court in the course of a trial may have the defendant psychiatrically examined if there is any doubt regarding his mental condition. It is appropriate to mention that in the Court of General Sessions in New York City all offenders are given a psychiatric examination between trial and sentence, and if it is deemed necessary, a psychometric and a psychological one also. These reports, as well as probation reports, accompany the offender to the institution or prison. If the mental condition of the defendant necessitates psychiatric observation, he is placed in the Psychiatric Division of Bellevue Hospital for a period up to four weeks.

As yet, a common rule for examining offenders has not been worked out for the different jurisdictions of the United States. Because of this, the kind of offenders to be examined will depend upon the psychological insight of the probation officers, the prosecuting attorney, or the court. Sometimes the court may be able to see some mental abnormality in the defendant which will necessitate psychiatric examination. In some cases the counsel for the defense will require that an examination be made.

There is no doubt that to a certain extent the type of crime expresses a certain make-up in the person. This fact then should be utilized in the selection of those offenders who ought to be examined psychiatrically, as long as we do not have a rule that provides that all offenders be given a psychiatric examination.

In any event, of those offenders without obvious psychotic manifestations, murderers and sexual offenders should be examined. Many of these are pathologic in nature. We find in many sexual offenders perversion, neurotic character disorders, borderline intelligence, senility, psychoses, and alcoholism.

How serious this problem is may be shown by a case that the Danish State Attorney, Harald Petersen, has referred to.[5] A laborer was charged with having killed his wife and one of their children, the apparent motive being jealousy. The defendant operated a crane in a great industrial concern, an occupation which required a great deal of caution. He received good testimonials from family friends and from his employer, who said that he was in every respect normal, an impression which he also gave at the trial. However, because of the cold-bloodedness of the homicide, he was given a psychiatric examination, which showed that he was mentally retarded—a moron. While in prison before the trial, his mental defectiveness was revealed, and he was later transferred to a special institution for this type of offenders.

[5] H. Petersen, "Mentalitetserklæringer i Straffesager," *Annuaire des associations de criminalistes nordiques,* Stockholm, 1940, p. 95.

All sexual offenders should be given careful psychiatric and psychological examinations, including psychometric and psychological tests. Since so many psychiatric factors are involved in the make-up of sexual offenders and since many of them present deviations from the normal, it would seem advisable to make psychiatric examinations of them compulsory by law.

In the group of sexual offenders, particular attention should be given to the prostitutes. At present, they are examined for venereal diseases, which is, of course, a wise policy. However, they should also be given a psychiatric examination, because this is the only way to reach an understanding of their personality problem and establish a possible treatment for their behavior. When it is recalled that want rarely compels a girl to become a prostitute, and it is stated that of 530 Danish prostitutes who were under the control of the police 8 per cent were idiots and 20 per cent mentally retarded, there is good reason to believe that a psychiatric examination of all prostitutes is as necessary as a venerealogical one.[6]

All those who have committed particularly serious crimes—pyromaniacs, murderers, and assaultists—should also be psychiatrically examined. Their acts may be due to some abnormality of the mind, and every effort should be made to prevent any recurrence. Such prevention makes possible the understanding of the causes and circumstances that have led to these types of crime.

In addition to these, middle-aged and aged offenders should be psychiatrically examined, if circumstances warrant. There is no doubt that the bodily weaknesses which are related to old age may cause difficult social conditions for a person, because he is not able to compete with his fellow men in the same way as he did previously. If an old man encounters difficulties he may react abnormally and antisocially. Since senility may be accompanied more or less by intellectual deterioration, poor ability to concentrate, poor memory, rigid and narrowminded thoughts which may be more pronounced than is readily surmised, changes which on the whole are brought about by hardening of the arteries in the brain and senile alterations in the brain cells, one will understand how an old man may act antisocially. This indicates the necessity of examining all offenders over the age of fifty-five.

6 Evensen, op. cit., p. 296.

For the sake of early rehabilitation and re-education, there is no doubt that psychiatric examination of young offenders is necessary. The same applies to persons who commit their first crime at thirty or forty, because such a sudden change of their behavior at this age may reflect abnormal minds.

These examinations will uncover, as we have seen heretofore, a great many offenders who are mentally abnormal without being insane in the legal sense. Because of their abnormality, these people in all probability will continue their criminal activities. But they should not be punished as normal persons are. They must be given special treatment in other and more gentle forms than punishment, and, if necessary, be treated in a psychiatric institution under medical care and be kept there for an indefinite time. You will recall that in recent years California, Illinois, Michigan, and Minnesota have to some extent followed this idea in regard to sexual offenders.

I am proud to say that the Penal Code of 1902 of my native Norway was the first in the world to incorporate the new ideas as outlined above.

Paragraph 65 of the Norwegian Penal Code provided that offenders dangerous to society might be given an indefinite sentence and incarcerated in a prison for a term not exceeding fifteen years. This law is not concerned with the theoretical separation between punishment and prevention. It goes further than that and ignores the century-old concept of retaliation.[7] The law says: "If any person is guilty of several accomplished or attempted crimes for which penalties are provided . . . (offenses against public safety, counterfeiting, sexual crimes, kidnapping, grand larceny, extortion and robbery, offenses against property) the court can decide to lay before the jury the question whether in view of the nature of the crimes, their motives, or the attitude of mind that they indicate in the criminal, he is to be regarded as particularly dangerous to society or to the life, health, or prosperity of individuals. If this question is confirmed, a sentence can be passed that the offender is to be kept in prison as long as it is considered necessary, the term however, not to exceed three times the fixed penalty and in no case to exceed fifteen years more than the fixed term."

[7] Hartvig Nissen, "Straffen og dens sociale fölger," Verneforeningens landsmöte i Bergen, Aug. 14–15, 1939, p. 14.

On the whole it may be said that the new ideas in the Norwegian Penal Code gave the judges freedom to fix the punishment liberally, and yet within certain limits, all giving due consideration to the individual's care.[8]

In 1929 a new law was passed in Norway which was concerned with the special treatment of mentally abnormal offenders who were not legally insane, those that the law defines as having a "weakened mind" (not mentally defective). This is the famous Paragraph 39.

This paragraph said that if a crime subject to punishment was committed by a person mentally weakened in his development or by a person with a permanently weakened mind, and there was a danger that the person would repeat such a crime, the court could decide that the person be placed in custody by one of the following means: (a) that he live at a certain place; (b) that he report regularly to probation officers; (c) that he abstain from the use of alcohol; (d) that he be given or secure private care; or (e) that he be confined in an institution such as a farming colony or a prison.

The apparent advantage of this law is that it takes care of those who are mentally abnormal but are not legally insane. But there are other advantages. When the offender is transferred to an institution, the original report of the psychiatrist is sent with him, so that the authorities have the opportunity to know his mental make-up and will therefore be more competent to treat him and judge his outlook. Further, when he is considered for release into custody, the Department of Justice considers this report and the information gathered in the institution about the offender, enabling one to estimate what type of custody has to be chosen.

The idea of segregating the different types of offenders into three large groups—legally insane offenders, mentally abnormal but not legally insane offenders, and those offenders with no apparent mental pathology—is aimed not only at dealing properly with the offenders but also at depopulating the prisons. Social considerations are also taken into account, and a great many of the offenders are kept in institutions other than prisons, even in private custody.

There is too often little conformity in the administration of the law, both here and abroad. In view of the fact that society must

8 *Ibid.*, p. 13.

maintain its security, an adequate administration of the criminal law is necessary. This necessitates a thorough knowledge of it, and those who want to specialize in the different types of work with offenders, such as prosecution, probation, and so on, should be given opportunity to devote much more time to the study of the criminal law and its administration than heretofore. Law schools should devote more time to the teaching of criminal law and the social and medical sciences than they do today. The study of crime is so extensive that every man who is fighting crime should be a specialist in the field, and this also extends to those who have to do with its administration.

Administration of criminal law has been improved considerably, and when one views the development, it can be seen that it progresses slowly in the right direction.

The outstanding fact regarding the administration of criminal law in America is that we have two sources of laws—state and Federal—which at times may conflict. It is a human trait that everyone wants to be his own boss, including the states, for which reason the Federal government may have a hard time enforcing its laws. The states have tried to make laws regarding the regulation of important elements like banking, business, food, and liquor. The Federal government has expanded its jurisdiction and thereby a greater conformity has been given to the administration of criminal law. The White Slave Act of 1910, the Extortion Act of 1932, the Kidnapping Act of 1934, and the National Firearms Act of the same year indicate that our authorities, generally speaking, are aware of the great need to regulate laws in order to obtain stability in society. The outstanding task to be accomplished is to try to bring the law into conformity with the progress of science.

The treatment of the offender in prison is a problem that must be seriously considered. Until recently, we have relied mainly upon the usual method of treating the offender—incarceration. By punishing him, we think that we can deter him from committing future antisocial acts. Hundreds of years of experience have shown how futile such treatment is. It has been assumed that between 60 and 80 per cent of the population of our penitentiaries are persons who have been incarcerated one or more times.[9] Thorsten

9 Waite, *op. cit.*, p. 2.

Sellin found that 50.5 per cent had already previously been incarcerated.[10]

Because of the principle of retaliation, there is a widespread and deep-rooted belief in most humans that every offender shall have to serve a sentence. They do not consider the fact that in prison the offender may contact dangerous or malicious criminals who may influence him so much that he, when released, might develop a definite antisocial pattern. However, lately this tendency has to some extent been counteracted. Our children's and juvenile courts have aimed at keeping children and juveniles away from the adult offenders, not only during the court procedure but by sending them to state training schools and reformatories.

The state of New York has promoted this purpose by enacting certain laws such as the Wayward Minor Act and the Youthful Offender Act. Correctional and penological authorities have for some time felt that an elimination of early criminal records and convictions should be brought about by new legislation. It has been the opinion that those adolescents between sixteen and nineteen, who after having been carefully investigated and psychiatrically examined are assumed to be capable of becoming law-abiding citizens, should be handled as youthful offenders, not as criminals. Several years ago Governor Thomas E. Dewey, then district attorney of New York County, the nine judges of the Court of General Sessions, and Mr. Irving W. Halpern, the chief probation officer of that court, agreed to initiate a new form of treatment under the Wayward Minor Act. This law provides that any person between sixteen and twenty-one who habitually associates with dissolute or disorderly persons, is disobedient to the commands of parents or guardians, or is in danger of becoming morally depraved can be handled as a wayward minor and not as a criminal.

After the Wayward Minor Act had been used in the Court of General Sessions for several years, it became apparent that while it filled the gap, it was not the best means of proceeding against youthful offenders, because in too many instances parents were forced to testify that their children had been habitually disobedient or wayward, when, in truth, they had only been involved in a casual offense. Because of this difficulty, the conviction grew that there

10 *Ibid.*, p. 23.

was a compelling need for a new category of the offender. New legislation was discussed, and a new law was passed by the legislature which authorized courts dealing with felonies and misdemeanors to treat young people between the ages of sixteen and nineteen as "youthful offenders" instead of as convicted criminals. This law, which became effective on Sept. 1, 1943, provides that youth courts shall be "youth parts" for the arraignment of such offenders.

Under the law the grand jury or the district attorney may in cases of felonies recommend to the court, or the court itself may determine, that the defendant shall be regarded as a youthful offender if he himself consents to such a procedure. If he does, the indictment is not filed by the grand jury, and the defendant is not placed in the criminal category. Fulfilling this aim, the youthful offenders shall be treated separately and apart from the sessions of the court reserved for adult trials. Also, the law provides that the defendant may be paroled to await the determination of the court. If he is to be incarcerated during the period of his examination, treatment, or investigation, he must be segregated from all persons over nineteen years of age who are charged with crime. The law provides that the maximum probation period for this type of offender shall be three years. In case the defendant is not fit for probation, the court can commit him for a term of not more than three years to any religious, charitable, or other reformative institution authorized by law to receive persons over the age of sixteen. The law states specifically that the record of a youth considered as a youthful offender shall be sealed and not open to inspection and that his being a youthful offender is no disqualification to public office or to employment or any other privilege.[11]

The law, as outlined here, represents an important contribution to progressive penology. It is implied that the authorities who have to deal with a young defendant must of necessity be aware of the personal and social factors and the educational ability of the offender, which can be determined only after psychiatric and psychological examinations and after an evaluation of the situational and vocational tests. Since maladjustment is often the result of an offender's not finding the type of work he is fit to do, rehabilitation

11 C. K. Simon, "A New Chance for Youth," *Survey Midmonthly*, Nov., 1943, p. 297.

and re-education can take place only when he finds his right occupation in society. That means that the judge, the court, and the probation department must have a thorough knowledge of the youthful offender.

The Youth Authority Act, which has been approved in California, is similar in its objectives to the Youthful Offender Act. It provides that a youth between sixteen and twenty-one shall be dealt with by a State Authority consisting of three persons, that he be detained in a proper place before trial, and that a simplified procedure be used during trial. Further, the power of sentence is taken away from the judge, except in serious cases like homicide. The offender is kept under supervision and treated and is only released when this is compatible with the security of society. Such an act repudiates the tradition of punishment and has as its objective the deterring of offenders from repeating their crimes.

The only apparent difficulty with the act is in the selection of the three members who constitute the State Authority. It goes without saying that they all ought to be well trained in the field and that at least one of them should be a psychiatrist experienced in criminal psychopathology. The act unfortunately did not provide for a psychiatrist. However, the state of California is to be praised for being the first in the Union to introduce such an act. It is also noteworthy that while in 1941 the state gave $100,000 to support the program, in 1943 it increased its allocation to $1,075,000.

Federal legislation along similar lines has also been drafted, and one may assume that if it is properly enacted, it will be of decisive value in rehabilitating offenders.

The Youthful Offender Act and the Youth Authority Act try to rehabilitate the offender, which should be the aim of all treatment. And yet, this is only part of the treatment; prevention is still more important.

Volumes have been written about the prevention of crime, all more or less overlooking the basic fact—the variety of the human mind and its overwhelming participation in crime. The theory of retaliation as a basis for punishment has shown its shortcomings; also, the theory of fear of punishment has been proved inadequate in preventing criminal acts. The greater number of petty larcenists or thieves do not think about being punished before they are

imprisoned. However, crimes such as embezzlement and petty larceny would probably increase if they went unpunished, which
means that certain types of humans will have to be reminded that
they will be punished if they transgress the law.

On the other hand, there are two types of criminals who are not
at all influenced by any threat of punishment. These are the habitual criminals, who because of a faulty development of their superego adhere only to their own criminal code, and those persons
generally called neurotics, who because of strong unconscious conflicts are unable to resist their inner drives.

Criminal law, then, will have to be realistic and rational. To our
mind this means that the law should take into consideration not
only the offenses but also the personality of the offenders as well. An
antisocial act can never be separated from its doer, as the act reflects something of his mind. Hence, only the man with an insight
into the human mind will have the necessary means to give possible
treatment to an offender. We might say that preventive treatment
should have started with the father or grandfather of the offender,
but this should not exclude treating him psychiatrically if this is
indicated. It should be stressed that a personal or social maladjustment, reflecting the offender's make-up, has occurred before the
offense has taken place. Because of this maladjustment there are
many people who in the course of time may commit crimes from
which they cannot free themselves. Psychiatry is able to detect their
difficulties and treat them.

Of course, psychiatry has heretofore concerned itself with curing
mentally sick people, but those who have maladjustments which
may result in crimes are also to an extent mentally sick, although
not necessarily psychotic. It is a great error for anyone to believe
that only psychotic people are mentally sick. There are a number
of other mental conditions which make the individual unable to
adapt to the demands of society.

Because of the complexity of personal elements intermingled
with social factors involved in crime, there exist neither universal
nor specific remedies for its treatment or prevention. Crime is a
part of psychological and sociological phenomena which interact.
Just as we will have a certain amount of mental diseases or a certain
amount of unemployment, so we will also have antisocial activ-

ities, because they are all part of the same manifestations of human life, having their root in the personality and being closely related to social conditions. The personality of the individual and the social life he takes part in are as intimately connected with each other as are the different organs of the body. If disease occurs in the heart, lungs, or any other organ, the body is ill, and, if seriously so, the individual may die. If crime or unemployment take place, the human and society become mentally and socially sick. Yes, so sick that society loses its structure and becomes disorganized.

The obvious differences among human minds regarding desires, needs, mental functioning, and abilities make it impossible that all people live under the same conditions. But even so, we may be able to alleviate living conditions to some extent and to relieve suffering, including that of a mental nature.

I doubt whether the psychiatrist, apart from treating the mentally sick, can find a more dignified and rewarding task than saving those people who themselves do not realize that they are personally and socially maladjusted, and whose conduct society does not fully understand. People who may turn to antisocial activities are in desperate need of psychiatric help.

It would be futile and foolish to claim that we could detect all those potential offenders. However, there are those persons who experience deprivations, frustrations, and inner conflicts which may lead to maladjustments and then to crime, the potentiality of which we would be able to detect if the subjects came for psychiatric advice and treatment.

Clinics should be established where maladjusted persons in conflict with society and with themselves would be examined and treated. The mental hygiene clinics throughout the country have, generally speaking, done a good job in helping mentally sick people. Offenders, however, require an extension and deepening of psychiatric care. Because of the war it might seem out of place to establish such clinics, but it is at a time like this that society becomes unstable and maladjustment occurs, bringing crime in its wake. This makes the establishment of such clinics more desirable than in normal times. If our present clinics for nervous and mental diseases and for mental hygiene were not inadequate in number and in facilities, they might be able to extend their services to include the potential offender. If the undertaking proposed here is to succeed, it will need financial support, because the clinics would have to be furnished with adequate and properly trained personnel experienced in dealing with offenders. Above all, the administration of these clinics should be given to qualified psychiatrists. If it is not, the results will be other than those expected. The value of such clinics must ultimately depend upon those individuals who can carry the plan into action.

The causes of crime are, as pointed out before, manifold, and treatment must be varied. There are no experts who can go into a community and eradicate crime by means which the community itself probably would not know. The treatment of crime has been compared to that of a bodily disease. In one case a certain type of treatment, such as psychoanalysis or psychotherapy, may help. In another type, transferring a boy to a foster home may be indicated, and some advice to the parents of the boy may be necessary. But, it should be stressed that criminal activities are not readily cured, because in a number of cases a cure may depend upon how easy it will be to modify the personality structure of the offender. Prevention of crime, then, varies with each individual and situation. Attempts at eradicating crime should begin with strengthening the system we have.

Further study of the offender from the psychiatric-psychologic point of view is one way of strengthening the system. We do not know all the reasons why an offense is committed, and we will certainly not know them until we understand all the complexities of the human mind. However, we will know some part of them if our attention is led in the right direction.

There is one weapon which from its inception has been a means of improving living conditions for mankind—science. However, science has not and will not be the means of bettering standards of living if it cannot transform its accomplishments in research into practical purposes for society.

The same holds true for psychiatry. In spite of the fact that psychiatry is a psychologically minded discipline, it is and must be social in its implications. Research within this field has to transform all possibilities into effectual actualities and make them useful to people. If not, research, here or in any other field of science, has no legitimate value. From this point of view all science is *social,* because ultimately the value of any science, besides a theoretical interest for the few, lies in its practical application to the various aspects of social life. It is this application of science to life that has caused the great changes in everyday living, not only culturally and socially, but mentally and spiritually.

This metamorphosis was produced by the technique which was founded upon science. But the establishment of the technique, which overnight, so to speak, totally changed the conditions of life by offering necessities not previously available, was and could only be created by those who had the faculty for unconditioned research. We see then scientific research as a whole continues to be the greatest contributor to the improvement of human conditions, being an expression of self-preservation, a tool in the struggle for life, a weapon for steady progress. This progress has always been— and always will be—dependent upon man's ability to familiarize himself with the very same conceptions that gave life to these tools in order that a better world might be created.

It would be an exaggeration to say that in the field of criminology methodological research on a purely scientific basis has taken place. The nature of criminological research up to now and the lack of understanding of the essential problem bring to mind a story about Charles Darwin.

Two boys once decided to play a trick on him. They took a centipede's body, a butterfly's wings, a grasshopper's legs, a beetle's head, and glued them all together. They then put the new species into a box and took it to Darwin.

"Please, sir, can you tell us what kind of a bug this is?"

The scientist examined the bug and then looked at the boys.

"Did it hum?" he asked.

"Oh, yes, sir!" answered the boys.

"In that case," declared Darwin, "I would say it's a humbug."

In the past one has tried to find the causes of crime and its remedies by patching and mending in odd places. This may sound exaggerated, and yet considering the unusual resistance that man has shown by only touching the problem, it is only a faint reflection of what has really taken place. The many able and painstaking investigations, faulty or insufficient as many of them might appear, had their merit, for they were performed in a true humanitarian spirit. People in general, however, not only had little understanding of the problem of crime but directly hampered its solution. Such hindrance had and still has deep psychological reasons. In man there still abides the principle of retaliation—the principle of revenge. "If you break the law, you shall be punished." Anyone claiming that society of today is something different from what it was one hundred years ago should be advised that man in his psychological structure is basically the same as he was then and even as he was thousands of years ago.

The man of today who is proud of belonging to an enlightened society harbors in his soul forces that drive him to regard the criminal as an enemy of society. Every human feels himself threatened to some degree by competition and is therefore more or less insecure, for which reason he must relieve his fears and aggressions. A way to rid himself of them is to inflict punishment upon the offender. The offender on his side also has fears and aggressions, and he gets rid of them by assaulting and punishing the law-abiding citizen.

In view of these circumstances, one is not surprised that society has been reluctant, to put it mildly, to accept the investigations and the proposed improvements for the criminal. As long as the talion principle exists in the mind of man, every step taken to arrive at a true solution of the problem of crime will be counteracted.

Our tools for determining the mental condition of the offender are still crude and may be compared to the binoculars used three hundred years ago in observing the stars. As psychiatrists, we are interested in knowing what bearing mental deviations or abnormalities have on criminal behavior, and we want to know whether or not an offender's personality consists of pathological traits to such an extent that we may say that they elicit antisocial activities.

As yet, we do not know anything about the delicate mental processes that take place when the criminal impulse is transformed into action. It would be worthwhile to initiate a research project to examine from the psychiatric, psychological, and physiological points of view a number of offenders. Since these examinations necessarily involve a great deal of subjectivity, they should be aided by electroencephalography. In the latter we have a rather objective method, though it is time-consuming and demands special apparatus. In this research attention should be paid to the fact that many of the disturbances present in nervous and mental diseases are in one way or another, as S. Bernard Wortis, among others, has pointed out, connected with some defects in brain tissue metabolism.[12] At present we do not know the biochemical reactions which may be assumed to be related to the brain's functioning.

By this five-pincered approach, one would probably be able to ascertain more accurately the nature of the mentally abnormal offender and thereby come upon a possible criterion of his abnormality. From such an investigation we might also establish a basis upon which we could distinguish between the normal and mentally abnormal offender. This would be of great value in the courts, for remember that the law, with few exceptions, only differentiates between sane and insane.

This research project would therefore give reliable statistics as to how many offenders are in reality mentally abnormal without being insane, and it would be especially necessary here that we obtain reliable figures. It will be only upon the basis of such facts that we may possibly succeed in establishing general rules by which these offenders will be adequately taken care of by proper authorities.

Closely related to the mental make-ups of these offenders are their cultural patterns, which have not yet received full attention. We might be able to examine cultural patterns from two different approaches; first, consider those offenders whose crimes are directly or indirectly related to alcohol, and, second, those whose antisocial acts are perpetrated largely because of unconscious forces.

As has been said previously, a great number of offenders are intoxicated at the time of their crimes, making one think that the abolition of alcohol would reduce crime to a minimum. It has been said apropos of the interrelationship between personality traits and cultural patterns in crimes committed under alcoholic influence that many a crime would not have been perpetrated if the person had been sober. However, men of a high cultural standing do not

[12] S. B. Wortis, "The Metabolism of Brain Tissue," *Bulletin of the Neurological Institute of New York*, IV (April, 1936), No. 4, 595.

usually fight when under the influence of alcohol, while men of a low cultural level in the same condition are quite apt to use their fists. This may perhaps reflect behavior having its roots in their culture.

The same principle should be used in examining the relationship between the criminal pattern and crimes committed largely on an unconscious level. Such an examination would throw light upon the influence that bad companionship has upon the perpetrator and perhaps enable us to see what types of offenders are affected by their associates. Among the offenders with unconscious motivations who would be proper subjects for such examinations are those suffering from kleptomania, pyromania, dipsomania, and so on.

The connection between physical diseases or deformities and criminal activities could also be included in the examination of cultural patterns. Research should be undertaken in areas where delinquent boys and girls live, and in juvenile courts, child guidance clinics, and city hospitals. Investigations of this type might yield some clues to an understanding of the psychological mechanisms in children, adolescents, and adults as well.

It would be worth while to remember that before starting a research project, the worker must spend considerable time poring over literature in the field so that techniques that have failed will be avoided and successful research will not be needlessly duplicated. This is tiresome but if the investigator knows how to read only the essential material, his task will be lightened.

It is impossible to go into all the research problems that are pertinent to all the factors which determine the relationship between the offender's make-up and his act. It is sufficient to say that if more adequate research were done in psychiatric criminology, a better understanding of the mental functioning and of the setup in which the offender works would result. We would then have better tools for dealing with personality maladjustment and one of its offspring—criminal activity.

However, study of the offender himself is not enough. Research can only prove its value if its results are applied to practical purposes and taught properly. For this reason it would be a sound idea in the larger cities of the country to choose an experienced psychiatrist with training in clinical psychiatry and criminal psychopathology to take care of the research and teaching.

It is important that medical students, law students, social workers, probation officers, and prison personnel be taught the findings in psychiatric criminology. To the student the various aspects of crime are so complicated that he may feel at a loss when he first tries to gain some information about it. The lectures should therefore proceed along rather elementary lines.

Also, since crime is acted out in a society where economic, political, and religious forces exist, it is necessary that the psychiatrist be familiar with these forces which may influence the conduct of humans. He must therefore study sociology, anthropology, law, and philosophy if he is to be able to understand the propensities of crime.

It should be borne in mind that, regrettable as it is, too few students choose this type of work. To overcome this indifference the students should be given stimulating subjects illustrated by clear-cut cases. For this purpose such cases should be worked up and kept on file, thereby making them easily available for teaching in other cities and states.

To meet the demand of research and teaching in psychiatric criminology, the establishment of a Department for Research of Criminal Behavior should be considered. This body would try to contact persons engaged in criminological work, for instance, the courts, child guidance clinics, parole boards, probation departments, other public agencies, the Section on Forensic Psychiatry of the American Psychiatric Association, the Orthopsychiatric Association, the Osborne Association, the American Prison Association, and the Section on Criminology of the American Sociological Society.

If established along proper lines, the Department for Research of Criminal Behavior could take upon itself responsibility for criminological research, act as a place for research information, instigate investigations, and be a repository of research material.

In view of the progress made up to the present, one would think that the treatment of the offender has changed decisively. We have now for some time had children's and juvenile courts, child guidance clinics, and reformatories, but not much has been done regarding the treatment of the prisoner. He is still treated as a custodial case. Mental patients were first placed in hospitals not for treatment but for the protection of society. The same is true of most offenders today. Prisons were built to provide housing for the prisoners with little or no treatment available. How the prisoners themselves feel has been admirably described by Oscar Wilde in his *De Profundis:*

For us there is only one season, the season of sorrow. The very sun and moon seem taken from us. Outside, the day may be blue and gold, but the light that creeps down through the thickly-muffled glass of the small iron-barred window beneath which one sits is grey and niggard. It is always twilight in one's cell, as it is always twilight in one's heart. And in the sphere of thought, no less than in the sphere of time, motion is no more. The thing that you personally have long ago forgotten, or can easily forget, is happening to me now, and will happen to me again to-morrow. Remember this, and you will be able to understand a little of why I am writing, and in this manner writing . . .

Usually we are not concerned about those individuals kept in prisons. Those of us who have spent some time in working with offenders in the prisons are shocked by the waste of human material and human happiness. To me the incredible thing is that not far from us are sitting thousands of people in prisons with hardly anyone caring about it. I do not want to speak about the mismanagement and neglect we see in many institutions here and abroad. I only wonder how it is possible that humans can see their kind imprisoned and, practically speaking, not do anything about it. Most people today take it for granted that if anyone is a transgressor, he is to be punished and put into prison, and perhaps the individual's only crime was that he was caught. So ingrained are the retaliatory principles that man not only demands that the offender be imprisoned, but also forgets that he is imprisoned.

It is regrettable to see what a futile job it is to mobilize people's interest in prison problems, and the more regrettable when we know that in general, they are highly interested in the sensational crimes played up by the tabloids. It is deplorable that criminal acts are so often utilized for commercial purposes. It is true that people want news and that newspapers have to secure it for them, but education will not progress as long as people continue to satisfy their desire for sensational news. Much of life is sport, but crimes are certainly not, even if they may appear so on the surface. One cannot fail to see that there is a certain amount of admiration for the offender or the gangster.

The large headlines and pictures about criminal acts cannot avoid impressing the reader. One cannot say that it is the newspapers, with a few and honorable exceptions, which are at fault here. It is more the public itself. A newspaper which does not furnish its readers with the latest news, including news of criminal acts, is in the eyes of the population a poor one. It has to match other newspapers in order to survive. If people only knew how many crimes are committed that are not mentioned in newspapers and knew what lies behind the offenders' antisocial acts, the behavior and suffering involved, then they would have another and truer picture of what crime means and the lesson it teaches—that crime never pays.

Because a great number of people admire some criminals, there has even been competition among the criminals themselves to get the largest headlines and the most prominent photographs. As there is a hierarchy in society, there is also a hierarchy among criminals in which that man who has committed the most sensational crime is most admired by the others.

Prevention of crime is then much of a problem of education. What is education? It is learning the lines of a mighty play, or the rules of a mighty game. When an individual does not adhere to the rules of a game, he forfeits it. The same applies to social rules. When they are transgressed, the perpetrator becomes an outlaw because the rules of society have to be maintained. If they are not, society loses its structure and its power to protect its members. Education should, then, be the instruction of the intellect and the adaptation of the personality to the laws of society.

While our technique has made our means perfect, our goals as to how to instruct society in general and how to deal with offenders in particular have become confused. We have failed to approach a scientific or realistic attitude toward producing an integration of our goals. This integration of goals must have its ultimate aim in a stabilization of society and of the mental equilibrium of its members. We will certainly not overcome this disintegration of society until we think in terms of those apparently intangible matters which make life worth living.

But it will certainly not help to ask people to work or fight whole-heartedly for axioms such as right, justice, and truth if these very humans are not assured a right to live as human beings—that means if their biological requirements are not fulfilled. The old spiritual formulae of the French Revolution—Liberty, Equality, and Fraternity—were taken from their spiritual sphere and put into an economic frame around 1850. While the economic demands are still most important, they are not an end in themselves but a means, and a means to acquire a certain biological minimum. There are certain elementary biological demands that in one way or another have to be satisfied. They are the biological drives; nutrition as a biological process, depending upon the situation, is fundamental in the same way as the sexual drive is.[13]

Science has progressed so far today that it has provided for the biological requirements of every human. These are not fulfilled not only because men find themselves unable to obtain their needs but even more because society has its own shortcomings. Integration of all human and social forces necessitates stabilization, which can be reached first when biological minima quanta are achieved. Society is responsible to the individual because some of the causes of injustice are inherent in it. In the same way society is at least to some extent responsible to the offender, because some of the causes of antisocial activities are ingrained in it.

But the offender is also responsible to society. One may ask how he or any other individual can feel responsibility to or have interest in a society which, odd as it may appear, denies him access to participation in the maintenance of society. No structure reared by man, even if it is only a squalid hut, can be devoid of human interest.

If the offender is to be changed, the ethical axioms that govern human conduct at all times must be translated into realistic terms. What then does it mean to be realistic? It does not only mean to see life as it actually appears. To be realistic requires, paradoxical

13 The structure and bonds of a family in a primitive society are determined to a very large extent by the fundamental biological need of food. A. I. Richard, *Hunger and Work in the Savage Tribe*, p. 212.

though it may sound, having dreams that nourish and inspire our thoughts to realistic action and behavior.

We see then that the ethical principles that control human behavior must be translated into terms that will have a meaning and a significance to everyone, including the offender. His mind has to be psychologically prepared for a new attitude, a new life, or a new change, in perhaps the same way that people in general must be psychologically prepared to meet the change from wartime to peacetime conditions. Such a change for the offender carries with it a moral significance.

It is the same with society at large. In the protection of its members from enemies outside and within lies its moral significance. The behavior of the individual, be it a personal or a social maladjustment, is only a reflection of how disorganized society is. A high social order can be reached only when mental and social abnormalities are at a minimum. On his character depends man's greatness, and on society's character depends its primacy and prestige.

This primacy and prestige can be reached and maintained only when law and science go hand in hand in establishing concepts by which society can be governed. But the law and the legislators will have to reckon with the concepts of truth and justice that live within the people. Then the law, based upon the knowledge of the human mind, can guide and educate the public about the meaning behind it. Then will the law succeed in its supreme task.

BIBLIOGRAPHY

Abraham, Karl. Selected Papers. London, 1927.

Abrahamsen, David. "Den psykiatrisk-psykologiske bakgrunn for et barnedrap begått av en vanför," in Frihet Sannhet; festskrift til Johan Scharffenberg, Oslo, 1939, pp. 404–19.

—— Discussion in the Archives of Neurology and Psychiatry, XLIX (April, 1943), No. 4, 631 ff.

—— "Mass-Psychosis and Its Effects," The Journal of Nervous and Mental Disease, XCIII (Jan., 1941), No. 1, 63–72.

—— "Psychodynamics in Criminal Behavior," address delivered at the annual meeting of The Association for Psychoanalytic and Psychosomatic Medicine, New York, June 6, 1944.

—— "The Dynamic Connection Between Crime and Personality," Journal of Criminal Psychopathology, V (Jan., 1944), No. 3, 481–88.

—— "The Function of Language and Its Development in Early Childhood," Acta psychiatrica et neurologica, Copenhagen, XIII (Jan., 1938), 1–9.

—— Videnskapens fremtid. Oslo, 1938.

Achille-Delmas, François. Psychologipathologique du suicide. Paris, 1932.

Adler, Alfred. The Individual Criminal and His Cure. New York, National Committee on Prisons and Prison Labor, 1930.

—— "Zur Psychologie der primitiven Menschen," Internationalen Zeitschrift für Individualpsychologie, Berlin, 1936.

Alexander, Franz, and Hugo Staub. The Criminal, the Judge and the Public. New York, Macmillan Co., 1931.

Alexander, Franz, and William Healy. Roots of Crime. New York, Alfred A. Knopf, 1935.

Aschaffenburg, Gustav. Beiträge zur Kriminalpsychologie und Strafrechtsreform. Heidelberg, 1926.

—— Crime and Its Repression. Boston, Little, Brown & Co., 1913.

Bard, Philip. "The Neuro Humoral Basis of Emotional Reactions," Chapter VI in A Handbook of General Experimental Psychology. Worcester, Clark University Press, 1934.

Beccaria, Cesare Bonesana. An Essay on Crimes and Punishment. Dublin, 1777.

Bender, L. "Behavior Problems in the Children of Psychotic and Criminal Parents," Genetic Psychology Monographs, XIX (1937), 229–338.

Bender, L., and F. J. Curran. "Children and Adolescents Who Kill," Journal of Criminal Psychopathology, I (April, 1940), No. 4, 297–322.

Bender, L., and P. Shilder. "Aggressiveness in Children," Genetic Psy-

chology Monographs, XVIII (Oct.–Dec., 1936) , Nos. 5 and 6, 410–525.

Birnbaum, Karl. Die psychopathischen Verbrecher. Leipzig, 1926.

Bjerre, Andreas. The Psychology of Murder. London, 1927.

Bleuler, Eugen. Dementia Praecox oder Gruppe der Schizophrenen. Berlin, 1911.

Bloch, Iwan. The Sexual Life of Our Time. London, 1940.

Bon, Gustave L. Psychologie des foules. Paris, 1934.

Borgstrom, C. A. Eine Serie von kriminellen Zwillingen. Munich, 1939.

Brahn, Max. Klinische Wochenschrifft. Berlin, 1931.

Breuer, F., and Sigmund Freud. Psychic Mechanism of Hysteric Phenomena. Vienna, 1893.

Brill, A. A. Psychopathology of Crime; Its Psychiatric and Social Implications. Pamphlet reprinted from *The Journal of the American Institute of Homeopathy,* March, 1929.

Brown, J. F. Psychology and the Social Order. New York, McGraw Hill Book Co., 1936.

Brown, J. F., and K. A. Menninger. Psychodynamics of Abnormal Behavior. New York, McGraw Hill Book Co., 1940.

Burt, Cyril. The Young Delinquent. London, 1931.

Bychowski, Gustav. "Zur Psychopathologie der Brandstiftung," *Schweizer Archiv für Neurologie und Psychologie,* V (1919), 29–56.

Cassity, John Holland. "Personality Study of 200 Murderers," *Journal of Criminal Psychopathology,* II (1942), No. 3, 296–304.

Catton, Joseph. Behind the Scenes of Murder. New York, W. W. Norton & Co., 1940.

Chassell, Clara Frances. The Relation between Morality and Intellect. New York, Teachers College, Columbia University, 1935.

Comte, Auguste. Annale medicale psychologie. Paris, 1901.

Conklin, Edwin Grant. Heredity and Environment in the Development of Men. Princeton, Princeton University Press, 1915.

Conn, Jacob H. "The Aggressive Female 'Psychopathic Personality,'" *The Journal of Nervous and Mental Disease,* XCV (March, 1942), No. 3, 316–34.

Damon, Albert. "Physique in Heredity Mental Defect: An Anthropometric Study of 97 'Old American' Female Morons," *Human Biology,* XIII (Dec., 1941), No. 4, 459–72.

Darrow, Clarence. Clarence Darrow's Plea in Defense of Loeb and Leopold. Chicago, Haldeman Julius Co., 1926.

Davis, Oliver, Charles Minty, and F. A. Wilshire. Mentality and the Criminal Law. Bristol, England, 1935.

Dawson, George Ellsworth. "A Study in Youthful Degeneracy," *The Pedagogical Seminary,* 1896.

Dearden, Harold. The Mind of the Murderer. London, 1930.

Dession, George H. "Psychiatry and the Conditioning of Criminal Justice," *Yale Law Journal,* XLVII (Jan., 1938), 319–40.

Diethelm, Oskar. Treatment in Psychiatry. New York, Macmillan Co., 1936.

Dollard, John, Neal E. Miller, Leonard W. Doob, O. H. Mowrer, and Robert R. Sears. Frustration and Aggression. New Haven, Yale University Press, 1939.

Dugdale, Richard L. The Jukes; A Study in Crime, Pauperism, Disease, and Heredity. 4th ed., New York, G. P. Putnam's Sons, 1910.

Durkheim, Émile. De la division du travail social. Paris, 1893.

——— Le Suicide. Paris, 1930.

Ellis, Havelock. Studies in the Psychology of Sex. 2 vols., New York, Random House, 1940.

Evensen, H. Prostituerte. Oslo, Den Rettsmedisinske Kommisjons Beretning for Året, 1938.

Federal Bureau of Investigation. Uniform Crime Reports, 1938–1943.

Fenichel, Otto. Outline of Clinical Psychoanalysis. New York, The Psychoanalytic Quarterly Press and W. W. Norton & Co., 1934.

Ferenczi, Sandor, and Otto Rank. The Development of Psychoanalysis. Washington and New York, Nervous and Mental Disease Publishing Co., 1925.

Ferrero-Lombroso, Gina. Criminal Man, according to the Classification of Cesare Lombroso. With an introduction by Cesare Lombroso. New York and London, G. P. Putnam's Sons, 1911.

Ferri, Enrico. Criminal Sociology. Translated by Joseph I. Kelly and John Lisle, edited by William W. Smithers, with introductions by Charles A. Ellwood and Quincy A. Myers. New York, Little, Brown & Co., 1917.

Fink, Arthur Emil. Causes of Crime. Philadelphia, University of Pennsylvania Press, 1938.

Flinker, Robert. Die Psychologie und Psychopathologie der Hysterie. Leipzig, 1938.

Foxe, Arthur N. "Psychiatric Classification in a Prison," The Psychiatric Quarterly, XII (Oct., 1938), 617–28.

Fredrich, Julius. Die Bedeutung der Psychologie für die Bekampfung der Verbrechern. Hanover, 1915.

French, Lois Meredith. Psychiatric Social Work. London, 1940.

Freud, Anna, and Dorothy T. Burlingame. Report on Hamptead. London, April, 1942.

Freud, Sigmund. Beiträge zur Psychologie des Liebeslebens. Leipzig, 1924.

——— Collected Papers. Authorized translation under the supervision of Joan Riviere, 4 vols., New York and London, The International Psychoanalytical Press, 1924–25.

——— Drei Abhandlungen zur Sexualtheorie. Leipzig and Vienna, 1915.

——— Massen-Psychologie und ich Analyse. Leipzig, 1921.

Freud, Sigmund. New Introductory Lectures on Psychoanalysis. Translated by W. J. H. Sprott. New York, W. W. Norton & Co., 1933.

—— Sammlung kleiner Schriften zur Neurosenlehre. 3 vols., Leipzig and Vienna, 1906–13.

—— "Selected Papers on Hysteria and Other Psycho-neuroses," The Journal of Nervous and Mental Disease, 1920.

—— The Ego and the Id. Authorized translation by Joan Riviere. London, 1927.

Frosch, Jack, and Walter Bromberg. "The Sex Offender—A Psychiatric Study," The American Journal of Orthopsychiatry, IX (Oct., 1939), No. 4, 761–76.

Gault, Robert H. Criminology. New York, D. C. Heath & Co., 1932.

Gellhorn, Ernst. Autonomic Regulations: The Significance for Physiology, Psychology and Neuropsychiatry. New York, Inter Science Publisher, Inc., 1943.

Gillespie, Robert Dick. Psychological Effects of War on Citizen and Soldier. New York, W. W. Norton & Co., 1942.

Glueck, Sheldon. "Psychiatric Examination of Persons Accused of Crime," Yale Law Journal, March, 1927.

—— State Legislation Providing for the Mental Examination of Persons Accused of Crime. New York, National Committee for Mental Hygiene, Inc., 1924.

Glueck, Sheldon and Eleanor T. 500 Criminal Careers. New York, Alfred A. Knopf, 1930.

—— Juvenile Delinquents Grown Up. London, 1940.

—— Later Criminal Careers. London, 1937.

Good, Rankine. "Malingering," British Medical Journal, Sept. 26, 1942, pp. 359–62.

Goring, Charles. The English Convict. London, 1913.

Goring, M. M. Kriminalpsychologie. Munich, 1922.

Groddeck, Georg Walther. Book of the Id. Washington, Nervous and Mental Disease Publishing Co., 1928.

Guthne, Malcolm. Spencer's Formula of Evolution. London, 1879.

Hall, G. S. Adolescence. 2 vols., New York, D. Appleton and Co., 1904.

Halpern, Irving W. A Decade of Probation. A study and report for the Court of General Sessions of New York City, 1936.

Hamburger, Christian. "Studies on Gonadotropic Hormones from the Hypophysis and Chorionic Tissue," Acta pathologica et microbiologica, Supplementum XVII, Scandinavica, 1933.

Harrington, Milton. A Biological Approach to the Problem of Abnormal Behavior. Lancaster, Pa., Science Press Printing Co., 1938.

Hart, Bernard. The Psychology of Insanity. Cambridge, England, 1929.

Healy, William, and Benedict S. Alper. Criminal Youth and the Borstal System. New York, The Commonwealth Fund, 1941.

Healy, William, and Augusta F. Bronner. Delinquents and Criminals, Their Making and Unmaking. New York, Macmillan Co., 1926.

—— New Light on Delinquency and Its Treatment. New Haven, Yale University Press, 1936.

Heinemann, F. Neue Wege der Philosophie. Leipzig, 1929.

Henderson, D. K. Psychopathic States. New York, W. W. Norton & Co., 1939.

Hendrick, Ives. Facts and Theories of Psychoanalysis. 2d ed., rev. and enl., New York, Alfred A. Knopf, 1939.

Hoffman, Frederick Ludwig. Suicide Problems. Newark, Prudential Press, 1927.

—— The Homicide Problem. Newark, Prudential Press, 1925.

Hoffman, Herman. Über Temperamentvererbung, Grenzenfragen des Nerven und Seelenleben. Berlin, 1923.

Hooton, Earnest Albert. Crime and the Man. Cambridge, Harvard University Press, 1939.

—— The American Criminal: An Anthropological Study. With the collaboration of the Statistical Laboratory of the Division of Anthropology, Harvard University. 3 vols., Vol. I, The Native White Criminal of Native Parentage, Cambridge, Harvard University Press, 1939.

Hoover, J. Edgar. Persons in Hiding. Boston, Little, Brown & Co., 1938.

Hrdlicka, Ales. "The Criminal," Journal of Criminal Psychopathology, I (Oct., 1939), No. 2, 87–90.

Husserl, E. Vorlesungen zur Phänomenologie des inneren Bewusstseins. Halle, 1928.

Isaacs, S. S. Social Development in Young Children. New York, Harcourt, Brace & Co., 1933.

Janet, Pierre Marie Felix. Les Neuroses. Paris, 1909.

Jaspers, Karl. Allgemeine Psychopathologie für Studierende, Artze und Psychologen. Berlin, 1923.

—— "Kausale und verständliche Zusammenhang zwischen Schicksal und Psychose bei Dementia Praecox," Zeitschrift für die gesamte Nerologie und Psychiatrie, XIV (1913), 158–263.

Jones, Ernest. "Anal Erotic Character Traits," in his Papers on Psychoanalysis. New York, Wm. Wood & Co., 1923.

Jung, Carl Gustav. The Psychology of the Unconscious. Authorized translation, with an introduction, by Beatrice M. Hinkle. New York, Dodd, Mead & Co., 1916.

Kahn, Eugen. Psychopathic Personalities. Translated from the German by H. Flanders Dunbar. New Haven, Yale University Press, 1931.

Kallmann, Franz Josef. The Genetics of Schizophrenia. New York, J. J. Augustin, 1938.

Kallmann, Franz Josef, and Eugene S. Barrera. "The Heredoconstitutional Mechanisms of Predisposition and Resistance to Schizophrenia," *American Journal of Psychiatry,* XCVIII (Jan., 1942), No. 4, 544–50.

Karpman, Benjamin. The Individual Criminal. Washington, Nervous and Mental Disease Publishing Co., 1935.

Klein, Melanie. Psychoanalysis of Children. Authorized translation by Alix Strachey. New York, W. W. Norton & Co., 1932.

Knight, R. P. "The Dynamics and Treatment of Chronic Alcoholic Addiction," *Bulletin of the Menniger Clinic,* No. 1 (1937), 233–50.

Kretschmer, Ernst. Medizinische Psychologie. Leipzig, 1939.

—— Physique and Character. Translated from the 2d., rev. and enl., ed. by W. J. H. Sprott. New York, Harcourt, Brace & Co., 1925.

Kubie, Lawrence Schlesinger. The Practical Aspects of Psychoanalysis. New York, W. W. Norton & Co., 1936.

Lange, Johannes. Crime and Destiny. New York, C. Boni, 1930.

Lange-Eichbaum. Genie-Irrsinn-und Ruhm. Munich, 1928.

Lehrman, Philip R. "Some Unconscious Determinants in Homicide," *The Psychiatric Quarterly,* XIII (Oct., 1939), No. 4, 605–21.

Levy, David M. "A Method of Integrating Physical and Psychiatric Examination," *American Journal of Psychiatry,* IX (July, 1929), No. 1, 121–94.

Lévy-Bruhl, Lucien. How Natives Think. Authorized translation by Lilian A. Clare. New York, Alfred A. Knopf, 1926.

Lewis, Nolan D. C. A Short History of Psychiatric Achievement. New York, W. W. Norton & Co., 1941.

—— Research in Dementia Praecox. New York, The National Committee for Mental Hygiene, 1936.

—— The Constitutional Factors in Dementia Praecox. Washington, Nervous and Mental Disease Publishing Co., 1923.

Lilienthal, K. V. "Frantz von Liszt," *Zeitschrift für die gesamte Strafrechtswissenschaft,* XL (1919), 535 ff.

Liszt, Franz von. Lehrbuch des deutschen Strafrechts. Berlin, 1891.

—— Strafrechtliche Aufsätze und Vorträge. 2 vols., Berlin, 1905.

Lombroso, Cesare. Crime, Its Causes and Remedies. Translated by Henry P. Horton. Boston, Little, Brown & Co., 1918.

—— The Female Offender. New York, D. Appleton and Co., 1911.

Luxemburger, Hans. Die erbbiologische Stellung der schizophrenen Psychosen. Stuttgart, 1939.

McKernan, Maureen. The Amazing Crime and Trial of Leopold and Loeb. Chicago, Plymouth Court Press, 1924.

Malamud, William. Outlines of General Psychopathology. New York, W. W. Norton & Co., 1935.

Malinowski, Bronislaw. Crime and Custom in Savage Society. New York, Harcourt, Brace & Co., 1926.

Malinowski, Bronislaw. Sex and Repression in Savage Society. New York, Harcourt, Brace & Co., 1927.

—— The Life of Savages in North-Western Melanesia. London, 1922.

Mangum, C. W. "The Destiny of the Psychopathic Criminal," *Proceedings of the 69th Annual Congress of the American Prison Association,* 1939, pp. 307–14.

Mannheim, K. Mensch und Gesellschaft im Zeitalter des Umbaus. Leiden, 1935.

Mead, Margaret. Sex and Temperament in Three Primitive Societies. New York, William Morris & Co., 1935.

Menninger, Karl A. Man against Himself. New York, Harcourt, Brace & Co., 1938.

—— The Human Mind. New York, Alfred A. Knopf, 1937.

Meyer, Adolf. "The Aims and Meanings of Psychiatric Diagnosis," *American Journal of Insanity,* LXXIV (Oct., 1917), No. 2, 163–68.

Moll, Albert, Untersuchungen über die Libido sexualis. Berlin, 1897.

Monrad-Krohn, G. H. The Clinical Examination of the Nervous System. New York, Paul B. Hoeber, Inc., Medical Book Department of Harper & Brothers, 1938.

Montassut, M. La Dépression constitutionelle. Paris, 1938.

Murchison, Carl. Criminal Intelligence. Worcester, Clark University Press, 1936.

Newman, H. H., F. N. Freeman, and K. J. Holzinger. Twins: A Study of Heredity and Environment. Chicago, University of Chicago Press, 1937.

Nissen, Hartvig. Alkohol og forbrydelse. Oslo, 1933.

—— "Strafferetsutviklingen i Tyskland," *Tidskrift for rettsvidentskap,* 1938, pp. 243–64.

Nissen, Ingjald. Max Weber og den tyske kultur. Oslo, 1937.

Noyes, Arthur R. Modern Clinical Psychiatry. Philadelphia and London, W. B. Saunders Co., 1939.

Overholser, Winfred. "Psychiatry and Crime," *Year Book of the National Probation Association,* 1930, pp. 1–11.

—— Psychiatry and the Law—Cooperators or Antagonists? Pamphlet reprinted from *The Psychiatric Quarterly,* XIII (Oct., 1939), 622-38.

—— "Some Possible Contributions of Psychiatry to a More Effective Administration of the Criminal Law," *The Canadian Bar Review,* Nov., 1939, 638–55.

—— The Practical Operation of the Massachusetts Law requiring the Psychiatric Examination of Certain Persons Accused of Crime (the "Briggs Law"). Pamphlet reprinted from the *Massachusetts Law Quarterly,* XIII (Aug., 1928), No. 6, 2–16.

—— "What Immediate Practical Contribution Can Psychiatry Make to Criminal Law Administration?," *Reports of the American Bar Association*, LV (1930), 594–614.

Planck, Max. Where Is Science Going? London, 1933.

Quetelet, L. A. J. Physique sociale; ou, essai sur l'homme et le développement des facultés de l'homme. Brussels, 1869.

Raoul, Allier. The Mind of the Savage. London, 1929.

Ray, Isaac. A Treatise on the Medical Jurisprudence of Insanity. Boston, Little, Brown and Co., 1838.

Reckless, C. W. The Etiology of Delinquent and Criminal Behavior. Bulletin 507 of the Social Science Research Council, New York, 1943.

Reik, Theodor. The Unknown Murder. London, 1936.

Rhodes, T. F. Genius and Criminal. London, 1932.

Richards, Audrey I. Hunger and Work in the Savage Tribe. London, 1932.

Rorschack, Hermann. Psychodiagnostik. Berne and Berlin, 1932.

Rosanoff, Aaron J., Lena M. Handy, and Isabel Avis Rosanoff. "Criminality and Delinquency in Twins," *Journal of Criminal Law and Criminology*, XXIV (Jan.–Feb., 1934), No. 5, 923–34.

Rush, Benjamin. Sixteen Introductory Lectures to Courses of Lectures upon the Institute and Practice of Medicine. Philadelphia, Bradford and Innskeep, 1811.

Scharffenberg, Johan. Pamphlet containing his discussion before The Norwegian Association of Criminology. Oslo, 1935.

Sellin, Thorsten. Culture Conflict, and Crime. Bulletin 41 of the Social Science Research Council.

——— The Criminality of Youth. Philadelphia, The American Law Institute, 1940.

Selling, Lowell S. "The Psychopathology of the Hit-and-Run Driver," *American Journal of Psychiatry*, XCVIII (July, 1941), No. 1, 93–98.

Shaw, C. R., and H. D. McKay. Social Factors in Juvenile Delinquency. Vol. II, No. 13 of Reports on the Causes of Crime, Washington, D.C., National Commission on Law Observance and Enforcement, 1931.

Shaw, C. R., and others. Brothers in Crime. Chicago, University of Chicago Press, 1938.

Sheldon, W. H. The Varieties of Human Physique: An Introduction to Constitutional Psychology. New York and London, Harper & Brothers, 1940.

Singer, Harold Douglas, and W. O. Krohn. Insanity and Law. Philadelphia, P. Blakiston's Son & Co., 1934.

Skjerbaek, Oluf J. "Krigen og kriminaliteten hos ungdommen," *Nordisk tidsskrift for strafferet*. Vol. II, Copenhagen, 1917.

Solomon, Harry C., and Joseph V. Klauder. "Trauma and Dementia Paralytica," *Journal of the American Medical Association*, XCVI (Jan., 1931), No. 1, 1–7.

Speer, Ernst. Vom Wesen der Neurose. Leipzig, 1938.

Spranger, E. Lebensformen. Halle, 1927.

Stekel, Wilhelm. Sadism and Masochism. New York, Liveright, 1929.

Strecker, A. E., and F. B. Baugh. Practical Clinical Psychiatry. Philadelphia, F. Blakiston's Son & Co., 1931.

Stumpfl, Friedrich. Die Ursprünge des Verbrechens. Leipzig, 1936.

———— Studien über Vererbung und Endstehung geistiger Storüngen. Berlin, 1935.

Sutherland, Edwin H. Principles of Criminology. Philadelphia, J. B. Lippincott Co., 1934.

Suttie, I. D. Origin of Love and Hate. London, 1935.

Taft, D. R. Criminology. New York, Macmillan Co., 1942.

Talbot, Eugene. Degeneracy, Its Causes, Signs and Results. London, 1898.

Thompson, Charles B. "A Psychiatric Study of Recidivists," *American Journal of Psychiatry*, XCIV (Nov., 1937), No. 3, 591–604.

———— "Trigant Burrow's Theory of Human Conflict," *American Journal of Sociology*, XLIII (Jan., 1938), No. 4, 632–34.

Tulchin, S. H. Intelligence and Crime. Chicago, University of Chicago Press, 1939.

Tulin, L. "The Problem of Mental Disorder in Crime," *Columbia Law Review*, XXXII (1932), 933–62.

Vines, H. W. C. The Adrenal Cortex and Intersexuality. London, 1938.

Waite, J. B. The Prevention of Repeated Crime. Ann Arbor, University of Michigan Press, 1943.

Wallack, Walter M. The Training of Prison Guards in the State of New York. New York, Teachers College, Columbia University, 1938.

Weber, Max. Witschaft und Gesellschaft. 2 vols., Tubingen, 1925.

Wechsler, David. "Nonintellective Factors in General Intelligence," *Journal of Abnormal and Social Psychology*, XXXVIII (Jan., 1943), No. 1, 101–3.

———— The Measurement of Adult Intelligence. 3d. ed., New York. The Williams & Wilkins Co., 1944.

Wechsler, Israel S. A Textbook of Clinical Neurology. 4th ed. rev., Philadelphia, W. B. Saunders Co., 1939.

Weihofen, H. Insanity as a Defense in Criminal Law. New York, The Commonwealth Fund, 1933.

Wertham, Frederic. Dark Legend; A Study in Murder. New York, Duell, Sloan & Pearce, 1941.

Westermarck, Edvard. Origin and Development of the Moral Ideas. 2 vols., London, 1906–08.

———— The Goodness of Gods. London, 1926.

White, William A. Crimes and Criminals. New York, Farrar & Rinehart, 1933.

———— Insanity and the Criminal Law. New York, Macmillan Co., 1923.

Whitehorn, J. C. "Concerning Emotion as Impulsion and Instinct as

Orientation," *American Journal of Psychiatry*, XI (May, 1932), No. 6, 1093–1106.

Willemse, Wilhelmus Antonus. Constitution Types in Delinquency. London, 1932.

Witmer, Helen Leland. Psychiatric Clinics for Children with Special Reference to State Programs. New York and London, Oxford University Press, 1940.

Young People in the Courts of New York State. Legislative Document No. 55, 1942.

Zilboorg, Gregory. Mind, Medicine and Man. New York, Harcourt Brace & Co., 1943.

—— "Misconceptions of Legal Insanity," *American Journal of Orthopsychiatry*, IX (July, 1939), No. 3, 540–53.

—— "Some Sidelights on Psychology of Murder," *The Journal of Nervous and Mental Disease*, LXXXI (April, 1935).

Zilboorg, Gregory, and others. One Hundred Years of American Psychiatry. New York, published for The American Psychiatric Association by Columbia University Press, 1944.

Zondek, B., and H. V. Euler. Archiv fur Physiologie. 1934.

INDEX

Abnormal children, treatment, 143

Abnormality, mental: bearing on criminal behavior, 17, 67, 215; in murderer, 157; difficulty of detecting, 158; of offenders, 187, 192, 194 ff.; legal provision for, 189

Abortion, age groups, 128

Abraham, Karl, 108

Accessibility, of offender to examiner, 80

Accidental offenders, 94, 95; chronic, 103, 196

Accidents, in case history, 72

Acute offenders, see Momentary offenders

Adjustment to society: failure, 51, 58, 61; lack of, in schizoid personality. 103; juvenile, 59, 130, 135; see also Maladjustment

Adolescence, crime in, 129

Age groups: arrests by, 42 (tab.); of psychopaths, 113; of types of crime, 128 f., 205; of English juvenile delinquents, 133

Age of consent, 199

Aged, sexual offenses by, 204

Aggression, antisocial behavior as expression of, 27 f.; measurement of, 89; in offenders with neurotic personalities, 107; as related to murder, 148, 161, 168-73

Aggressive behavior, in children, 58; causes, 89

Alcohol, as factor in crime, 50, 122 ff., 201, 216

Alcoholic murder, 161, 168 f.

Alcoholics, family history, 123; personality, 124 f.; treatment, 200

Alcoholism, as expression of aggression, 28; among chronic offenders, 104; in neurotic offenders, 115

Alertness, of offender, 80

Alexander, Franz, 16, 107; introduced concept of neurotic character, 108

Ambivalent feelings, 130

Ambulatory schizophrenia, 101

American criminology, 13 f.

American culture, 47 f.

American Prison Association, 218

American Psychiatric Association, 190, 218

American Sociological Association, 218

Anal sadistic level, 107

Anatomical types, see Criminal types

Anethopathy, 114

Ankle clonus, 78

Anthropology, methods used in psychiatry, 8; criminal, 14; see also Biological criminology

Antisocial activities, partly conscious, partly unconscious, 33; American culture as soil for, 48; as escape from family conflict, 49, 141; alcoholism and, 125; faulty development of superego and, 125; result of tension between ego and superego, 137; many may be attributed to inner forces, 147; resulting from sense of guilt, 194; have roots in personality, 211, 212

Antisocial behavior, 24, 27; among many members of family, 38 ff.; tests for, 89; of psychopaths, 114; no abnormal significance to offender, 192

Antisocial children, treatment, 142 ff.

Antisocial pattern, 208

Antisocial persons, clinics for, proposed, 175

Antisocial tendencies, 7; prompted by sexual conflicts, 42

Apfelberg, Benjamin, 116, 117

Aphasia, 78

Argyll-Robertson's sign, 76, 77, 78

Arson, age group, 128

Aschaffenburg, Gustav, on causes of crime, 12; on types of criminals, 40; on sexual offenders, 116; on alcohol and crime, 122

Assault, expression of aggression, 28; among alcoholics, 122; alcohol and, 168

Assaultists, should have psychiatric examinations, 204

Associational offenders, 94, 95, 217; chronic, 103 f., 196

Astasia-abasia, 79

Australia, homicide in, 149

Autism, 97